On the Threshold of the Holocaust

GESCHICHTE - ERINNERUNG - POLITIK

POSENER STUDIEN ZUR GESCHICHTS-, KULTUR- UND POLITIKWISSENSCHAFT

Herausgegeben von Anna Wolff-Powęska und Piotr Forecki

BAND 11

Tomasz Szarota

On the Threshold of the Holocaust

Anti-Jewish Riots and Pogroms in Occupied Europe

Warsaw – Paris – The Hague –
Amsterdam – Antwerp – Kaunaus

Translated by Tristan Korecki

Bibliographic Information published by the Deutsche Nationalbibliothek
The Deutsche Nationalbibliothek lists this publication in the Deutsche Nationalbibliografie; detailed bibliographic data is available in the internet at http://dnb.d-nb.de.

Library of Congress Cataloging-in-Publication Data
Szarota, Tomasz, author.
  [U progu zaglady. English]
  On the threshold of the Holocaust : anti-Jewish riots and pogroms in occupied Europe : Warsaw, Paris, The Hague, Amsterdam, Antwerp, Kaunas / Tomasz Szarota ; translated by Tristan Korecki – First edition.
    pages cm. – (Geschichte, Erinnerung, Politik, ISSN 2191-3528 ; Band 11)
  ISBN 978-3-631-64048-7
  1. Pogroms–Europe. 2. Jews–Persecutions–Europe. 3. World War, 1939-1945–Atrocities–Europe. 4. Antisemitism–Europe. 5. Holocaust, Jewish (1939-1945)–Europe. I. Korecki, Tristan, translator. II. Title.
  DS135.E83S9713 2015
  940.53'1844–dc23
                    2015034018

Publication of this book was funded by the Ministry of Research and Higher Education of the Republic of Poland within the scheme of the National Programme for the Development of the Humanities, 2012-2013 project.

 NARODOWY PROGRAM
ROZWOJU HUMANISTYKI

Cover illustration :
© Musée Juif de la Déportation et de la Résistance, Mechelen - Belgique

ISSN 2191-3528
ISBN 978-3-631-64048-7 (Print)
E-ISBN 978-3-653-02440-1 (E-Book)
DOI 10.3726/978-3-653-02440-1

© Peter Lang GmbH
Internationaler Verlag der Wissenschaften
Frankfurt am Main 2015
All rights reserved.
Peter Lang Edition is an Imprint of Peter Lang GmbH.

Peter Lang – Frankfurt am Main · Bern · Bruxelles · New York ·
Oxford · Warszawa · Wien

All parts of this publication are protected by copyright. Any utilisation outside the strict limits of the copyright law, without the permission of the publisher, is forbidden and liable to prosecution. This applies in particular to reproductions, translations, microfilming, and storage and processing in electronic retrieval systems.

This publication has been peer reviewed.

www.peterlang.com

Table of Contents

Foreword 7

Chapter 1 Warsaw 19
Anti-Jewish excesses after the German invasion..................................19
March 1940: The Easter occurrences. The sequence of incidents 23
The Poles: organisers and participants of the riots 35
The conduct and attitudes of Varsovians..59
The role of the Germans: Instigators, or organisers and active
participants of the incidents?..66

Chapter 2 Paris 75
Anti-Semitic propaganda and first anti-Jewish incidents
at the threshold of the occupation..75
French anti-Semites and their German counterparts...........................84
The incidents on Champs-Elysées of 20th August 1940.......................96
Excesses continue. Competition amongst anti-Semitic
organisations. Anti-Jewish legislation 105
The Parisians' attitude 105
A *Kristallnacht* in the city on the Seine. Paris synagogues
attacked in the night of 2nd/3rd October 1941.................................... 121

Chapter 3 The Hague and Amsterdam. Antwerp............................ 135
The two capital cities of the Netherlands 135
Antwerp... 148

Chapter 4 Kaunas/Kovno 159
From an independent state to a (forcedly established) Soviet republic............ 159

The Lithuanian Activist Front in Berlin and the Underground at home 159

"Self-cleansing actions": a task of the *Einsatzgruppen*
and a stage in the Holocaust 165

Kaunas in Lithuanian hands, 23rd–24th June 1941: A national
uprising, or a settling of accounts with the "Judeo-commies"? 172

A five-day a pogrom under German oversight (25th to 29th June, 1941) 179

A German offer to the Jews: continued pogroms or the ghetto 211

Foreword

What we normally associate the Holocaust with is genocide. The destruction of the Jewish nation has enshrouded the anguishes, sufferings, and humiliations the Jews experienced before being annihilated. Anti-Jewish riots tend to be neglected by authors of general studies concerning the history of the Second World War; similarly, they are not to be found in the works describing the Shoah. Likewise, not much would be found in the publications about the pogroms witnessed after 22nd June 1941 by Ukraine, Poland, Lithuania, Latvia, Belarus, and Moldavia.[1]

Studies authored by historians from the countries where these occurrences took place tend to pass them over in silence for one more reason. To embark on this subject, a sore point as it really is, calls for courage as it implies that infamous and ignominious, or viciously brutal deeds could have been perpetrated not only by the Germans but also by the researcher's compatriots. It is true that anti-Jewish disturbances – incidents, excesses, riots – sometimes turning into pogroms in which the Jews were getting beaten and in many cases killed, were not infrequently inspired by the German occupiers. It is, however, no less true that such incidents tended to occur here and there on the initiative of the local population – before the Germans entered. It should be borne in mind that the Germans might afterwards have persuaded or encouraged local people to take part in the persecutions or extermination of their Jewish neighbours, but as a rule they did not force them to do so.

Let us make a fair point: it was not the Germans who originally invented pogroms; pogroms did not first occur during the Second World War, or even in the twentieth century. The anti-Jewish disturbances and excesses of the 1930s rank among the black chapters in Polish history. According to Jolanta Żyndul's findings, in 1935–1937 alone, about a hundred fairly remarkable anti-Jewish incidents took place in Poland, with some 2,000 victims beaten and a dozen-or-so

---

[1] What I have in mind are books such as: R. Hilberg, *The Destruction of European Jews*, London 1961 (and its numerous subsequent British and U.S. editions; French ed.: idem, *La destruction des Juifs d'Europe*, Paris 1988); idem, *Täter, Opfer, Zuschauer: Die Vernichtung der Juden 1933–1945*, Frankfurt am Main 1992; M. Gilbert, *The Holocaust. A history of the Jews of Europe During the Second World War*, New York 1985; a re-edition of the latter: idem, *The Holocaust. The Jewish Tragedy*, Glasgow 1987; L. Yahil, *Überlebenskampf und Vernichtung der europäischen Juden*, Munich 1998.

killed.² Fatalities – appallingly – occurred in Poland after the war as well, just to recall the pogrom of Kielce of 4ᵗʰ July 1946.³

As the title of this book clearly suggests, I will not deal with anti-Jewish occurrences in countries allied with the Third Reich, Slovakia being one of them.⁴ Having focused on countries occupied by the Third Reich, I have decided to take a closer look at Warsaw, Paris, The Hague and Amsterdam, Antwerp, as well as Kaunas. My choice was based on the existing literature as well as on the possibility for me to get to the sources, such as police reports, press releases or articles, and eyewitness accounts. It is for this particular reason that I have quit, having considered the gathered resources unsatisfactory, the idea of writing a separate chapter on the anti-Jewish incidents in Prague in March and May 1939.⁵ The same is true for Lwów/Lvov, where a bloody pogrom occurred twice in July 1941.⁶ Since I have

---

2   J. Żyndul, *Zajścia antyżydowskie w Polsce w latach 1935–1937*, Warsaw 1994, pp. 42, 54.
3   Cf. B. Szaynok, *Pogrom Żydów w Kielcach 4 lipca 1946*, Warsaw 1992; K. Kersten, *Polacy, Żydzi. Komunizm: anatomia półprawd 1938–68*, Warsaw 1992 (esp., the essay *Pogrom Żydów w Kielcach – znaki zapytania*, pp. 89–142); *Antyżydowskie wydarzenia kieleckie 4 lipca 1946 roku. Dokumenty i materiały*, vol. I, ed. by S, Meducki and Z. Wrona, Kielce 1992; vol. 2., ed. by S. Meducki, Kielce 1994.
4   Allow me here to mention a book on anti-Semitic incidents in Slovakia: E. Nižnansky, *Židovská komunita na Slovensku medzi československou parlamentnou demokraciou a slovenským štátom v stredoeurópskom kontexte*, Prešov 1999, of which I have learned, and received copies of its excerpts, from Mr. Jerzy Tomaszewski. Apart from the pogroms committed in the summer of 1941 in Moldavia, the conscience of Romanians is charged with the killing of some 35,000 Jews in Odessa on 23ʳᵈ–25ᵗʰ October 1941; cf. D. Litani, "The Destruction of the Jews of Odessa in the Light of Romanian Documents", *Yad Vashem Studies*, vol. 6, 1967, pp. 135–154.
5   20ᵗʰ March 1939 saw a fire set in a synagogue, whereas 25ᵗʰ and 26ᵗʰ May witnessed anti-Jewish street riots organised in Prague by two fascist organisations: *Vlajka* (The Flag), run by Jan Rys-Rozsévac, and *Národní obec fašistická* (National Fascist Community) led by Gen. Radola Gajda. A biography of the latter, by A. Klimek and P. Hofman, titled *Vítěz, který prohrál: generál Radola Gajda* (Prague and Litomysl 1995), mentions this episode in one sentence (p. 277). I thank Messrs. Witold Nawrocki and Jiří Kořalka for their guidance in gathering materials regarding this unwritten chapter.
6   The first pogrom took place on 30ᵗʰ June and lasted until 3ʳᵈ July 1941, killing approx. 4,000 Jews. The second, referred to as "the Petlura Days", entailed some 2,000 Jewish casualties; cf. F. Friedman, *Zagłada Żydów lwowskich*, Lodz 1945; English ed.: idem, "The Destruction of the Jews of Lwow 1941–1944", [in:] idem, *Roads to Extinction: Essays on the Holocaust*, New York 1980, pp. 244–321; reprinted in: M.R. Marrus (ed.), *The Nazi Holocaust. The "Final Solution" Outside Germany*, vol. 2, Westport and London 1989, pp. 659–736; also, cf. *Enzyklopädie des Holocaust*, Bd. II, Berlin 1993, pp. 851–3.

found it impossible to complement the information given by Andrzej Żbikowski in his *U genezy Jedwabnego*. *Żydzi na kresach północno-wschodnich II Rzeczypospolitej, wrzesień 1939 – lipiec 1941* (Warsaw 2006), the reader is kindly referred to this study, which discusses the occurrences taking place between September 1939 and July 1941 in the Eastern Borderland of what was the Second Republic of Poland (it was found that Jews were killed in thirty-one localities of the region). In spite of my endeavours, I have not managed to learn the details of the anti-Jewish incidents in Oslo in July 1941[7], or in Copenhagen in December 1941.[8]

I initially intended to deal in the introductory section with the events of *Kristallnacht* witnessed by the Third Reich in November 1938. Having become acquainted with a considerable portion of relevant publications,[9] I have discarded the idea, as it would have gone beyond the framework of this study. However, I have found my acquaintanceship with the course of the events in Germany quite useful as it has allowed me to determine the extent to which those occurrences were viewed elsewhere as a model to follow – just to mention here the

---

7   I have found a single mention of these incidents in the microfilmed files of the British Public Record Office (materials prepared based on the analysis of censored letters, of which I availed myself at the Institut für Zeitgeschichte in Munich (ref. no. MA 1492/17)).

8   As Leni Yahil tells us, the Danish fascists first attempted to destroy the monument of Jewish writer Meïr Aaron Goldschmidt and afterwards, on 20th December 1941, set fire to a Copenhagen synagogue. In response to New Year's wishes he received from Dr Marcus Melchior, a rabbi, King Christian X wrote: "… it is with regret that I have learnt of the fire of the synagogue, but I am glad that the damages caused have proved not overly significant." Let us add that the perpetrators were caught and sentenced on 3rd February 1942 to three years in prison; *The Rescue of Danish Jewry. Test of a Democracy*, Philadelphia 1969, pp. 48, 63.

9   I should, first of all, mention in this context the following books: W.H. Pehle (ed.), *Der Judenpogrom 1938. Von der "Reichskristallnacht" zum Völkermord*, Frankfurt am Main 1988; K. Pätzold and I. Runge, *"Kristallnacht". Zum Pogrom 1938*, Cologne 1988; D. Obst, *"Reichskristallnacht". Ursachen und Verlauf des antisemitischen Pogroms vom November 1938*, Frankfurt am Main 1991; W.-A. Kropat, *"Reichskristallnacht". Der Judenpogrom vom 7. Bis 10. November 1938 – Urheber, Täter, Hintergründe*, Wiesbaden 1997 (a study that throws new light on the occurrences, showing that they were not limited to one night); H. Graml, *Reichskristallnacht. Antisemitismus und Judenverfolgung im Dritten Reich*, Munich 1998 – being the third edition of this classic study; 'Zeitschrift für Geschichtwissenschaft' – a special issue entitled *Novemberpogrom 1938. Reaktionen und Wirkungen*, 1988, no. 11. A study by Karol Jonca, *„Noc kryształowa" i casus Herschela Grynszpana*, 2nd ed., Wroclaw 1998, can be deemed an achievement in Polish historiography.

breaking of windows in Jewish shops, the devastation and arson of synagogues, or the guidelines to protect nearby "Aryan" establishments and houses.

The comparative approach proposed in this book has proven to be successful as it enables us to discern the similarities, sometimes quite astonishing, among the occurrences taking place in the different countries. If we take a closer look at the groups or formations organising the anti-Jewish incidents, whose members were from the local population, we will easily notice that the origins of a definite majority of those formations dated back to the pre-war years, their background being the political activities of extreme rightist groups. Some of those formations were banned by their respective governments in the late thirties, their journals suspended. The new situation offered them an opportunity to resume activity and implement their programme, which was, in any case, close to the national-socialist ideology of the German occupiers. Attempts were made to obtain consent from the Germans for reactivation of a party or organisation. Even though the activists could not count on a proactive attitude, such as (for instance) financial assistance, they could at least assume that the Germans would favour their actions aimed against the Jews (and freemasons), thus ensuring a degree of impunity to the perpetrators and contributors. Some of the leaders of such local fascists were hostile to the Germans and tried to take advantage of them to fulfil their own political goals; such people, arguably, believed that they were driven by patriotic motives. Andrzej Świetlicki in Poland or Robert Hersant in France are, seemingly, examples of such an attitude.[10]

When one looks closely at the anti-Jewish disturbances described in this book, the role played by hit squads – consisting mostly of young people, sometimes even children – becomes apparent and striking. This is particularly true for Warsaw, where assaults on Jews were carried out by "gangs of striplings", and for Paris – where the fascist youth organisations Gardes Françaises and Jeune Front stood out as the most active groups in the anti-Jewish excesses. Since fighting squads have been mentioned, it should be emphasised that at least some of them had emerged before the war, in addition to the fact that many of them followed the model of the German Sturm-Abteilungen. Such was definitely the case with the Dutch "*Weer Afdeling*" ("Defence Division") or the Flemish "*Zwarte Brigade*"

---

10 A like view of these collaborators, at least some of them, has been proposed by David Littlejohn in his book (whose title is meaningful in this respect): *The Patriotic Traitors. A History of Collaboration in German-Occupied Europe 1940–1945*, London 1972. German historian Franz W. Seidler, author of the biographical dictionary *Die Kollaboration 1939–1945* (Munich and Berlin 1995), moves toward a similar concept.

("Black Brigade"); I should suppose that the same would be true for the Lithuanian "*Gelezinis Vilkas*" ("Iron Wolf").

Comparative studies offer a really valuable tool as along with the similarities, they enable us to identify essential differences. The residents of Prague, Warsaw, Brussels, Paris, The Hague, Oslo, or Athens perceived the Germans encroaching on their cities as enemies, invaders and occupiers that denied the independent status of their country. On the other hand, the Germans encountered an enthusiastic welcome in places such as Kaunas or Lvov – seen there as rescuers and liberators from the alien yoke of the hated "Bolsheviks". The hope was entertained that the Germans were bringing the freedom they so much desired, and it was expected that they would contribute to reestablishment of an independent Lithuania and, likewise, a *samostiyna* Ukraine. Putting it otherwise, insofar as the local collaborationist formations could hardly count on any support from public opinion from the Czechs, or in Poland or Western Europe, they expressed the opinion of a significant portion of the society in Lithuania, Latvia, Belarus, and Ukraine on the eve of the occupation. In certain cases, the collaborationist groups' attitude toward the Germans and the hopes associated with them were an even more complex issue – for example, the aspirations expressed by separatist movements, such as the Belgian Flemings or the French Bretons. In Poland, for that matter, the Germans were the invaders – but not the only ones; hence the concept of joining together with one of the enemies against the other, a proponent of which was the National Radical Organisation, an organisation brought into being by activists of the pre-war National Radical Camp. Those advocating this idea presented it as a revisited concept of Józef Piłsudski from the period of the First World War.

Let us resume the thread of similarities, though. Probably all the activists and instigators who embarked on political activity with the consent of the German occupational authorities had two points of their agenda in common: anticommunism and anti-Semitism, usually merged into the slogan of "combating the *Judeo-commies*". The forms and methods applied by them were quite similar too: Jewish passers-by were attacked, beaten, and humiliated; their possessions were robbed; leaflets were posted and distributed calling to boycott Jewish shops, workshops, manufactories, and eating places; storefronts were smashed; threats of setting fire to dwellings or blowing them up were made. This is what happened, at least, in Western Europe, where local anti-Semites exerted pressure on the Jewish people so that, seeing the hostility surrounding them and the menacing perils, they would resolve on their own to leave their country and emigrate. Let us bear in mind that even in the Third Reich, at least by the end of 1940, plans to resettle the Jews to Madagascar – or to send them off to Siberia in cooperation with the Soviets – were still quite seriously considered.

Although the Lithuanian anti-Semites received instructions from their agency in Berlin (where the Lithuanian Activists' Front was formed on 17th November 1940) to create an atmosphere in their home country which would force the Jews to leave Lithuania, no such exodus occurred until the outbreak of the German-Soviet war. After the outbreak, events followed so fast that most of the local Jews remained where they were. In this situation, no-one could any longer count on the Jews escaping on their own, or their being efficiently expelled. In Kaunas, the Lithuanians drew their own conclusion, or were perhaps prompted to this end by the Germans: the Lithuanian fascists simply decided to kill the local Jews. The Ukrainian fascists in Lvov, as well as in a number of towns and villages in western Ukraine, took a similar decision. In Western Europe efforts were made to fuel anti-Semitic sentiments, the Jewry there being accused of the war disaster suffered; in Kaunas, not only were the Jews identified by the Lithuanian "patriots" with Soviet rule and the NKVD tormenters, but gossip and rumours were spread about Jews poisoning the drinking water in the wells, or Jewish villains shooting out of hiding. In Lvov, where the Soviets had murdered a vast number of detained prisoners before withdrawing from the town, the call to take revenge for the victims soon gained popular support in the local community, which focused on the Jews as the scapegoat.[11]

When one embarks on analysing the course of anti-Jewish incidents, riots, and pogroms in occupied Europe, it turns out that the part played by the German authorities in each of these cases is hard to define. There were various institutions, outposts or "stations", crews, and formations operating within the occupied territories, all of which represented the Third Reich's interests but were engaged in competence contests against one another. Alongside the military authorities, civil occupational administration bodies functioned, and beside these, police structures or representatives of departments, such as the Propaganda Ministry led by Goebbels or the Foreign Ministry run by Ribbentrop, which formally (and formally only) reported to those bodies. It is a rare opportunity that, based on the surviving documents, such as official reports, we are able to reveal the behind-the-scenes mechanisms of the specific occurrences and show the role

---

11 Cf. K. Popiński, A. Kokurin and A. Gurjanow, *Drogi śmierci. Ewakuacja więzień sowieckich z Kresów Wschodnich II Rzeczypospolitej w czerwcu i lipcu 1941*, Warsaw 1995, pp. 8-10, 28, 162-168, 176, 220-232, quoting estimates of killed prisoners of 2,000 to 7,000; also, cf. B. Musial (ed.), *"Konterrevolutionaere Elemente sind zu erschiessen". Die Brutalisie- rung des deutsch-sowjetischen Krieges im Sommer 1941*, Berlin and Munich 2000.

played by the Germans – or, even more specifically, which German authority ordered specifically whom to act in a specified way. One such occurrence was the attack on the Paris synagogues in the night of 2nd/3rd October 1941; another, and an even more peculiar example is the Kaunas pogrom, to which the German term "self-cleansing action" was attached.

It has proven impossible to determine the connections and contacts of local fascist and anti-Semitic formations with the persons acting on behalf of occupational authorities (of whatever sort) in Warsaw, between autumn 1939 and spring 1940; in Paris, in the summer of 1940; in The Hague and Amsterdam, in February 1941; and in Antwerp, in April 1941. Either the relevant documents have been destroyed, or the connections and contacts have left no trace in writing. Hence, a historian willing to delve into this problem has no choice other than to resort to conjecture and look for circumstantial evidence. There also are, however, arguments confirming the contributions of the "German factor" in the preparation of anti-Jewish incidents. It is an ascertained fact, for that matter, that anti-Semitic formations were allocated locales for organisational purposes by the German authorities, these often being apartments owned by Jews or the premises of Jewish institutions. It is also known that the Germans financially subsidised anti-Semitic journals such as the Paris weekly *Au Pilori*. It was solely from the Germans that the Flemish fascists could have obtained a copy of the anti-Semitic film *Der ewige Jude*, after the projection of which anti-Jewish riots erupted in Antwerp. The Paris police were forced to release the organisers and participants of excesses directed against the local Jewry as a result of intervention from the Germans. What is more, the extant reports of the police in this case tell us that those taking part in the incidents asserted, when interrogated, that their leaders had been promised exemption from punishment. Who exactly had guaranteed their immunity – we are, regrettably, not told. Certainly, none of the military command, as this circle was completely surprised by the street incidents in Paris. General Alexander von Falkenhausen, the military occupational governor in Belgium, was astonished by the anti-Jewish disturbances in Antwerp.

There are many indications that the anti-Jewish actions in occupied Europe were initiated or supported primarily by one institution – local branches of the Security Police (Sipo) and Security Service (SD), subordinated to their Berlin headquarters, the Reich Security Main Office (RSHA). Paris was the only place where the situation was different during the first months of the occupation, and this was due to the thoroughly unique position enjoyed there by Ambassador Otto Abetz. Apart from Sipo and SD, crews of the Nazi Ministry of Propaganda played a critical role everywhere, among whose tasks was photographing and filming the anti-Jewish incidents.

Regardless of whether these disturbances emerged as the spontaneous undertakings of local fascist formations without prior coordination or instruction from German principals, the Sipo and SD, as well as the Propaganda-Abteilung or Propaganda-Staffel, realised that such developments could be of use for their own political and propagandist purposes. Anti-Jewish riots created an excellent opportunity to show that not only the Germans were anti-Semitic; and that societies were hostile toward the Jews everywhere, expressing that hostility through the allegedly spontaneous manifestations, attesting that further coexistence with Jews was impossible, regardless of the country. Taking advantage of the opportunity, they could also present a negative picture of the defeated opponents of the Third Reich – featuring people committing violent acts and banditries, violating law and order, which could only be reinstated by the "law-respecting" German occupiers. Anti-Jewish incidents provided arguments in favour of introducing special discriminatory regulations with respect to the Jewish population that differentiated them from the remainder of the society and were aimed at isolating them. Thus, the incidents in Warsaw and Kaunas – and probably also those in Amsterdam – can be seen in the context of the plans to establish ghettoes in these towns. The Germans proposed the ghetto to the Jews as a beneficial solution, their only rescue from the aggression of those anti-Semitic Poles, Lithuanians, or Dutchmen.

In Warsaw, the ghetto wall construction works started almost overnight after the local anti-Jewish excesses had ceased, all of a sudden (and, doubtlessly, on command). In Kaunas, the commander of the Nazi *Einsatzkommando 3*, SS-Standartenführer Karl Jäger, overtly told the delegation of Jewish elders he received on 7th July 1941: continued pogroms or the ghetto! The anti-Jewish riots in occupied Europe, whether fomented or merely supported afterwards, served an additional purpose; they were used as a lever coercing the German military or civil administration to proactively join in the "solving of the Jewish question" on the territory of the country they ruled. By demonstrating the "savage" and "barbaric" conduct of the local anti-Semites, the Sipo/SD highlighted their own role as an agent that ensured or, rather, reinstated law and order, one that could offer different methods to implement the *Endlösung* programme.

The anti-Jewish incidents and, to a much greater degree, the pogroms carried out in the East of Europe show the capacity of human nature – what man is capable of doing to his fellow man,[12] what baseness he can resort to, and what

---

12   We may recall here the famous epigraph from Zofia Nałkowska's book of short stories *Medaliony* (*Medallions*), which has been translated into several languages: "People dealt this fate to people."

immense reservoirs of sadism he can draw from. The Germans were not, after all, the only participants in the beatings and killings of Europe's Jews – which should serve as additional proof that there are no "criminal" nations, or nations that are incapable of committing such crimes.[13] Laying blame on entire nations for felonious acts makes no sense, after all. While Poles, Frenchmen, Lithuanians, or Ukrainians joined and participated in anti-Jewish excesses and pogroms, there were those amongst their compatriots who condemned the persecutions of Jews and protested against racial discrimination. There were those in the lands where the genocide was carried out who looked on in fear and dismay, whilst the most courageous and, indeed, the best among them rushed to help the Jews.

When Jews became the object of attack from the mob during the street disturbances, they most often sought shelter or escape from the area of threat. Sometimes, however, they would organise self-defence patrols or squads and try to tackle the attackers – as in Warsaw, Paris, or Amsterdam. In the latter case, they were helped in their struggle with the local fascists by Dutch communists; in the Polish capital, the actions of the Jewish Bund were supported by Polish socialists. In the course of the pogroms in Lithuania and Ukraine, exceptionally few Jews undertook to fight to save their lives. The image of a group of Jews who did not stop saying their prayers while dying made a profound impression on a German soldier who witnessed the pogrom in Kaunas.

---

13 In Poland, the awareness that the Poles were not completely without sin was raised by, among others, the publication in 2000 of Jan T. Gross's book *Sąsiedzi* (English version: *Neighbors. The Destruction of the Jewish Community in Jedwabne, Poland*, Princeton 2001; translations into other languages have been published as well). The book triggered a national debate in the mass media, one of the outcomes being the publication of a two-volume collection *Wokół Jedwabnego*, P. Machcewicz and K. Persak (eds.), Warsaw 2002, comprising related essays written by historians, accounts and testimonies of witnesses, and archival materials. Essays by E. Dmitrów, P. Machcewicz and T. Szarota have been published also in German: *Der Beginn der Vernichtung: Zum Mord an den Juden in Jedwabne und Umgebung im Sommer 1941*, transl. (from the Polish) by B. Kosmala, Osnabrück 2004. Also, cf.: A. Polonsky and J.B. Michlic (eds.), *The Neighbors Respond. The Controversy over the Jedwabne Massacre in Poland*, Princeton and Oxford 2004. For my own stance, see: T. Szarota, "Mord w Jedwabnem. Udział ludności miejscowej w Holokauście", [in:] idem, *Karuzela na placu Krasińskich. Studia i szkice z lat wojny i okupacji*, 2nd ed., Warsaw 2007, pp. 172–186.

Back in 1993, when I delivered a paper on anti-Jewish incidents and pogroms in occupied Europe[14] at a scholarly conference held on the fiftieth anniversary of the Warsaw Ghetto Uprising, I did not expect to resume the topic years afterwards, finally writing a book on those occurrences. This would have not been possible without support from the Alexander-von-Humboldt-Stiftung, which has enabled me to carry out additional research in Germany (primarily, at the Munich-based Institut für Zeitgeschichte (IFZ) and the Zentrum für Antisemitismusforschung in Berlin). Assistance has also come from the Commissariat général aux Relations internationales de la Communauté française de Belgique, who enabled me to do research at the Centre de recherches et d'études historiques de la Seconde Guerre mondiale in Brussels, as well as at the Nederlands Instituut voor Oorlogsdocumentatie in Amsterdam. Finally, a grant received from the French Ministère de l'Enseignement Supérieur et de la Recherche allowed me, during the several months of my stay in Paris, to make use of the collections of, among others, the Archives Nationales, the Institut d'Histoire du Temps Présent (IHTP), and the Archives de la Préfecture de Police.

This book would have no doubt been much more limited if not for the invaluable help from: Mr. Jean Astruc, the admirable librarian of the IHTP; Ms. Paule René-Bazin, who facilitated my access to the Paris archives; Ms. Elke Fröhlich of the IFZ; Mr. José Gotovitsch, Director of the Brussels World War 2 research centre; Mr. Gerhard Hirschfeld, Director of the Bibliothek für Zeitgeschichte in Stuttgart; Mr. Johannes Hoffmann, Head of the Forschungsstelle Ostmitteleuropa in Dortmund; Ms. Beate Kosmala of the Zentrum für Antisemitismusforschung, Berlin; Messrs. Piotr Łossowski and Henryk Wisner, my colleagues from the Institute of History, Polish Academy of Sciences, who made it possible for me to use the relevant texts in Lithuanian; Mr. Knut Stang, researcher with the University of Göttingen, an eminent expert in the history of Lithuania in WW2 period; and, Ms. Karen Taieb, responsible for the archives with the Centre de Documentation Juive Contemporaine in Paris, who has provided me with photocopies of several documents of relevance.

The grant received under the National Programme for the Development of the Humanities in Poland has enabled the production of a translation of this book into English, thus giving it the opportunity to reach the reading public worldwide.

---

14 The paper was subsequently published in the collection: D. Grinberg and P. Szapiro (eds.), *Holocaust z perspektywy półwiecza. Pięćdziesiąta rocznica powstania w getcie warszawskim*, Warsaw 1994, pp. 153–175; English version: "Anti-Jewish Pogroms and Incidents in the Occupied Europe", [in:] D. Grinberg (ed.), *The Holocaust. Fifty Years After*, Warsaw 1994, pp. 109–123.

I was fortunate to have Tristan Korecki, an excellent translator, hired for this purpose. Wherever possible, I have endeavoured to complement the source material for this particular edition and make use of the most recent literature, particularly with respect to the occurrences in Warsaw and Kaunas.

Chapter 1 Warsaw

Anti-Jewish excesses after the German invasion

Emanuel Ringelblum, the legendary creator of the Warsaw Ghetto Archives who later tried to save his life hiding on the "Aryan" side, wrote bitterly in his study, *Polish-Jewish Relations During the Second World War*, in the autumn of 1943 and the winter of 1943–4:

> After the German invasion, there was a revival of anti-Semitism in the full sense of the term. It was manifested in the relief work carried out by the NSV (*Nationalsozialistische Volkswolhlfahrt* – National Socialist Social Welfare). In the public squares, enormous NSV trucks distributed free bread and soup (made from commandeered Polish produce) to the starving population of Warsaw. For the first few days, the Jews were not excluded from this relief. But this was primarily for the sake of the films that were being made in the newly conquered capital. On Muranowski Square I witnessed how the Jews who had been given free bread and soup for the sake of the filming were immediately afterwards beaten by the German soldiers and how the queue, which the Germans themselves had caused to be formed, was made to disperse. The anti-Semitic mob would pick out the hungry Jews standing in line before the NSV trucks and would point out who was a *Jude* – the one German word the hooligans learned at once.
>
> Very soon round-ups began for the various military formations that needed skilled workers for jobs of various kinds. As the Jews were not yet wearing special badges, it was difficult for the German blood-hounds to distinguish between Jews and non-Jews. The anti-Semitic scum came to their aid and obligingly pointed out the Jews to the Germans. Thus was the first bond sealed between the Polish anti-Semites and the Nazis. The platform that united them was, as usual, the Jews. The first performances of the Polish anti-Semites came as a severe shock to the Jews."[15]

When writing this, Ringelblum had no access to any relevant documents, and could only trust his own memory; sometimes he perhaps all too hastily generalised certain individual observations. That the Jews were not excluded from the charity

---

15 E. Ringelblum, *Polish-Jewish Relations During the Second World War*, edited and with footnotes by Joseph Kermish and Shmuel Krakowski, translated from the Polish by Dafna Allon, Danuta Dabrowska, and Dana Keren, Evanston, Illinois 1992, pp. 37–38. For reasons completely incomprehensible to me, neither the Introduction (by J. Kermish) nor the Foreword (by Yehuda Bauer) mention the earlier Polish edition, compiled by Artur Eisenbach (Warsaw 1988).

action in its first few days is not true. They were in fact eliminated, although nothing like this was officially stated in the capitulation arrangement. Józef Dąbrowa-Sierzputowski noted down in his diary on 30th September 1939: "Today, they were distributing dinner at Broni Square. They are treating the local people in a kind fashion. First, they gave pea-soup to the Polish soldiers, then, to the women, and finally, to the men. *What they are doing to the Jews is just chasing them away* [emphasis – T.S.]."[16] The German brochure, *Mit der NSV nach Polen*, an account of a participant of the events, is an important source of information. The author, Walter Hebenbrock, describes an encounter of 30th September 1939 between the crew of the NSV-Hilfszug Bayern with a troop of Blue Police (*Granatowa policja*), a formation which was tasked to guide the Germans and act as interpreters: "When *Parteigenosse* Janowsky was giving them some directions, and remarks that by no means shall the Jews be taken into account in the welfare actions, they accept this with great applause, and from then on are badmouthing the Jews terribly. We agree with them, but are of the opinion that it would have been better, had they made their anti-Semitic attacks somewhat earlier." Hebenbrock made an observation on how the charity action proceeded in the following days: "Wherever the Jews appear, they are removed. The Poles themselves are looking after it now. That the Jews are trying to introduce themselves as *Volksdeutschen* is an instance of turpitude only the children of Israel are up to." To recapitulate, it was the Germans who had ordained the discrimination of the Jews, but there were Poles who appeared and lent them a hand in its delivery. Hebenbrock produces a facsimile of a notice dated 15th October 1939 to the people of Warsaw, co-signed by Janowsky as a special representative of the NSV for Warsaw, and Lord Mayor Stefan Starzyński (in office until 26th October 1939). The notice concerns the taking over of charity functions by the municipal services and the Capital-City Committee of Social Self-Help, and is concluded with the phrase: "The Jewish people shall be excluded from the welfare being offered," added on demand of the Germans, without a shade of doubt.[17]

It is true that before badges for Jews with the Star of David were introduced in the *Generalgouvernement* on 1st December 1939, the Germans had considerable difficulty recognising them in the street – the Star-of-David armband was to facilitate the task for them.[18] With its appearance, the mark ensured the local anti-Semites to act with impunity. In his *Chronicle of the War and Occupation*

---

16 *Wspomnienia wojenne*, ms, the Archives of the Capital City of Warsaw, ref. no. 40, c. 25.
17 W. Hebenbrock, *Mit der NSV. nach Polen*, Berlin, 1941, pp. 49–50, 58, 95 (published by Zentralverlag der NSDAP).
18 Cf. T. Szarota, "The Reaction of Occupied Europe to the Stigmatization of the Jews with the Star of David", *Acta Poloniae Historica*, vol. XC, 2004, pp. 97–111.

Years, Ludwik Landau noted, as of 8th December 1939: "The armbands devised for the Jews are mostly being worn already – although a certain number of persons who are actually subject to the instruction are trying, driven by considerations of some sort, not to put on this signage. [...] Those wearing the armbands come across unpleasantness at times, be it from the Germans – there have reportedly been cases of armband-wearing individuals being thrown out of a tram, not to mention the constant 'catching for [forced] labour'; or, from the locals – in the form of assaults by striplings, etc.; what prevails, however, is an indifferent attitude, and as they say, kindness is manifested sometimes indeed."[19] It is a pity that signs of compassion and solidarity were so scarce then, while we regrettably see recurring assaults by juvenile hooligans on the Jews.

There is a line in the *Diary* of Adam Czerniaków, who led the Jewish religious community of Warsaw, dated 28th December 1939: "On the street a madwoman (!) in a white hospital gown is beating Jews."[20] The chronicler Emanuel Ringelblum noted, as of 2nd–3rd January 1940: "In Warsaw within the last two days, the Jews were getting beaten for failing to wear their armbands";[21] we are not told who did the beating, the Germans or the Poles. But we have no such doubt when it comes to reading a record made by Czerniaków on 4th January 1940: "Rinde [Bote] came to the office black-eyed from Nalewki Street and Wasserman arrived with a bloody nose that a street mob gave him at Teatralny Square when he came to the rescue of a Jew tormented by the crowd." On 27th January 1940, the same chronicler observed: "Jews were beaten up on Marszalkowska [Marszałkowska] and Poznanska [Poznańska] Streets during the day and in the evening"; and, on the following day: "At 2 p.m., a gang of teenage hooligans, which for the last several days had been beating up Jews, paraded in front of the Community offices breaking the windows in the houses on the other side of the street. An emissary

---

19 Edited by Zbigniew Landau and Jerzy Tomaszewski, vol. I, Warszawa, 1962, pp. 121–122.
20 *The Warsaw Diary of Adam Czerniaków. Prelude to Doom*, edited by Raul Hilberg, Stanislaw Staron, and Josef Kermisz, translated by Stanislaw Staron and the staff of Yad Vashem, New York, 1979, p. 103. This edition is not to be found in the National Library of Warsaw or in the Jewish Historical Institute. I have used a photocopy made available to me by Dr Marcin Urynowicz.
21 The fact that there is no complete English-language edition of the Ringelblum diary is hard to understand. *Notes from the Warsaw Ghetto*, published by Jacob Sloan (New York 1958), only contains fragments of the diary, with the notes of March 1940 missing. I have used the Polish edition, *Kronika getta warszawskiego: wrzesień 1939 – styczeń 1943*, edited and with an introduction by Artur Eisenbach, translated from the Yiddish by Adam Rutkowski, Warsaw 1983, p. 69.

of the Community, Engineer Friede, was beaten up by a second group at Elektoralna Street until he was bleeding." On that very same day, 28th January 1940, Ludwik Landau remarks as follows in his *Chronicle*: "The other method of political struggle applied by the occupiers is *inciting* anti-Semitic brawls [emphasis – T.S.]. These brawls, combined with the beating and robbing of Jews, have been lasting for a few days now, but assumed enormous proportions today. The people are unfortunately proving easily provoked, through which attitude the 'paving-of-the-way' by the former Polish governments is obviously expressed." Let us once again refer to the notes of the man who was later on to create the Ghetto's underground archive: "Yesterday, on 28th January, Polish gangs were roaming around: people were dragged out of the droshkies and beaten with *nahajkas* [whips] and 'bulls' [i.e., cowhides]. The beating took place on Leszno, Elektoralna, Orla, Królewska, Marszałkowska Streets, and elsewhere." Another record reads: "Today, the 30th, we have had a tough day to survive. In the Saxon Gardens [*Ogród Saski*], a gang of Polish hooligans aged fourteen to fifteen spotted me wearing an armband. I had a narrow escape from them, half-dead. [...] There is a Christian madwoman (a Russian, seemingly) still prowling on Marszałkowska St. She's running at the head of a gang of nippers. She assaults out of the blue, and beats severely. Yesterday, a few were heavily wounded, resulting from these rowdy assaults. [...] The anti-Semitic assaults *are organised by somebody* [emphasis – T.S.]. Young hooligans, nine, ten years old take part in them. They are afraid of repulsing them duly, although there are places (Karmelicka St.) where they are stood up to. *One of the Germans drove the gang* [emphasis – T.S.] that was pounding around."

In my opinion, the most perceptive commentary to these events is in the diary of Chaim Aron Kapłan, the outstanding pedagogue, Hebraist, and man of letters. Here is a record he made on 1st February 1940:

> No nation lacks hooligan elements, and the conquerors have paved the way for them. They have hinted that the Jews are expendable, that the government will not adhere to the letter of the law when the victims are Jews. And a hint is enough for hooligans. In the past few days there has been no end to attacks upon Jews in public places in broad daylight. The conquerors' eyes look on, but they are struck with blindness.[22]

Let us take a look again into Ringelblum's diary. Here is a record from 1st–2nd February 1940: "The assaults on Jews are happening on various streets; on Chłodna, Żelazna Sts. Assaults combined with robbery." As Adam Czerniaków noted, on

---

[22] *Scroll of Agony. The Warsaw Diary of Chaim A. Kaplan*, translated and edited by Abraham I. Katsh, New York–London 1965, p. 114.

4th February 1940: "I received a reply to my complaint about the incident of Jews being beaten up (tormented) by a madwoman, etc., from Kommandantur der Ordnungspolizei für den Distrikt Warschau: *'Ich teile mit, dass ich die mir erforderlich erscheinenden Anweisungen gegeben habe'* [I am informing you that I have issued the instructions that appeared necessary to me] (Feb.2.1940)." In his Polish edition of Czerniaków's *Diary*, Marian Fuks comments on this passage based on what he had learned from Julian Kulski, the then "commissary mayor". As Kulski recollects, "When I once interceded in writing with the German overseer (I cannot remember the date) about the assault by some dregs on the Jews in Długa St., I received from there a reply similar to that quoted by Czerniaków: 'The instructions for reinstating the order have been issued.' The other thing is that in this very case, the group of rogue men, no doubt inspired to assault by the Germans, had dispersed before then. There were no victims recorded at the time."[23] Four days later, the Judenrat chairman would inscribe the following record in his diary: "In the morning at the SS. They informed me that the madwoman in the streets will be restrained." But this was either delayed, or the anonymous anti-Semite began acting again, as we find in the Ringelblum diary this piece of news: "the madcap is rummaging again, she was picking on those who wore no armband." However, afterwards, for the next two weeks, there are no mentions in the sources of any other anti-Jewish actions whatsoever. The next piece of information is from Czerniaków's diary, dated 26th February 1940: "During evenings on Grzybowska Street, etc., teenagers are beating [people] up and extorting ransom." Early in the last ten days of March is when the next such mentions appear. This time, they concerned occurrences taking place on a much larger scale, reminding many observers of pogroms.

March 1940: The Easter occurrences. The sequence of incidents

For Christians, Easter is, on the one hand, a commemoration of the Crucifixion of Christ, and on the other, a feast of the miraculous Resurrection and Ascension. Since the Passion is chiefly associated with the persecutors, identified as the Jews insulting Jesus on his way up to Golgotha, it was easy to make references to anti-Jewish sentiments during Easter. In 1940, Good Friday, the day commemorating the Crucifixion, fell on 22nd March. On the following day, Ludwik Landau remarked in his diary: "It's Holy Saturday today, Easter is tomorrow. [...] Incidents

---

23 *Adama Czerniakowa dziennik getta warszwskiego, 6 IX 1939–23 VII 1942* [Adam Czerniaków's Diary of the Warsaw Ghetto, 6th September 1939–23rd July 1942], edited and with footnotes by M. Fuks, Warsaw 1983, p. 83.

of youngsters assaulting Jews, particularly women, are taking place, these being particularly used as opportunities for robbery, for that matter; but there are sometimes incidents of resolute response in defence of Jews on the part of non-Jewish passers-by." On that same day, 23rd March 1940, Emanuel Ringelblum noted: "On Leszno Street, on Żelaznej-Bramy Square, young hooligans were robbing people – eight-, nine-year-olds." These two notes do not differ much from those from the preceding months which I have already cited. On Easter Sunday, 24th March 1940, Adam Czerniaków wrote in his diary: "In the afternoon, on the Jewish streets, beatings of the Jews and window-breaking. A sort of pogrom."

This time, anti-Jewish disturbances occurred on a large scale indeed. "Beginning with Friday, [22nd] March," Ringelblum tells us in his diary, "until today, Thursday, [28th] March, excesses against the Jews have been taking place on nearly all the Jewish streets, in particular, on the streets bordering on the Jewish ghetto: on Leszno, Rymarska, Żabia Sts., Bankowy Sq., Graniczna St., Żelaznej-Bramy Sq. (a rally was held there the day before yesterday, at which anti-Jewish invectives were heard shouted), Grzybowska, Rynkowa, Żelazna, Chłodna, Mazowiecka Sts., and elsewhere. Jewish shops were plundered everywhere. [...] The stalls were robbed, the largest iron bars broken out. In the first days, they satisfied themselves with cracking the panes, later they began pillaging."

Before I refer to more chronicle notes, let me quote a fragment from the article "*Nie naśladować Niemców*" ("The Germans Must Not be Imitated"), published in what was probably the most popular conspiratorial periodical in occupied Warsaw, *Polska Żyje!*, an organ of the Headquarters of the Defenders of Poland.[24] This text is worthy of our attention for a number of reasons. It is the only source of information explaining the reasons behind the incidents. We read, "In the week after [probably, *before* – T.S.] Easter, the following incident occurred in Warsaw: A boy pinched an apple from a Jewish [orig., "jewish"] tradeswoman's stall. A few Jews rushed for him. Hunted him down. Thumped him to death. They killed a kid because he had stolen an apple. The Jews committed a crime. Today we cannot know whether the crime was committed thoughtlessly, or some 'other Satans were involved' and the happening was an act of tragic provocation. In any case, the crime did not elicit any punishment on the part of the authorities, whereas it triggered an outburst of spontaneous mob rule. They started breaking windows in Jewish shops, beating Jews, and looting the content of the smashed outlets. The striplings were throwing bricks at the throngs of Jews ['jews'] driven to labour. From the Jewish district, the riot moved to almost

---

24 Nos. 41–42, undated, of 27th March 1940 (according to my calculation).

the whole of the town. Excesses were going on all day long, without counteraction from the German authorities, who moreover offered them wide-ranging support." Further fragments of this text will be referred to as the story unfolds.

The news of the death of a Christian child will probably remain unverified. In all probability, the boy simply was beaten, but the rumour spread like wildfire that he had fallen victim to a murder that called for revenge and for the perpetrators to be punished. When exactly it happened is hard to determine. "In the week after Easter" seems to suggest it was Tuesday, 26th March, or any of the following days; based on Ringelblum's notes, one concludes that the incidents began earlier – on Friday, 22nd March. According to Czerniaków's note, the riot began on Sunday, 24th March. This same date – Easter Sunday and, simultaneously, the Jewish feast of Purim for the year 5700 – is referred to as the date the anti-Jewish riots began in Warsaw by Rabbi Szymon (Shimon) Huberband in his notes taken down during the war.[25] In his diary entry of 4th April, the novelist Stanisław Rembek, who resided near Warsaw but often visited his friends in the city, wrote: "I was told that on Holy Saturday, on Sunday, and on Monday, a pogrom against the Jews, *organised by the Germans* amongst some pretty little boys [emphasis – T.S.] was taking place in their quarter on Mirowski Square. They were dragged out of the trams and beaten to the extent that the streets were full of blood."[26] The date the pogrom began, as given by Ringelblum, is confirmed in a very important document – a memo sent on 5 April 1940 by the Polish Embassy in Rome to the Vatican's Secretariat of State. The relevant passage reads: "As we have been informed by various and completely reliable sources, certain groups organised, paid, and protected by the Gestapo attempted to rob Jewish shops in Warsaw, on Friday, 22nd March. The plunder was arranged on Good Friday in order to reaffirm the German legend whereby Catholic institutions during the Holy Week would have it as their purpose to provoke hatred toward Jews amidst Christians."[27]

---

25 Rabbi Shimon Huberband, *Kiddush Hashem. Jewish Religious and Cultural Life in Poland During the Holocaust*, edited by Jeffrey S. Gurock and Robert S. Hirt, translated by David E. Fishman, 1978, p. 55. I am indebted to Jacek Leociak, PhD, for having drawn my attention to this particular book.
26 S. Rembek, *Dziennik okupacyjny*, Warsaw 2000, p. 43.
27 *Le Saint Siège et la situation religieuse en Pologne et dans les Pays Baltes 1939–1945*, première partie 1939–1941, Città del Vaticano, 1967, p. 234 (series *Actes et Documents du Saint Siège relatifs à la Seconde Guerre Mondiale*, ed. Pierre Blet et al.). I am indebted to Dariusz Libionka, PhD, for having drawn my attention to this particular book.

Let us return to the information gathered by the chroniclers as the events unfolded. On Monday, 25th March 1940, Landau wrote: "The anti-Jewish riots continue and are growing. Today, a gang of striplings, mostly aged 14–15, went around the Jewish shops in the area of Marszałkowska Street, breaking the storefronts and robbing the goods. The passers-by kept a passive stance, fearing, probably, that any act on their part would cause them resentment, or even peril; there were no police, neither Polish nor German, to be seen anywhere around. It is hard to imagine that such incidents could be taking place contrary to the will of the German authorities. And if this is occurring with their knowledge, it is no less plausible that it is on their initiative."

Czerniaków, as usual, merely briefs us on what happens: "Pogroms on the streets. At the corner of Żurawia Street beatings and window-breakings. The hag that was beating the Jews is again roaming the streets." In the diary of Professor Stanisław Srokowski, a geographer, we read a description of the incidents that took place on that Monday on Elektoralna Street, near Hale Mirowskie ("Mirów Halls" – this name applied to a trade centre and/or its surrounding area, the Mirowski Market Square): "It was riff-raff with knives that took part in it, the Jewish shops were being destroyed, the Jews were beaten mercilessly. The Germans, who had staged it, were passively looking at all those things, needless to say." A note in the same diary, dated 26th March–3rd April 1940, reads: "The [anti-]Jewish riots, which began during Passion Week and reappeared after Easter, exhibited a scary view. Gangs of striplings were scampering around the half-Jewish districts, armed with sticks looking [all] the same, or with rubber batons, and, having broken the storefronts in one Jewish shop or another, did the robbing. They were often presided over by a German in uniform, summoning the rabble, while the other Germans were filming these scenes of plunder. Those filming were filmed too, so they say."[28]

Returning to the conspiratorial press, here is some news on the occurrences from *Biuletyn Informacyjny* of 29th March 1940: "Beginning with the second day of Easter [i.e., Monday, 25th March 1940 – T.S.], the several quarters and streets of Warsaw have every day been the scene of anti-Jewish disturbances. Children and striplings (aged 9 to 14) and suspicious individuals are breaking windows, initiating the pillage of shops, beating bloody any Jews passing by. The German authorities are not responding. The Polish police are trying to control the situation, to no avail. On Marszałkowska St. and in Wola [district], *filming of the incidents by*

---

28 *Zapiski Stanisława Srokowskiego. Wrzesień 1939 – sierpień 1944*, the Archives of Polish Academy of Sciences, Warsaw, typescript, ref. no. III-22, c. 62.

the Germans [emphasis – T.S.] has been confirmed. What we are dealing with are the typical dealings of German agents exploiting Polish anti-Semitism and the under-sophistication of the Polish masses – the action's goals are: (a) distraction of the masses from the occupiers; (b) 'sublimation' of the accumulated hatred for the Germans by shifting it against the Jews; (c) undermining the pro-Polish sentiments in the Allied countries and in the U.S.; (d) the splintering of the anti-German front within the country into groups fighting amongst themselves."

Szaniec, an underground magazine published by a formation of pre-war National Party activists, informed on 9th April 1940: "Beginning with 26th March 1940, the occupiers have been *arranging* [emphasis – T.S.] pogroms against the Jews in Warsaw. On a larger scale, such pogroms took place at the bazaars on Stalowa and Ząbkowska Streets, at Hale Mirowskie, at Kercelego Square, on Krochmalna Street, in the Old Town. Individual Jewish shops and apartments were smashed all around the town. Only one pattern was visible everywhere: gangs of street dregs were transported by lorries to the site of the pogrom, who under the leadership of the '*Volksdeutsches*' set about doing 'their work' in presence of the police and German gendarmerie. The gendarmes themselves attentively dressed the beaten and bloodied Jews in the street. The whole scene having been filmed, thee gangs were packed onto the vehicles and carried further on. Films of this sort, with an appropriate commentary, will go to America and the neutral countries so as to show the world how the 'bestial Polish gangs' treat the Jews and what Christian care is extended by the Germans to the Jews."[29]

On Tuesday, 26th March 1940, the already-quoted diary by Chaim Aron Kapłan contains the following passage:

> This year is a Jewish leap year, and so Easter comes about a month before Passover. The end of winter. Sun and ice. And now their holiday of Resurrection has turned into a time of panic for us. The eve of their desire has been made a time of trembling. But this is not the conquerors' doing. Whoever is successful has his work done for him by others, and therefore this is not the conquerors' doing. But it is done with their knowledge and consent, and according to some, under their "lofty" supervision. Never before have there been such days of chaos, upheaval, and confusion in the Polish capital as on the holiday of Easter, which this year fell on March 25. Christian "ethics" became conspicuous in life and then – woe to us! Someone organised gang after gang of hooligan adolescents, including also little ones who have not yet left their grade-school benches, to attack Jewish

---

29 Wojciech Jerzy Muszyński was the first to quote this article in his book *Duch młodych. Organizacja Polska i Obóz Narodowo-Radykalny w latach 1934–1944. Od studenckiej rewolty do konspiracji niepodległościowej*, Warsaw 2011, p. 242 (mentioning the issue but not specifying the date, which otherwise is important).

passers-by and give them murderous beatings. It was simply a hunt, in which Jews were hunted like animals in the forest. And what is there to deny? We are cowards! In cases such as this we have only one choice – to run away. And running away only adds courage to the attacking toughs. There is much ugliness in these attacks in broad daylight, in full view of the authorities who stand at a distance enjoying the sight of our torments.

On that same day, Adam Czerniaków noted: "More street beatings (at the vegetable market). I am forwarding a report to the proper authorities." We regrettably do not know who was to receive the letter of intervention. A few hours after writing this, Czerniaków was in Krakow leading a delegation of the Jewish Council, and where he took further steps in order to keep the Warsaw incidents in check. Yet, they continued, for the time being.

On Wednesday, 27th March 1940, Landau wrote: "The anti-Jewish incidents have not come to an end: yesterday, today, again these same gangs pillaged the shops in various regions of the town. A gang of quite small boys was led, it is said, by some older youth, a student, or something of the sort. Some observers of these incidents say they have seen a German car nearby, which was observing the course of the fracas." On that same day, the first and only news item about the riot was published in a "rag" – the German-published *Nowy Kurier Warszawski*. A text titled "Victims of brawls and assaults", featured in the column *Wczoraj w Warszawie* [Yesterday in Warsaw] informed its readers as follows: "On the second day of Easter [i.e., 25th March – T.S.], a total of six persons fell victim to brawls or assaults in various points of the city. These are: Wolf Gingold (29 Pawia St.), Abram Frydman (49 Stawki St.), Henoch Arensztajn (15 Nowolipie St.), Leon Łobżowski (77 Leszno St.), Edward Podlasin (60 Leszno St.), and Tadeusz Dąbrowski (58 Leszno St.). All the brawl and assault victims were aided at the Emergency Service dispensary." What this tells us is that the Jews defended themselves against the attackers, and clashes occurred at times. Before I resume this thread, some diary notes of relevance, from Thursday, 28th March 1940, will be quoted.

The author of *Chronicle of the War and Occupation Years* wrote as follows:

> Anti-Jewish incidents is the matter that has come to the fore in Warsaw most recently. These incidents have unfolded to a great extent, and so, the Jewish populace are living under threat again, and they are afraid of appearing in the streets in the main Jewish quarters. The shops are especially robbed – windows broken, appliances destroyed, and, primarily, commodity looted; but alongside these, apartments are falling victim to the attacks, and, all the more frequently, passers-by, who, recognised by their armbands, are beaten and robbed. All this is perpetrated by gangs roaming across the town, in the Jewish quarters and in the downtown area alike: on Franciszkańska St., on Leszno St., on Marszałkowska St., in Powiśle [district], in Praga [district]. The gangs are forces of up to 500 people, usually young striplings and various dregs. That *the Germans are staging*

these incidents [emphasis – T.S.] becomes increasingly clear. The taking of photographic and motion pictures by the Germans is commonly observed, and they are not concealing it at all; it happens that there is a German vehicle initially coming along, the film operators get off it, and only afterwards a crowd of robbers appears. Also Polish policemen were taken to participate in the action: at one spot, a policeman ordered that a closed shop be opened, and then told the awaiting crowd to take whatever they wanted; in any case, there has been no instance, anywhere, of the police intervening whatsoever. The same is true, after all, for the German police, quietly gazing at the action. [...] The goal of the actions is to incite the Christian and Jewish populace against each other, as well as to procure documents meant to excuse – well, put on a pedestal as the defenders of order, the avengers of the oppressed! – the Germans in the territory of Poland in the eyes of the foreign countries. This end will be served by the photographs and footage; also, this end will be served by the Jews calling on the Germans to protect them against the assaults of the Polish Christian people. The Germans have reportedly issued a secret instruction to the Jewish communities to officially request assistance; otherwise, the Germans have warned, the occurrences will be assuming increasingly considerable dimensions. These incidents are, besides, taking place not only in Warsaw but in various provincial towns. [...] As for the Jews, they are trying to defend themselves by organising self-help, a militia of a sort – weaponless, clearly enough – which is meant to defend the people and their possessions against the aggressors; but is that enough, or will the Jews finally find themselves forced to request the Germans, as the latter has demanded?

That the Germans exerted pressure on the Jews to "officially request assistance" from them is confirmed by a declaration submitted in Jerusalem, as of 12th May 1940, by a certain Doctor S.S., a fugitive from Warsaw. His account goes as follows:

> The chief of the labour office in the Jewish Community, Mr. Rozen, went to Brandt, the chief official of the Gestapo who is in control of the Jewish Community, asking him to intervene in the pogrom. Brandt assured Rozen that he would give an order to stop the disturbances, and that he could quietly return to the Community office. But when Mr. Rozen was on his way, just in front of the building of the Jewish Community, the hooligans dragged him from his car and began to beat him, breaking his hand and ribs.

As Adam Czerniaków's notes tell us, Hilel Rozen was beaten on 27th March 1940; the subsequent part of his account is crucial:

> When the Gestapo was again asked to give orders to stop the pogrom, the Germans demanded that the Jewish Community should send a written request asking the German authorities to act against the Poles. The Jews understood that the Germans wanted to obtain an anti-Polish document from the Jews and the Community refused to send such a request.[30]

---

30 This very important report was published in 1943 in the United States, in: *The Black Book of Polish Jewry. An Account of the Martyrdom of Polish Jewry Under the Nazi*

Some provincial regions indeed saw incidents similar to those in Warsaw. As the article "*Żydzi w 'Guberni'*" ["The Jews in the {General}gouvernement"] published in *Biuletyn Informacyjny* tells us, "At the same time when the pogrom provocations were taking place in Warsaw – identical incidents were found to appear in Piaseczno, Parczew, Lubartów, Międzyrzecz, etc. In one small town in Podlasie, Germans in civil attire used threats to force Jewish youth to throw snowballs at the people exiting a church."

Let us once again take a look at Ringelblum's diary. In a note dated 28th March 1940, we can read:

> Today, they did the pillaging on Karmelicka, Franciszkańska Streets. A genuine battle took place there between Jews and the hooligans. A Christian got killed there, supposedly. Stories are being told that many unregistered Jews were taken from that street. Today, whole gangs of detained hooligans were being led away. […] All were armed with sticks and twisted wires. Who is behind these excesses? It is believed that these incidents could have been prevented had there been a will to do so; or aborted, in the worst case. The best proof is that today in the afternoon the excesses were interrupted. The event was filmed, they filmed the moment the [German] soldiers were running out and driving the hooligans away. It often happened that soldiers would jump out of the trams to drive away the hooligans.

The news that the incidents came to an end turned out to be premature: in both Landau's and Ringelblum's diary, there appears, on Thursday, 28th March, a mention of Jews defending themselves. Perhaps Marek Edelman was the first to have said a little more about it. In his brochure *Getto walczy (udział Bundu w obronie getta warszawskiego)* [The Ghetto Fights. (How the Bund participated in the defence of the Warsaw Ghetto)], with an introduction penned by Zofia Nałkowska, we read:

> The world was to be shown that not only the Germans hated the Jews. Thus, during the Easter Holidays of 1940, pogroms lasting several days were instigated. The German Air Corps engaged Polish hoodlums for 4 zloty per "working day". The first three days the hooligans raged unopposed. On the fourth day the Bund militia carried out revenge actions. Four major street battles resulted in the following localities: Solna Street–Mirowski Market Square, Krochmalna Street—Grzybowski Square, Karmelicka Street–Nowolipie Street, and Niska Street–Zamenhofa Street. Comrade Bernard [Goldsztejn/Goldstein – T.S.] commanded all of these battles from his hide-out.

Occupation, Editor: Jacob Apenszlak, Co-Editors: Jacob Kenner, Dr. Isaac Lewin and Dr. Moses Polakiewicz, pp. 30–31. This collection of documents, almost forgotten today, was published as a result of the efforts of the American Federation for Polish Jews and the Association of Jewish Refugees and Immigrants from Poland.

The fact that none of the other active political parties took part in this action is significant as an example of the utter misconception of existing conditions common to Jewish groups at the time. What is more, all the other groups even opposed our action. It was, however, our determined stand that momentarily checked the Germans' activities and went on record as the first Jewish act of resistance.[31]

To comment on just two details: While German pilots did indeed participate in the riots, they certainly did not organise them or pay the attackers. And, although the end of these riots coincided with the appearance of Jewish self-defence groups, this was not the reason the excesses were unexpectedly interrupted.

In 1949, Bernard Goldstein, one of the self-defence organisers and member of the underground Central Management of the socialist Bund organisation, spoke through his memoirs *The Stars Bear Witness*, published in New York. We read:

> Groups of hooligans, mostly youths, stormed through the Jewish sections of Warsaw. They charged down the streets shouting, "Beat the Jews! Kill the Jews!" They broke into Jewish homes and stores, smashed furniture, seized valuables, and beat the occupants. In the district near the Polish Handicraft High School at 72 Leshno [Leszno] Street, the older students joined the pogrom as soon as school was out. [...]
>
> The Germans did not intervene. They neither helped nor hindered the pogromists. We saw many smiling German camera men recording the scenes with relish. We later learned that the pictures appeared in German magazines. They were also shown in movie theaters as graphic evidence that the Poles were winning their freedom from Jewish domination.
>
> We were immediately besieged by requests from comrades that something be done. An emergency meeting of the Bund collective was held in my apartment at 12 Novolipya [Nowolipie Street], and we discussed the possibility of active resistance. Over us hung the danger of the German doctrine of collective responsibility. Whatever we might do to hinder the pogromists could bring terrible German vengeance on all the Jews of the city. Despite that danger, we concluded that we had no choice – we must strike back.
>
> We decided to fight back with "cold weapons" – iron pipes and brass knuckles, but not with knives or firearms. We wanted to reduce the danger that a pogromist might be killed accidentally. We hoped in this way to teach the hooligans a lesson and to minimize the possibility that the Germans would inflict some terrible punishment on the entire Jewish community.
>
> Every fighting contingent was mobilized – slaughterhouse workers, transport workers, party members. We organized them into three groups: one near the Mirovsky [Mirowski] Market, another in the Francis[z]kanska-Nalefky [Nalewki]-Zamenhof[a]

---

31 M. Edelman, *Getto walczy. Udział Bundu w obronie getta warszawskiego*, Warsaw, pp. 8–9. Although the text was republished several times afterwards, the full name of "Comrade Bernard" was never given.

[Streets'] district, and the third in the Leshno–Karmelitzka–Smotcha [Leszno–Karmelicka–Smocza] district. When the pogromists appeared in these sections on the following morning they were surprised to find our comrades waiting for them. A bloody battle broke out immediately. Ambulances rushed to carry off wounded pogromists. Our own wounded were hidden and cared for in private homes to avoid their arrest by Polish or German police. The fight lasted for several hours against many waves of hooligans and raged throughout a large portion of the Jewish quarter.

The battle kept shifting to various parts of the city. Our organised groups were joined spontaneously by other workers.[32]

A harrowing description of the Easter pogrom is contained in the aforementioned notes of Rabbi Shimon Huberband. Here is what he says:

> On Shushan Purim and the week after the holiday, the attacks by young *goyim* took on horrifying dimensions. Scores and hundreds of shops were robbed and vandalized on Zelazna [Żelazna], Graniczna, Zabia [Żabia], Zelaznej [Żelaznej] Bramy, and other streets. The attacks were of such broad scope in every neighborhood that on Zabia Street the Polish merchants placed Christian icons in their shopwindows and hung pictures of saints on their doors to show that these weren't Jewish shops. A large number of Jews were badly beaten and wounded in all parts of the city. There was also talk that a Jewish woman had been killed by the Poles at Zelaznej Bramy. Due to the current relations it is difficult to establish how much truth there is to this rumor.
>
> The young *goyim* were organised in groups of fifteen to twenty, and were armed with stones and clubs. It is noteworthy that a large number of women participated in the attacks. Every organized group of the attackers was followed by a mob of people who stole the merchandise from shops, after the display-windows were bashed in. There were also attacks on Nalewki Street, but to a lesser extent, because the *goyim* met resistance from the Jews there.

Rabbi Huberband tells us that the Jewish self-defence was organised "two days after Purim", i.e., on 26th March 1940; what we moreover learn from him is that the group of young Jews who tackled the attackers was formed by a certain Henryk Lublin. They received support on Franciszkańska Street, and there is where a real battle was fought:

> They attacked the *goyim* from all sides. Bricks, stones and pieces of concrete were thrown at them from the bombed-out buildings. Many Poles were wounded. All that remained on the "battlefield" were some sacks which the *goyim* and *shikses* had taken

---

32 B. Goldstein, *The Stars Bear Witness*, translated and edited by Leonard Shatzkim, New York, 1949, pp. 52–53. Let me point out that the French edition of these memoirs, i.e., *Cinq années dans le ghetto de Varsovie*, Bruxelles, 1962, pp. 23–25, is far from identical with the English version I quote herein.

along to fill with stolen Jewish goods, some clubs which they had brought to beat Jews, and one dead *goy*.[33]

In his already-quoted *Polish-Jewish Relations*, Emanuel Ringelblum quotes an account from an eyewitness of the Franciszkańska Street struggle:

> A crowd of 200 to 300 people, armed with sticks, clubs and crow-bars, moved along under the command of young airmen with guns in their hands. Older Aryans brought up the rear of the procession; they directed the disturbance, were in constant communication with the Germans and gave instructions to the band of rowdies. The mob broke plate glass windows on the way. Inside the entrances to blocks of flats stood groups of Jews armed with sticks and clubs, ready for defence. At the corner of Franciszkanska and Walowa [Wałowa] Streets, the herd of hooligans came up against a group of a few score Jewish workers, armed with the picks they use to break up ice. Fighting broke out in which one hooligan was killed and two Jews.

An obituary of the Christian Pole killed by the Jews ought to have been published in *Nowy Kurier Warszawski*, the newspaper issued by the Germans in occupied Warsaw. If someone like that had really been killed, such a fact would have without a doubt been used for propaganda purposes. In spite of my efforts, I have found no such obituary published.

Let us look at the chroniclers' notes once again. Here is Ludwik Landau's entry for Friday, 29th March 1940:

> Anti-Jewish riots have formed a whole train of incidents. They keep on occurring, growing increasingly ferocious. The shops in the Jewish districts have been smashed to a pulp. [...] There are many wounded people, some reportedly have been killed – in any case, there was some Christian boy from the group of attackers killed, struck by a stone somewhere on Franciszkańska St. or Bonifraterska St. The Jewish Community was mobbed for a few hours by an enormous crowd, so the Community workers could only leave their offices under the protection of German gendarmes. Thus, the Germans' activity as defenders of the Jews against the Polish Christian populace has already commenced. Other places, too, have reportedly seen incidents of German actions brought against gangs they had themselves organised – such actions being coupled with merciless beating. And these actions were photographed – as examples of German actions in defence of order (in a few cases, rare as they were, Polish policemen trying to intervene were beaten by the German police; the police have for the most part, admittedly, shown all their good will toward the "Jew-busters"). But this is not the point where it ends. There have been, it is said, numerous detentions amidst the intelligentsia milieu. All the men from several houses on Złota St. were reportedly arrested – there are rumours about the discovery of some radio-station.

---

33 Huberband, op. cit., pp. 56–57.

In reality, what we are dealing with in this particular case are the consequences of a clash at 3 Sosnowa Street – "the first," according to Tomasz Strzembosz, "better recognised skirmish between representatives of the Underground and the Nazi police";[34] in parallel, this marked the beginning of the ill-famed *AB-Aktion*, directed at representatives of the Polish leadership classes, a subject I shall return to later on.

In his note dated 29th March, Landau remarks that "there are rumours again about building up the ghetto in Warsaw." As Ringelblum noted on the same day, "It was [...] quiet today, just some rare, isolated assaults on Jews. 16 skull trepanations were carried out at the Jewish hospital. Many Jews were arrested on Franciszkańska St., for some Christian had got killed in a tussle." This comes as a confirmation of the news about one fatality in the riots. Ringelblum, moreover, makes a note on the rumours about the ghetto: "Today, rumours were arriving that the fences around the ghetto will be replaced by walls." On Friday, 29th March, early in the morning, Adam Czerniaków returned from Krakow, and noted in his diary: "After the arrival, I stopped at the SS. In the Community new Instructions about the walling up of the ghetto, preparing a shelter for 3,000 persons expelled from the Reich."

On the following day, the chroniclers wrote down as follows. Ringelblum: "Today, 30th of March, the news has been confirmed that the Jewish Community received an instruction to have walls built in the places where barbed wire had hitherto been, separating the *Seuchengebiet* from the other areas. [...] Pertinacious rumours about the ghetto." Czerniaków: "From the very morning, rumours about the ghetto. [...] Later with Leist, I submitted Richter's instructions about establishing the Jewish postal service, the shelter for the 3,000 expellees from the Reich and our own letter about the virtual impossibility of building a wall (damaging the water installations, electric and telephone cables, etc.)." This information about the visit at the SA-Oberführer Ludwig Leist is very important, as four days earlier Leist had been appointed "plenipotentiary of the Head of the District for the City of Warsaw"; the Head of the District, Dr Ludwig Fischer, the Governor, assumed the function of "*Stadthauptmann*". I will revisit the issue of competence disputes amongst the German occupational authorities, that is, the civil administration, the military, and the police.

I would like to quote now a record in Ludwik Landau's *Chronicle* from Saturday, 30th March 1940: "The anti-Jewish disorders came to a halt as suddenly as is only

---

[34] T. Strzembosz, *Akcje zbrojne podziemnej Warszawy 1939–1944*, 2nd ed., Warsaw 1983, pp. 117–118.

possible with occurrences staged by the authorities. Detentions began in parallel, in massive size. [...] Individually selected persons are getting arrested: political activists from PPS [Polish Socialist Party], from the former *Falanga* [a faction of the extreme rightist organisation National Radical Camp (ONR), led before the war by Bolesław Piasecki – T.S.] (a certain Świetlicki and a certain Kozłowski, the organisers of the anti-Jewish gangs on behalf of the Germans), physicians, [...] attorneys, teachers. But besides these, there reportedly were, as they tell us from various points, mass-scale detentions, [the inhabitants of] entire buildings being taken prisoner. [...] Round-ups were carried out in the streets as well. [...] About the source of these detentions, there exist most varied interpretations. Due to the coincidence in timing, one of the versions ties this case with the anti-Jewish disturbances: they apparently would be repressive measures for the fighting, particularly, for the killing of the Christian boy, repressive measures targeted at the two sides. The arrest of the ONR-men, among other things, points to this possibility. But it does not seem that such extensive detentions in this connection and with this origin of the occurrences would make sense." Landau is obviously right. The German AB-Aktion, the extraordinary pacification action (*Ausserordentliche Befriedungsaktion*), was rooted completely somewhere else. On 1st April 1940, the day following the cessation of the anti-Jewish riots in Warsaw, Czerniaków mentions the following in his diary: "On orders of the *Ordnungspolizei*, we started digging the ditches in preparation for wall construction at 7 a.m.. [...] The walls must be built in several parts of the city." Three days later, the Germans told the Judenrat chairman, "The walls are being ordered to defend the Jews against excesses." A brilliant example of cynicism, that incidentally reveals the true purpose behind the pogrom.

The Poles: organisers and participants of the riots

The first mentions of the presumed organisers of the anti-Jewish disturbances in Warsaw that took place around Easter 1940 appear in Ludwik Landau's diary. As he wrote on 27th March 1940, "It is rumoured that these gangs have been organised by an association called '*Atak*' ['Attack'], specialising in anti-Semitic action, clearly totally favoured by the Germans, as attested by the inscriptions on the placards they are distributing for shops calling for the boycott of Jews." He adds on the following day: "The organisers of the gangs are reportedly: the anti-Semitic group '*Atak*' and the group of Prof. Cybichowski and his comrades – former ONR-men, etc."

We know very little of the mysterious "*Atak*" group. *Biuletyn Informacyjny* of 19th January 1940 was the first to mention it: "'*Atak*' – this is the name of an anti-Semitic publishing house (114 Marszałkowska St., apt. 5), which is apparently modelled after its 'fraternal' *Stürmer*. Its first work is window stickers featuring a drawing of a coupled axe and cross." Let us immediately rectify this: the model, if any, would rather have been *Angriff*, the name of a publishing house run by Joseph Goebbels, which in Polish would be "*Atak*", rather than Julius Streicher's weekly. If I am not mistaken, there is no occupation-period print preserved the public public collections that bearing the signature of "*Atak*" or sealed with an axe and a cross. Although this is rather improbable, one cannot exclude that prints of this kind might be part of a private collection.

Who were the members of "*Atak*"? What was their origin? Did the group emerge during the German occupation, or before the war? The solution to this puzzle came to mind as I read another related record in Landau's diary. As we learn from the note dated 1st April 1940, "*Atak*" continued its activities, "distributing placards featuring the *Krzyżtopór* symbol (an axe coupled with a cross) and the initials 'G.O.J. (*Gospodarczą organizujmy jedność* ['Organise Economic Unity!'; the acronym possibly also reads 'goy'] to dwellings and shops." I would have perhaps failed in my attempts to decipher the origins of all these names, signs, and symbols, had I not learned from Stanisław Potrzebowski's book on the pagan organisation *Zadruga* about the relations between the group's ideologist Jan Stachniuk and the outstanding sculptor Stanisław Szukalski, and about the publishing by the latter in 1920 of a brochure bearing the astonishing title *Atak Kraka* ("Krak's attack").[35]

Although the word "attack" immediately brought to my mind an association with the name of the anti-Semitic group of 1940, it was only when Dr. Anna Landau-Czajka drew my attention to the periodical *Krak*, published in the 1930s, that I was able to conclusively solve the enigma.[36] When I saw the issue of *Krak* from December 1937 at the National Library, I could not believe my eyes: the outer, title cover featured a drawing of a *Toporzeł* ("Axe-and-Eagle"), whereas the back cover displayed not only the word *Topokrzyż* ("Axe-and-Cross") but also a drawing of the symbol with the initials "G.O.J." (See Fig. 1) – which was precisely the acronym, and its explication, as quoted by Landau, with an additional explanation that it is "The sign of Christian establishments, shops, and residences." The following accompanying text was attached: "We have not been allowed to

---

35 S. Potrzebowski, „Zadruga': eine völkische Bewegung in Polen, Bonn, 1982, pp. 46–47.
36 The brochure *Atak Kraka* can be regarded as the first issue of *Krak* magazine. Its subsequent issue was published in June 1930, mentioning as places of publication: Krakow, Warsaw, Lwów, Poznań, Łódź, and Wilno. The periodical's publication was discontinued two years later and was afterwards reinstated in Katowice in 1937; its 1938 vignette reads "Katowice–Warsaw–Poznań".

mark the Jewish shops, to make them distinct from the Polish ones. What we therefore propose is to label Polish companies with the emblem of the *Topokrzyż*, a specimen of which is reproduced above. The effect will be the same. […] So, let's fight Jewry under the slogan 'G.O.J.' – 'Organise Economic Unity!'"

Figure 1: A sign with the "Topokrzyż" ("Axe-and-Cross") symbol that Warsaw anti-Semites distributed for "Aryan" shops in early 1940

Figure 2: *The article* "Nie naśladować Niemców" *("The Germans Must Not be Imitated") from the underground publication Polska Żyje! (no. 41–42, most likely of 27th March 1940)*

Nr. 41 - 42

POLSKA ŻYJE!

Biuletyn informacyjny Obrońców Polski

NIE NAŚLADOWAĆ NIEMCÓW!

W tygodniu poświątecznym w Warszawie zaszedł następujący wypadek: Chłopiec ściągnął handlarce żydówce jabłko ze straganu. Kilku żydów pognało za nim. Dopadli. Zatłukli na śmierć. Zabili dziecko za to, że ukradło jabłko.

Żydzi popełnili zbrodnię. Nie dociekamy dziś, czy zbrodnia ta została popełniona bezmyślnie, czy też „inni szatani byli tam czynni", a całe zajście stanowiło tragiczną prowokację? W każdym bądź razie, zbrodnia nie wywołała kary ze strony władz, natomiast pociągnęła wybuch odruchowego samosądu tłumu. Jęto tłuc szyby w sklepach żydowskich, bić żydów i grabić zawartość rozbitych sklepów. Wyrostki obrzucali cegłami gromady żydów pędzonych na roboty. Z dzielnicy żydowskiej rozruchy przeniosły się na całe prawie miasto. Przez cały dzień trwały ekscesa, którym władze niemieckie nie tylko nie przeciwdziałały, lecz okazywały daleko idące poparcie. Niemieccy oficerowie przystawali by fotografować i filmować zajścia. (zdjęcia te odpowiednio zmontowane obiegną niewątpliwie w najbliższych dniach różne ekrany i prasę neutralną). Żołnierze niemieccy zachęcali rozjuszony tłum: bierzcie, bierzcie sobie. Po co mają to mieć „Juden". (Podobno Niemcy płacą po 5 zł. na głowę za wszczynanie awantur).

I to stanowisko okupantów, te słowa życzliwej zachęty, powinny były niby strumień zimnej wody natychmiast otrzeźwić i opamiętać manifestantów. Tych rzeczy bowiem czynić nie wolno! Wszelkie pogromy muszą być kategorycznie potępione przez całe polskie społeczeństwo. Podobne zajścia są szkodliwe, zarówno

z punktu widzenia etyki chrześcijańskiej, jak interesu narodowego. Zbrodnia była straszna i należało domagać się za nią najsroższej kary, lecz kary słusznej, spadającej na istotnych winowajców, nie samosądu, połączonego z grabieżą. Grabież nie może być nigdy narzędziem sprawiedliwości. Samosąd jest ślepy i dlatego jest zawsze Złem. Samosąd nie zamyka sprawy, lecz otwiera długi łańcuch zemsty i bezprawia.

A przedewszystkiem: Nie wolno nam naśladować Niemców! Nie wolno czynić nic co uzyskuje ich poparcie i pomoc. Nie wolno nam przejmować ich zasad, metod, poglądów. Nie zamykamy oczu na niebezpieczeństwo żydowskie. Wiemy jakie stanowisko zajęli Żydzi względem Polaków pod okupacją sowiecką. Wiemy i pamiętamy. W odbudowanym wolnym domu ojczystym, nie będzie miejsca i dla tych okupantów. Potrafimy uwolnić się od nich. Nie będziemy jednak nigdy uciekać się do niemieckiego systemu okrucieństwa i grabieży. Nie staniemy się mordercami i złodziejami. Karać będziemy sprawiedliwie. Walczyć jak ludzie, nie jak zbrodniarze.

Precz z metodami niemieckimi!

After becoming acquainted with the periodical *Krak*, it was time to find out more about Stanisław Szukalski (1895–1987), his life and artistic output, and the artistic group he led – *Szczep Rogate Serce*.[37] The designer of a national temple of *Duchtynia*, modeled after the Germanic Walhalla, and of the national emblem of *Toporzeł*,[38] an artist who incessantly referred to Poland's Slavic and pagan past, Szukalski felt underappreciated in Poland. He believed the reason was the cosmopolitan stance of the local art critics, whom he saw as centred on the West, believing that Jews or people of Jewish descent prevailed among them. At some point, the following slogan appears in his political commentaries: "Down with communism – in the world; with the old – in social life; with the Jews – in Poland; with the clergy – in politics!"[39]

Lechosław Lameński, Szukalski's biographer, helped me to make contact with one of "Stach of Warta's" two remaining students. Marian Konarski, a painter, wrote me in a letter of 16th March 1993: "When the slogan came into being to defend Polish trade in Polish society, especially small-scale trading, against the well-organised supremacy of Jewish trade, he [Szukalski – T.S.] drew, on someone's request, the so-called *Topokrzyż* with the abbreviation 'G.O.J.'. And that's it. He never partook in any action – he left for America after the defeat of Warsaw in 1939." I have not managed to discover who commissioned the symbol. In his next letter, dated 25th March 1993, Mr. Konarski added: "I assert that neither in late 1939, nor during the occupation at all, were any of the members of *Szczep*, myself included, in Warsaw. And before the war, there were ten of us still alive. [...] A few were mobilised for the army, the rest worked for the conspiracy. I was with the ZWZ [Union of Armed Struggle] – later on, with the AK [Home Army] – with the Kedyw ["Directorate for Subversion", an underground movement, part of the AK] of Krakow."

Thus, the sign of the *Topokrzyż*, as composed by Szukalski and featured in his periodical *Krak*, can be seen as a kind of paid announcement of some anti-Semitic group, which used the slogan "Organise Economic Unity!" to implement racial segregation. Since *Krak* was published in Katowice, it might be presumed that the group in question operated in Silesia, associated, perhaps,

---

37 Of great help to this end is Szukalski's extensive and very reliable biography penned by Lechosław Lameński, *Stach z Warty Szukalski i Szczep Rogate Serce*, Lublin, 2007, pp. 506.
38 M. Myśliński, "Toporzeł – nowy herb Polski projektu Stanisława Szukalskiego", *Biuletyn Polskiego Towarzystwa Heraldycznego*, June 2003, pp. 1–7; and, *ibidem*, S.K. Kuczyński, "Jeszcze o znaku Toporła", pp. 8–10.
39 *Krak*, December 1937, p. 10; cf. Lameński, op. cit., p. 223.

with the *Kuźnica* periodical; its members, possibly displaced by the Germans, continued their activity in early 1940 in Warsaw. If I am not mistaken, nobody used the *Topokrzyż* in the following years or after the war.[40] There was, however, another sign, also designed by S. Szukalski: *Toporzeł* became the name of a publishing house set up in 1990 in Wroclaw to reedit and publish the writings of Jan Stachniuk and popularise the ideas of the pagan *Zadruga*.[41]

Let us come back, however, to the note of 28th March 1940 in Landau's diary. Along with "*Atak*", the organisers of the anti-Jewish riots in Warsaw he mentions included "the group of Prof. Cybichowski and his comrades – former ONR-men." The following day, *Biuletyn Informacyjny* found that the German agency delivering the invader's political and propagandist goals "is the part of *Falanga* which for a long time now has been endeavouring to become the nucleus of a Polish national-socialist party. Its supervisor: Andrzej Świetlicki, organiser of ONR armed bands, a German contract agent. Its patrons: the Rev. Trzeciak, a pathological anti-Semite, and Cybichowski, former prof.[essor] at the University of Warsaw, known from the trial regarding examination bribery at the Faculty of Law."

I will first present the last of these three figures. Professor Zygmunt Cybichowski (1879–1945) was a world-renowned scholar specialising in international law who had lectured at Warsaw University since 1916. He studied in Berlin, Paris, and Strasburg, where he obtained his doctoral degree. He had lectures at a number of European universities to his credit, and held a honorary doctorate from New York's Columbia University.[42] He was considered a Germanophile; he attended a nationalists' convention in Berlin in 1934. Although he rejected Nazi racist ideology, he opted in a book published in 1939, for a "separation of the Polish Nation

---

40 The last mention of the emblem I encountered was in E. Ringelblum's notes of 20th April to 1st May 1940: "A new association, 'Topór i Krzyż' ['Axe and Cross'], has been established in Warsaw and tasked with releasing the Polish community from the Jewish influence." Should we conjecture that the aforesaid *Atak* association continued to operate under a new name after the anti-Jewish incidents?

41 Published as reprints, entitled *Dzieje bez dziejów* and *Zagadnienie totalizmu*, respectively.

42 Cf. S. Łoza, *Czy wiesz, kto to jest*, Warsaw, 1938, p. 114; *Wielka Encyklopedia Powszechna PWN*, Warsaw, 1962, vol. 2, p. 643. For the most precise information on Z. Cybichowski's career as a scholar, cf. A. Śródka, P. Szczawiński, *Biogramy uczonych polskich*, part I: *Nauki społeczne*, Warszawa, 1983, pp. 240–242. Neither these authors, nor K. Pol, author of a text on Cybichowski within a "lexicon of Polish lawyers" series, published in the *Rzeczpospolita* daily (14th October 1999), mention the occupation-period of this character's biography. Cybichowski was the Pole who on the 7th of November, 1939, gave Hans Frank a tour of Wawel Castle: H. Frank, *Im Angesicht des Galgens*, Munich 1953, p. 427.

from the Jews," and the emigration of the latter. He considered communism to be a "degenerated form of cosmopolitism." Based on what the Polish Underground could learn about him, his attitude after Germany's invasion of Warsaw aroused much objection. Making use of his acquaintances from before the war, he was said to have proposed to them that they establish a judicature, procuring the post of a judge with the Court of Appeals, and obtaining an apartment for himself, which had retrieved from professor Stefan Baley.[43]

In connection with the anti-Jewish riots in Warsaw, Emanuel Ringelblum noted in his diary on 30th March 1940: "It is said they have talked to Prof. Cybichowski, the leader of *Falanga*, who reportedly declared that assaults on Jews are part of an age-old Polish tradition." Let me recall that the name *Falanga* has already appeared in this context, when Ludwik Landau noted the arrest of some activists of "the former *Falanga*" on the same date, 30th March 1940. The name refers to an organisation that was formed in 1934 and managed by Bolesław Piasecki, in the aftermath of the dissent that had occurred within what was called the National Radical Organisation (the other faction of which was named ONR–ABC). Even if the ideology professed by *Falanga* could meet Prof. Cybichowski's expectations, he was not connected with the organisation before the war: for instance, his name is missing in Prof. Szymon Rudnicki's fundamental monograph on the history of the ONR.[44]

Jerzy Cybichowski, Zygmunt's son, was definitely a member of *Falanga*; he will reappear in this story. Ringelblum's afore-quoted description of Prof. Z. Cybichowski as "the leader of *Falanga*" clearly does not refer to the pre-war organisation but rather to a follow-up entity formed by some of *Falanga*'s former activists, patently, in agreement with the occupiers.

In his note of 7th March 1940, Ludwik Landau remarks that on behalf of former ONR-men, "Prof. Cybichowski – disgraced a few years ago in the ugly case of fees charged for unofficial examinations, an expert in international law, whilst, apart from that, an outstandingly narrow-minded man, a megalomaniac who

---

43 In 2004, Prof. Szymon Rudnicki found in the archives of the National Remembrance Institute [IPN] documentation (not used to date by historians) concerning the "detailed inquiry" of former members of "the pro-German organisation 'NOR'" (ref. no. 0644/421, cc. 1–7). An extant Underground report dated 27th March 1940 lists the names of members of the Central Board; Prof. Z. Cybichowski is mentioned first. There are later-dated reports on him as well. I will come back to this very important documentation.
44 S. Rudnicki, *Obóz Narodowo-Radykalny. Geneza i działalność*, Warsaw 1985.

strives at any cost to perform a political role – is to create a Polish national-socialist party." Another note regarding him was put down on 18th March: "For some time, […] persistent, though it seems to me not-quite-plausible, rumours have been circulating amongst us about the invaders' intents to create, right now, a 'Polish government' and about parleys being held with various persons on these matters. Among others, the name of Cybichowski is mentioned, who, according to other news, has been nominated leader of a Polish Hitlerite party." Here is a note from *Biuletyn Informacyjny* of 5th April 1940: "Amongst those arrested on 30th March is Prof. Cybichowski, member of the Central Board of the National Radical Organisation [NOR], a group formed in Warsaw by the Germans, as a 'Polish' edition of national socialism. We cannot say whether this results from non-harmonised activities of the German authorities mutually clashing against one another, or is proof of some transformation. The closing by the Gestapo of the NOR office at 20 Ujazdowskie Ave. in the middle of March supports the latter possibility." Professor Cybichowski was released some time afterwards, but his stay in prison had apparently cured him of any belief in the possibility of cooperation with the occupiers. Let me point out that the last quoted entry mentions the name of the National Radical Organisation for the first time; as it will soon become apparent, this entity can be seen as an attempt at a continued functioning of the former ONR–*Falanga*, under the occupation. The conspiratorial magazine *Polska Żyje!* noted in its issue no. 45–46 of April 1940, that Prof. Zygmunt Cybichowski was "collaborating with the Germans and arousing indignation among the public by his conduct."

No one would have dared say anything like this about Jerzy, the professor's son. A student before the war, he was a member of ONR's Combat Section, and the one who prevalently contributed to unmasking Stanisław Brochwicz-Kozłowski as a German agent. The latter was set free in September 1939, and around 10th December 1939 caused the young Cybichowski's arrest, having met him in the street. On 2nd May 1940, he was deported to the Oranienburg-Sachsenhausen concentration camp, and after a few weeks was transported back to Warsaw and put in Pawiak prison; soon afterwards, he was released, probably on the intervention of his father. He soon afterwards joined the ranks of underground fighters and became editor of the conspiratorial magazine *Do broni!* He was killed in a skirmish on 13th May 1943.[45]

---

45 Cf. Z. Przetakiewicz, *Od ONR-u do PAX-u. Wspomnienia*, Warsaw 1984, p. 38; R. Domańska, *Pawiak. Więzienie Gestapo*, Warsaw, 1978, pp. 53, 68; also, posthumous reminiscence penned by Mieczysław Kurzyna, in: *Dziś i Jutro*, no. 43 (49) of

The Rev. Stanisław Trzeciak (1873–1944) is no doubt a figure that deserves a reliable scholarly biography.[46] The son of a peasant, he got his PhD in Theology in 1900 at the Jagiellonian University in Krakow, and subsequently deepened his knowledge in the university hubs of Freiburg, Bern, Rome, Vienna, and Munich. From 1907 to 1918, he held the Chair of the Holy Scripture of the New Testament at the Saint Petersburg Theological Academy. In the 1930s, he published a few unambiguously racist and anti-Jewish books, of which *Program światowej polityki żydowskiej* [A programme for the international Jewish policy] of 1936 would be mentioned years later by Tadeusz Mazowiecki as a "classical reading of Polish anti-Semitism."[47] In parallel, this priest proved himself to be prolific author of articles demanding that Jews be disenfranchised in Poland, barred from official employment, the military, the press and the film industry, or purchasing land – and ultimately, removed from Poland following expropriation. In 1939, he did not hesitate to propose that the Jews be marked with a "yellow patch" and that ghettos be built for them.[48] Hitler's activities in the Third Reich were for him the fulfilment of a "providential mission"; even Stalin won a favourable verdict from him, as he had eliminated Trotsky, the Jewish "criminal brawler".[49] These utterances came to be perceived, at some point, as symptoms of an outright pathological obsession, with one of the Catholic magazines urging him to undergo treatment.

3rd November 1946. See also a biography of Jerzy Cybichowski, in: Kunert, A.K., *Słownik konspiracji warszawskiej*, vol. 3, Warsaw 1991, pp. 57–58.

46 The most comprehensive text on the Rev. Stanisław Trzeciak is by Jarosław Rokicki, "Ks. dr Stanisław Trzeciak (1873–1944). Szkic biograficzny", [in:] *Biuletyn Żydowskiego Instytutu Historycznego*, 1999, no. 2 (190), pp. 43–54; cf. R. Żebrowski, "Trzeciak Stanisław", [in:] *Polski Słownik Judaistyczny*, vol. 2, Warsaw 2003, p. 741.

47 The article "Antysemityzm ludzi łagodnych i dobrych" was first published in the *Więź* monthly in 1960 and, afterwards, in the book *Druga twarz Europy*, 2nd ed., Warsaw 1990, p. 63.

48 A number of texts by S. Trzeciak have been quoted and discussed by Anna Landau-Czajka, PhD, in her *W jednym stali domu... Koncepcje rozwiązania kwestii żydowskiej w publicystyce polskiej lat 1933–1939*, Warsaw 1998, p. 240. He had the book *Ubój rytualny w świetle Biblii i Talmudu* [On ritual slaughter in light of the Bible and the Talmud], 1935, and *Talmud o gojach a kwestia żydowska w Polsce* [On what the Talmud says about the goyim, in the context of the Jewish question in Poland], 1939, published to his credit.

49 J. Tazbir, *Protokoły mędrców Syjonu. Autentyk czy falsyfikat*, Warsaw 1992, p. 96. The author points out that S. Trzeciak was among "perhaps the most zealous defenders of the claim" that the *Protocols of the Elders of Zion* was an authentic document.

A year before the war broke out, the Rev. Stanisław Trzeciak was moved by Church authorities from St. Hyacinth's Church to St. Anthony's Church, his former parish being entrusted to the Rev. Kazimierz Puder, a priest of Jewish descent. Those from the extreme right were indignant about this; in the atmosphere that had developed around it, on 3rd July 1938, a shoemaker called Rafał Michalski slapped the priest in the face as he was holding a service in the church. This incident strongly reverberated in almost the entire press of the period. *Dziennik Ludowy* of 5th July alluded that "the Rev. S. Trzeciak nowise concealed his hatred toward the Rev. T. Puder, he did his best to impede his successor's priestly service."[50] Let us hope, though, that there was no relation between Trzeciak and the shoemaker, who apparently was simply mentally ill.

Knowing Stanisław Trzeciak's views, and knowing the fact that he travelled in the thirties to Nazi Germany where he was recognised as a specialist in "Jewish matters" and, above all, in the Talmud, it is really no surprise that his name appeared among those making an attempt at establishing a Polish counterpart of the NSDAP. It is, however, not certain and it may even be deemed doubtful that he would have contributed to the organisation of the anti-Jewish actions in the spring of 1940. It should be pointed out that in 1937 he published an article entitled "Potęga Polski bez Żydów. Nie gwałtem lecz odseparowaniem się wywalczy sobie Polak niezależny byt" (A powerful Poland without Jews. Poles to gain independent existence not by violence but by separation), where he described anti-Semitic wrangles as the work of the Jews themselves, who desired to arouse compassion for themselves in Polish society.[51] It cannot, however, be precluded that someone, the Germans perhaps, could have persuaded him that anti-Jewish

---

50 The book by the Rev. H. Linarcik, *Ks. Tadeusz Puder (1908–1945). Świadectwo życia kapłana katolickiego pochodzenia żydowskiego*, Wrocław, 2010, does not mention such a fact; quoted after: J. Rokicki, op. cit., p. 45. There is an important text on the case of the Rev. T. Puder: J. Leociak, "Sprawa księdza Pudra", *Gazeta Wyborcza*, 30th/31st January 1993. Also, cf. T. Puder's bio, by Jan Wysocki, in: *Polski Słownik Biograficzny*, vol. XXIX, Wroclaw 1986, pp. 340–341. It is significant that Józef Bedrycki, author of a pamphlet entitled *Tragedia ks. Trzeciaka. Kulisy sprawy ks. Pudra*, Warsaw, 1938 (whose title suggests a "tragedy" of the Rev. S. Trzeciak), has stood up for the reputation of this priest. Włodzimierz Sznarbachowski mentions a J. Bedrycki, without quoting his first name, as a member of NOR, an organisation formed during the occupation to the knowledge of the Germans; see his *300 lat wspomnień*, London 1997, p. 192.

51 As J. Rokicki tells us, S. Trzeciak attended conferences organised in Erfurt by the Institut zur Erforschung der Judenfrage; cf. op. cit., p. 45. In Julian Tuwim's poem *Kwiaty polskie* (Warsaw 1993, p. 110) we read: "Trzeciak the priest, for his part, in Nurnberg, // Paid homage to *Parteitag*s inimical, // Whilst at that time, the Reverend Puder // Was

riots could facilitate the establishment of a ghetto in Warsaw. Did the occurrences that took place in the last week of March 1940 on the streets of Warsaw change the opinions, sentiments, or stance of this Catholic priest? Probably, partly yes; but not completely.

On the one hand, we have an account from Wanda Gorczyńska, a nun, Mother Superior of an Ursuline Sisters' institute and boarding school in Warsaw, who has told a story about Stanisław's intercession, as he claimed that "little famished Jewish girls" ought to be given priority when received by the institute.[52] On the other hand, Zofia Zaks, who lived outside the ghetto in Warsaw, could remember what this priest said at one of the May services in 1943, speaking of "the Jews getting burned in the ghetto like bedbugs."[53] Maria Szletyńska told me in a letter, based on what she had learned from Kazimierz's mother, Jadwiga Puder, that her other son Tadeusz learned from a Gestapo officer interrogating him that the reason he had been arrested was a denunciation from the Rev. S. Trzeciak.[54] The circumstances of Trzeciak's death during the Warsaw Uprising on 8th August 1944 are not clear; he was probably shot dead by a German officer near an insurgent barricade.

One more figure that appears among the main organisers of the Polish counterpart of the NSDAP (i.e., the NOR, to be covered at length in a moment), and also as a co-organiser of the anti-Jewish riots in Warsaw, was Andrzej Świetlicki (1915–1940). Before the war, he studied at the Warsaw University Faculty of Law and ran the Warsaw branch of ONR–*Falanga*, cooperating closely with Bolesław Piasecki. Zygmunt Przetakiewicz, who knew Andrzej well, wrote of him: "Andrzej Świetlicki was a mysterious figure. A tall and slim man, his aspirations and ambitions were great. His commander's inclination was nothing of a secret. When managing the Warsaw organisation of the National Radical

---

getting slapped in front of the altar [...]." (In my opinion, there is no evidence that Trzeciak travelled to Nurnberg at the time.).
52 This account has been passed on by Zuzanna Sienkiewiczowa, *Ten jest z ojczyzny mojej*, ed. by W. Bartoszewski and Z. Lewinówna, 2nd ed., Krakow 1969, pp. 808–809.
53 This account was shared with me by Zofia Zaks, PhD, on 28th December 2000; she had spoken about it earlier at a meeting of the Association of "Children of the Holocaust".
54 In her letter to me of 10th February 2001. Realising the menace to Rev. T. Puder, Archbishop Stanisław Gall appointed him chaplain in Białołęka near Warsaw (today, within the city limits), where he was arrested on 24th April 1941; he was successfully snatched out of the hospital on 7th November 1942. He thereafter remained in hiding till the end of the occupation, but was eventually killed in an accident in Warsaw when he was hit by a vehicle on 27th January 1945.

Movement, he formed his own 'storming parties' composed of the lumpenproletariat, among others."[55] Gustaw Potworowski's remarks on this man seem of utmost relevance to me: "Andrzej Świetlicki was a schoolmate of mine, we shared a bench at school, and I can assert that he was an excellent Pole, a genuine patriot. He would look at Piasecki, the leader, with admiration and got involved with the radical-national organisation [...] which gave the Left one more argument for accusing the ONR of collaboration."[56]

Włodzimierz Sznarbachowski's remarks are no less important: he knew Andrzej very well before the war and met him repeatedly during the first weeks of the occupation. As Włodzimierz wrote in his memoirs, "always with a headman's ambition, Andrzej Świetlicki was among those close to Bolesław who could alongside him pursue their own policy, and he had at his disposal a supportive and loyal group of members and combatants who did not accept the authority of Przetakiewicz. The NOR, as appointed by Świetlicki, suited both the Wehrmacht and Mr. Piasecki."[57] In an earlier text, Sznarbachowski recalled the rule of political tactics Piasecki had elaborated when at Bereza-Kartuska, the camp where political prisoners were detained; he was placed there in 1934 after the delegalisation of ONR by the Polish Government of the time. The rule claimed: "Rather than be fought, a stronger opponent ought to be penetrated." During the occupation, he apparently applied this tactic, "making use of the National Radical Organisation – NOR (which he had probably initiated before then), created in October by Andrzej Świetlicki, upon consent of the Wehrmacht." Evidently, Bolesław Piasecki was the conceiver, since Andrzej did not have "the ability of historical vision such that he would put them forth on his own. What he could do was to take them over from Piasecki for execution."[58]

In the already quoted memoirs of Zygmunt Przetakiewicz, we find a completely different depiction: "Bolesław informed me of the actions one of our former members, Andrzej Świetlicki, had taken. In arrangement with the German military authorities, he instituted the National Radical Organisation [NOR],

---

55 Przetakiewicz, op. cit., p. 16.
56 "Wspomnienia Gustawa Potworowskiego z działalności w Obozie Narodowo-Radykalnym i Narodowych Siłach Zbrojnych", [in:] W.J. Muszyński, op. cit., p. 481.
57 Sznarbachowski, op. cit., p. 191.
58 W. Sznarbachowski, "Bolesław Piasecki: od skrajnej antyniemieckości do projektów współpracy", *Zeszyty Historyczne* (Paris), fasc. 194, 1990, p. 91 (comprises a fragment of the author's reminiscences as well as a sort of review of the book by Antoni Dudek and Grzegorz Pytel, *Bolesław Piasecki. An attempt at a political biography*; Sznarbachowski had earlier shared with these authors information of interest to them.

which advocated common combating of Bolshevism and intended to act legally. Bolesław was openly agitated: 'This is crazy. He claims the Germans ought to be tactically used, we should get armed and, in a due moment, hit them from the back. I tried to explain to him', Bolesław said, 'that the concept was nonsensical, and harmful.' I said to Bolesław at that point that Świetlicki had always been overambitious, and now we had proof of it. 'I don't know what ending is going to come out of it', Bolesław continued. 'Do you know that they sing the *Rota* ["The Oath", a Polish patriotic song written during the Partition period by Maria Konopnicka in 1908, set to music by Feliks Nowowiejski – transl. note] at their office on Ujazdowskie Avenue, and do not conceal their attitude to the Germans at all?"'.[59] Considering that Piasecki was said to have apparently admired Piłsudski's conduct during World War One – the formation of the Legions, on the one hand, and of the Polish Military Organisation (POW), on the other – Świetlicki's actions would not seem "crazy" to him; all the more so since, by all indications, Świetlicki was delivering Piasecki's idea and concept. Zygmunt Przetakiewicz was assigned with the task of forming a clandestine organisation.

Before I resume the thread of the circumstances of the emergence of the NOR and discuss the organisation's objectives and its association with the anti-Jewish riots in Warsaw of March 1940, Andrzej Świetlicki's story, as tragic as it was, should be concluded. As we already know, he was arrested just after the riots came to an end on 30th March 1940, together with Professor Zygmunt Cybichowski. It is legitimate to presume that the German principals intended in this way to do away with the uncomfortable witnesses. However, their release on 16th April 1940 might be indicative of competence disputes between the German police authorities, military authorities (including the Abwehr), and administrative authorities – and, of an anyway strong position of their patrons (hard for us to identify today) playing a game with the Poles. While they managed to rescue Professor Cybichowski, Andrzej Świetlicki was put in prison again on 8th May 1940 and never left it: he was shot by a firing squad on 20th or 21st June 1940 in the series of executions that killed Maciej Rataj, one of the peasant movement leaders, Mieczysław Niedziałkowski, an outstanding socialist activist, and the eminent national movement activist Tadeusz Fabiani, among others.[60]

---

59 Przetakiewicz, op. cit., p. 37. W. Sznarbachowski recalled that *Jeszcze Polska nie zginęła*, the Polish national anthem, was sung after every meeting.
60 Domańska, op. cit., pp. 58, 68; L. Wanat, *Za murami Pawiaka*, 6th ed., Warszawa, 1985, pp. 172–173. When the *Dziś i Jutro* weekly informed its readers of a holy mass celebrated for colleagues murdered in Palmiry, A. Świetlicki among them, their execution date was given erroneously as 12th July 1941.

As far as the origins of the NOR are concerned, apart from the above-quoted accounts of W. Sznarbachowski and Z. Przetakiewicz, there are two more sources. One of them is the comments, dated 9th February 1942, to the report titled "Attempts at creating a Polish national-socialist movement in 1939–40", which were found by Czesław Madajczyk in the files of the Government Delegate's Home Office. Based on this document, Professor Madajczyk found that "In the attempts to create a Polish national-socialist party, three different milieus apparently took part, directly or indirectly: (i) some members of the former *Falanga*, with Świetlicki and Berdycki at the head; (ii) Germanophiles, with Cybichowski, W. Studnicki, and the Rev. Trzeciak; (iii) E. Samborski and Podgórski, members of *Pochodnia* Assoc."[61]

The three figures – Andrzej Świetlicki, Zygmunt Cybichowski, and the Rev. Stanisław Trzeciak – have already been described in some detail. We come across Józef Berdycki as the author of a 1938 anti-Semitic pamphlet denying the Rev. Tadeusz Puder, as a converted Jew, the right to officiate services in the Catholic Church. On the back cover of the pamphlet, he noted: "Ideological Distribution '*Atak*'. Publication of topical pamphlets bringing to the attention of Poles the forces bringing about the destruction of the nation."[62] Was that man, Józef Berdycki, one of the founders of the "*Atak*" organisation, whose operations were noted by the chroniclers as well as in the conspiratorial press?[63]

The question arises of how the illustrious politician Władysław Studnicki was related to NOR.[64] We know that Professor Cybichowski contacted him, asking him to intervene for the release of Bolesław Piasecki, who was detained at

---

61 C. Madajczyk, *Generalna Gubernia w planach hitlerowskich*, Warsaw 1961, p. 31 (footnote 96. An attempt to establish a Polish counterpart of NSDAP appears there in the context of the considerations of a "concept to form a residual Polish state (*Reststaat*)."

62 The pamphlet (see footnote 36) was reedited as *Tragedia ks. Trzeciaka. Ks. Pudra sprawy – część druga*. Both editions comprised a photograph of the Rev. S. Trzeciak wearing numerous distinctions, captioned "The Rev. Prof. S. Trzeciak, PhD, the valorous prelate. He successfully fights for a Poland without Jews." J. Bedrycki has also written a pamphlet on Cardinal Aleksander Kakowski, who died in December 1939, which included the following: "No mason and no Jew shall rip Poland out of our soul!"

63 In his brochure on "the case of the Rev. Puder", Berdycki quotes "the periodical *Krak*, which is fighting the Jewish invasion on our culture." A 1939–1940 directory for Warsaw has the entry: Berdycki, Józef, 'Atak', 35 Jerozolimskie [Ave.] (p. 25).

64 Mariusz Ryńca and Włodzimierz Suleja, authors of Studnicki's biography in *Polski Słownik Biograficzny*, have no doubt that he "collaborated with NOR [...] in agreement with the German occupation authorities"; vol. XLV, Wrocław 2007–2008, p. 131.

the time by the Germans.⁶⁵ And, one would not deny that that the content of his "Memorial for a reconstruction of the Polish Army and on the impending German-Soviet war", dated 20ᵗʰ November 1939, duplicated and submitted to the Germans, harmonised with a leaflet issued by NOR, of which more will be said in a moment.⁶⁶

The first name of the aforementioned Mr. Samborski was Erazm, the full name of the association he was a member of was "The Polish Society for Workers' Culture and Education" (*Polskie Towarzystwo Kultury i Oświaty Robotniczej*), with offices in Warsaw at 18 Grzybowska St. The crucial thing is that a Central Committee for the Eradication of Communism was affiliated with this organisation. Samborski's visiting the NOR office is mentioned also by W. Sznarbachowski.

The last individual mentioned, Podgórski, whom we are going to meet again soon, warrants special attention. While the aforesaid source mentions no first name, Sznarbachowski identifies him as Tadeusz, pointing out to a "homonym of the known PPS activist."⁶⁷ Before I move on to discussing the second of the sources useful in determining the origins of NOR, I should like to explain that Icchak (Henryk) Rubin, author of the work *Żydzi w Łodzi pod niemiecką okupacją 1939–1945* (The Jews in Łódź under the German occupation, 1939–1945), nowise had the information given by C. Madajczyk confirmed "based on his own research", but has simply quoted Madajczyk's findings in his book.⁶⁸

I have already mentioned the Polish Underground's reports on NOR in connection with Professor Zygmunt Cybichowski. We should note that these reports were taken over after the war by the Warsaw branch of the Security Office (secret political police, the "UB"), which in 1950 decided to deal with "members of the pro-German organisation 'NOR.'" The report dated 27ᵗʰ March 1940 and signed "Janusz" (i.e., Janusz Wilk), only using the initials of the individuals concerned (to be deciphered based on other extant reports and other sources), states: "After the capitulation of Warsaw, those 'younger' ones, under the star of P.B. [Bolesław Piasecki], led by P.Wł. [Władysław Puławski], following long deliberations at

---

65 W. Studnicki writes about it in his book, *Tragiczne manowce. Próby przeciwdziałania katastrofom narodowym*, Toruń, 2001, pp. 59–60 (being vol. IV of his *Pisma wybrane*, i.e., selected works); a German edition was issued in 1951: *Irrwege in Polen. Ein Kampf um die polnisch-deutsche Annährung*.

66 The text is in: *Tragiczne manowce* …, pp. 129–138.

67 Sznarbachowski, *300 lat* …, p. 192.

68 I. Rubin, *Żydzi w Łodzi pod okupacją niemiecką 1939–1945*, London 1988, pp. 141–142, and footnote 33 on p. 495; on Rubin's alleged own research, see: Dudek and Pytel, op. cit., p. 108, followed by Sznarbachowski, *Bolesław Piasecki* …, p. 88.

the Gestapo, set up a new pro-German organisation [under the name of] NOR. The Gestapo gave them an office, the former ZMP [Polish Youth Association] premises, at 20 Ujazdowskie Ave., completely furnished and equipped. Having determined the programme guidelines charted out at a dozen-or-so briefings with SS-Oberführer L. [?], the NOR Board was established, with the following cast of members: P. Wł. [see above] – Director; 1st Deputy – P.J. [Jan Podgórski] (National-Social Camp), 2nd Deputy – M.A. [Antoni Mucharski] (former official with the Ministry of the Treasury), Secretary – W.W. [Władysław Wójtowicz]." Before I move on to the further passages of this altogether sensational document, let me make a couple of indispensable remarks. In the first place, the information that the contacts were made not with the Wehrmacht but with the Gestapo is astonishing. The one holding the rank of SS-Oberführer (General) was Kurt Classen, who was in Warsaw in October and November 1939 as a "Chairman of the Police"; the higher-ranked SS-Gruppenführer was Paul Moder, Commander of the SS and the Police, who also was in Warsaw at the time.[69] Andrzej Świetlicki is not mentioned here, which is puzzling; another thought-provoking question is the role Władysław Puławski and Jan Podgórski would play with NOR. The other two named members of the organisation's Board appear in no other source known to me whatsoever. Let me also point that the premises offered to the organisation by the Germans before the war had been the office of the Polish Youth Association affiliated with the *Sanacja* Camp of National Unity. The office was later taken over by Jerzy Rutkowski, who acted on behalf of Piasecki and *Falanga*, but was regained by *Sanacja*, later withdrawing from cooperation, in 1938.[70]

Let us now take a look at the report again. Its author says that the General Council of NOR had some twenty members; he only cites the initials (sometimes noting just the surname) of ten individuals. Apart from Prof. Cybichowski and the Rev. S. Trzeciak, there is a former senator, "J." – i.e., Mieczysław Jakubowski.

---

69 I suspect that a mistaken rank is the case here: it is not impossible at all that contacts have been made with SS-Obersturmbannführer (Lieutenant Colonel) Johannes Müller, head of the Security Service for the District of Warsaw, reporting to Commander of the Police and Security Service (KdS), Josef Meisinger. Let me emphasise that W. Studnicki mentions talks with Müller in his *Tragiczne manowce* ..., pp. 59, 73, 76, 85, 94 (naming him a deputy head and then, head of the Gestapo).

70 Let me remind that the address "20 Ujazdowskie Avenue" (Aleje Ujazdowskie 20) is given in *Biuletyn Informacyjny* of 5th April 1940. W. Sznarbachowski says that apart from this office, the Germans handed over to NOR the former apartment of the poet Julian Tuwim which they had confiscated; see *300 lat* ..., p. 89 (the address, based on the directory, was 7 Mazowiecka St.).

As we read further on, "Presently, in mid-March of this year, the Gestapo sealed up the NOR office. [...] After the capitulation of Warsaw, P.Wł. offered himself to P.B. who proposed to P. cooperation with the Germans within the ONR. P. refused, and was, reportedly, consequently arrested and is kept in a prison today. Together with P., R.M. [Marian Reutt] is being gaoled – a very talented activist (holds three PhDs), and a few other eminent activists." That Bolesław Piasecki refused to cooperate with the Germans could be deemed sensational, if not for the fact that the reasons for his detention on 13th December 1939 had to do with the activity of Stanisław Brochwicz-Kozłowski, the German agent. Almost at that same time, Jerzy Cybichowski (of whose lot we have already learned), the said Marian Reutt, Wojciech Kwasiborski, and Tadeusz Lipkowski – all associated with Piasecki – were arrested. Save for Cybichowski, they were eventually killed by the Germans.[71]

The report under discussion concludes with the enumeration of ten initials of individuals who "often visited" the NOR office. Erazm Samborski and Edward Kozłowski appear among them; Ludwik Landau mentions the arrest of Kozłowski, together with Świetlicki, the latter as an organiser of the anti-Jewish riots, in a note made on 30th March 1940. As we can read in this fragment of the report, the premises were also visited by a "B., ed.[itor]" who "was (rightly) arrested before the war for espionage. He presently works for the Gestapo, and has many victims on his conscience." Beyond a shadow of a doubt, this is Stanisław Brochwicz-Kozłowski, who was unmasked by *Falanga* in June 1939. Let me point out, however, that the report does not mention his name. All the pre-war associates of Piasecki and the members of *Falanga* knew that he was a traitor whom the Polish court had sentenced to death, and thus it is simply impossible that he would have appeared at the NOR office – all the more so since, once released by the Germans, he paraded in Warsaw in a German uniform.[72]

---

71 Cf. A.K. Kunert, *Rzeczpospolita Walcząca. Wrzesień-grudzień 1939*, Warsaw 1993, p. 200; for a biography of Marian Reutt by Jacek Majchrowski, see: *Polski Słownik Biograficzny*, vol. XXXI, Wroclaw 1988–1989, pp. 162-163 (after he was released, he was active with the Underground; detained in 1944, he was murdered by the Germans at KL Gross-Born). W. Kwasieborski and T. Lipkowski were put in the Pawiak prison again on 19th June 1940, and were executed by firing squad, together with A. Świetlicki, in Palmiry, on 20th or 21st June 1940.
72 Cf. the article "'*Patriotyzm' szpiega*", *Biuletyn Informacyjny* of 12th December 1940; also, *Kronika Okupacji*, no. 6 (as reprinted in: Landau, L., *Kronika ...*, vol. III, Warsaw 1963, pp. 694–695). In the autumn of 1940, S. Brochwicz published a cycle of articles in *Nowy Kurier Warszawski*, under the penname "Henryk Zrąb", with the purpose of bringing

The Security Office also had other reports of the Polish Underground which referred to people associated with NOR. Another highly important report, regrettably undated, was compiled around the second half of April 1940 and focused on Jan Podgórski and Władysław Puławski. The former, born in the United States, arrived in Poland with General Józef Haller's army. We read in the report that he "is an inveterate anti-Semite, eradicating Jews with the use of any method, decent or nefarious," and we can learn that it is he who was the moving spirit behind the creation of NOR, "upon consent of the German authorities." However, the organisation was headed by Puławski instead, for this man "better suited the Germans' expectations." His military rank of Major and high post held with the POW Members' Association (*Związek Peowiaków*) were definitely assets.[73] One moreover learns that "Podgórski mistrusted the Germans, preferred to be less involved and, primarily, did not put himself at risk. [...] He was aware that the Germans cared much about establishing in Poland an apparently legal Polish government, which would obviously have been completely dependent upon them. Podgórski consented to this, and the relevant negotiations were carried out with the Germans on his inspiration. [...] All these plans have nevertheless been thwarted in the recent time, the organisation suspended, and a series of the organisation's persons detained." Those mentioned among the arrested members of NOR were: Andrzej Świetlicki, Prof. Cybichowski, W. Puławski, Mr. Bryc (no first name) – "former Reader in Botany at the University of Wilno, Podgórski's aide", and Mr. Czubiak.[74] After these events, Podgórski "will probably switch to conspiratorial work, and he

---

    shame to *Sanacja's* rule; he also authored a brochure, under his own name, titled *Bohaterowie czy zdrajcy. Wspomnienie więźnia politycznego*. Earlier on, in March 1940, Arnold Szyfman, a famous man-of-the-theatre of Jewish descent, happened to share a prison cell with him at Daniłowiczowska St. Brochwicz perceived his arrest as a mistake. As Szyfman recollects, he "always referred to Hitler as 'our Führer', whereas he besmeared Poland and splattered mud at her"; see: A. Szyfman, *Moja tułaczka wojenna*, Warsaw 1960, p. 71. Brochwicz was sentenced by the Underground on 17th February to death, and the verdict was executed by knifing; A.K. Kunert, "*Stanisław Brochwicz vel Stanisław von Brauchitsch*", *Kierunki*, 1985, no. 7.

73 In her chronicle of the Pawiak prison, R. Domańska lists a certain "Władysław Pułowski" among the prisoners transported on 2nd May 1940 to KL Sachsenhausen; see: op. cit., p. 56. Could a letter have been mistaken in the surname? I should point out that Jerzy Cybichowski was taken with the same transport.

74 My presumption is that the name of the said scholar employed at the Wilno University was Stanisław. In 1935, Stanisław Bryc formed and became editor-in-chief of a periodical *Nakazy Dnia*, which was remade a year later as *Nowe Drogi. Organ Polskiej Partji Radykalnej* (an organ of the Polish Radical Party). According to R. Domańska, Tytus

no longer can count on some agreement with the Germans." The report also mentions that Świetlicki, Cybichowski, and Puławski were released from detention.[75]

Let us now refer back to the information shared by Włodzimierz Sznarbachowski who closely observed the first stage of NOR's activities (until 23rd December 1939, the date he left Warsaw for Rome). In a 1968 broadcast of Radio Free Europe (which was his workplace at the time), he said: "Piasecki assigned for collaboration with the occupiers one of the managers of the action consisting in *outwitting* the Germans [emphasis – T.S.]."[76] In his text published in 1990 by the Paris-based *Zeszyty Literackie*, he wrote: "In November 1939, Piasecki entrusted me with the task to observe the NOR. [...] Piasecki requested me to look into there from time to time and, without getting involved, to find out how NOR was functioning in practice. I was also invited by Świetlicki. I visited the office on the [Ujazdowskie] Avenue a couple of times, meeting former *Falanga* men there; among them, Berdycki, Ryszard Oracz, Professor Cybichowski and his son Jerzy, Marian Reutt, and others."[77] He then mentions a few more names – seemingly, based on the document found by C. Madajczyk, as it is quoted in a footnote; yet, Puła[w]ski is also mentioned (with the wrong spelling of the surname and without a first name; a remark on him is added, "from the POW, I suppose"). To my mind, the mention of Marian Reutt is particularly important. As Sznarbachowski says elsewhere, in October 1939, "a few of his acquaintances from before the war" offered themselves to Reutt, "German staff officers, proposing to enter into talks" with him.[78] Let me remark that Reutt was arrested by the Germans, together with Piasecki, on 13th December 1939.

On leaving the country, Sznarbachowski took a leaflet issued by NOR in autumn 1939, which was a sort of policy paper of this organisation. Its content, as reconstructed from memory years afterwards, read as follows: "Polish Nation! It is owing to *Sanacja* that Poland has suffered a terrible defeat, losing its independence and its western lands. But not everything has been lost – the Polish

---

Jan Czubiak was gaoled at Pawiak on 16th April 1940; on 21st September 1940, this man was transported to KL Auschwitz; see: op. cit., pp. 49, 96.

75 As we already know, A. Świetlicki was arrested once again; as was, probably, Puławski.
76 The Polish Broadcasting Station of Radio Free Europe, broadcasting from Munich, issued in 1968, in London, a brochure *Prawda o PAX-ie i Piaseckim*, containing the texts of sixteen RFE broadcasts on these topics. Włodzimierz Sznarbachowski, then a contributor to RFE, was definitely the author; quoted after p. 9 thereof.
77 Sznarbachowski, *Bolesław Piasecki* ..., pp. 81, 89.
78 Sznarbachowski, *Bolesław Piasecki* ..., p. 92; also, *300 lat* ..., p. 190.

Army can still be rebuilt, so that it could take part in the inevitable war against Soviet communism. The lands conquered in the East will reinstate our territory seized by the USSR, whilst the other areas, further eastwards, will compensate us for the lost Pomerania, Silesia, and Poznań region, and be a contribution for the losses incurred due to the warfare. To fund the reconstruction [of the country] and its new army, we shall use the confiscated Jewish properties. Compatriots, join NOR now! Give us the chance to have the Homeland rebuilt, and for a Great Poland to emerge!" Sznarbachowski makes a clear statement that "Collaboration with the Wehrmacht was also meant to contribute to elimination of the Jewish question in Poland, with the use of German hands."[79]

In 1979, Jan Józef Lipski published a text on the then-late Bolesław Piasecki in *Biuletyn Informacyjny*, a newsletter of the Workers' Defence Committee (KOR). When recollecting NOR, he stated that "There is no evidence that Bolesław Piasecki would have taken part in that affair"; yet, responding to a polemic from Anka Kowalska, who defended the man who in the post-war years founded the PAX Association, he added: "I cannot believe that any *Falanga* activist could have taken a step as serious as collaboration without the leader being aware of it and offering his tacit consent, unless getting involved in a conflict and rebellion."[80] Wojciech Jerzy Muszyński, author of the most recent book on the National Radical Camp, presents a similar standpoint; when it comes to NOR, he believes that "the organisation was assumedly patronised, out of the closet, by Piasecki himself."[81]

Hanna Krahelska mentions in her diary, as of 9th March 1940, a "Polish national-socialist party" being formed in the early days of the occupation.[82] She tells us about a gathering convened in early March and that "the canvassing was done by a certain Puławski, former WP [Polish Army] officer." Krahelska's

---

79 Sznarbachowski, *Bolesław Piasecki* ..., p. 92; the leaflet's content is also quoted in *300 lat* ..., p. 192.
80 J.J. Lipski, "O Bolesławie Piaseckim", *Biuletyn Informacyjny* (a periodical of the Workers' Defence Committee), no. 1 (27), p. 32; "List otwarty do Jana Józefa Lipskiego", an open letter to J.J. Lipski, by Anka Kowalska, *Biuletyn Informacyjny*, no. 2 (28), pp. 64–65; therein, a reply to the said letter: "Odpowiedź Ance Kowalskiej", p. 66.
81 Muszyński, op. cit., p. 242.
82 H. Krahelska, *Pamiętniki z okresu okupacji* (a diary – not really a memoir, as the title would suggest), the Central Archives of Modern Records, ref. no. 383/II-3, c. 39. The note dated 28th February 1940 says that Bolesław Piasecki did not come to an agreement with the Germans and now is serving time in prison, whereas Andrzej Świetlicki is collaborating with them; ibidem, c. 25.

Kronika Agaty, record of 4th April 1942, offers a list of as many as thirteen individuals associated with NOR, which "was established by Świetlicki." Naming Puławski and Podgórski among them, she remarks that "Olpiński provided a contact with the German authorities."[83] And, one more piece of information on this milieu; here is what Stefan Rowecki, the ZWZ Commander under the German occupation, wrote in his report for 15th March to 2nd April 1940: "The *Falanga* group, organised within a Pol[ish] nat[ional-]social[ist] party, is used by the occupiers for diversionary actions (anti-Semitic excesses)." And, as we read therein: "In the last reporting decade, the strength of anti-Jewish action has intensified immensely, manifesting itself in organising pogroms which are assuming a mass character. Scenes of beating and pillaging are filmed by the Germans, presumably for purposes of external propaganda."[84]

We know today that the on day Colonel Rowecki was compiling this report, the riots had been over and it was quiet in Warsaw. The decision to discontinue the anti-Jewish excesses was made – probably, for a variety of reasons, as will be seen further on – obviously by the Germans. On 21st June 1940, *Biuletyn Informacyjny* published a very important article titled "*Zamilkły głosy o 'współpracy polsko-niemieckiej'*" ["Polish-German co-operation" advocates have withdrawn], stating that:

> It was already a few months [weeks, actually – T.S.] after the occupation of Warsaw by the Germans that attempts at making contact with the occupiers appear on the part of some mentally incompetent individuals in Polish society (Studnicki's independent action; the formation of the Radical National organisation – with Cybichowski, the Rev. Trzeciak, Podgórski, Maj. Puła[w]ski, Świetlicki, etc.; these latter doings have been patronised by the Gestapo). We witnessed the anti-Jewish pogrom, leaflets issued, etc. For almost two months now, all that has subsided, withered. There have been some arrests among the managers of the Radical National party. As it seems, *both sides have grown disappointed with each other* [emphasis – T.S.]. The German authorities soon withdrew from their planned "lenient policy" and now are resolutely and consistently eradicating culture, the Polish intelligentsia and nation, following a policy of complete lawlessness – as a result, any talks with Polish "politicians" have been discontinued. And vice

---

83 Ibidem, p. 165; "Ołpiński" is probably Stefan Ołpiński, an international swindler, who was in Warsaw in autumn 1939; Władysław Studnicki knew him and trusted him. Jerzy Rawicz wrote a book on him, entitled *Kariera Szambelana*, 2nd ed.: Warsaw 1974. (I am indebted to Prof. Szymon Rudnicki for having shared with me the information on S. Ołpiński and the book.).

84 *Armia Krajowa w dokumentach*, vol. I: *Wrzesień 1939 – czerwiec 1941* (September 1939 to June 1941), London 1970, pp. 194, 199.

versa: the milieu of Cybichowski, disheartened by the arrest of their own people and "incomprehension" on the part of their protectors, have withdrawn from their feeble and unpopular action. At present, "Polish-German contacts" are only expressed in the existence of a certain number of Poles – contract agents of the Gestapo, performing their commissioned tasks in their secondary positions.

Let us add that the same issue of the newsletter brought the following piece of news: "At the dwelling of Bol.[esław] Piasecki (the head of *Falanga*, imprisoned since October [actually, December – T.S.]), a severe search has been carried out. The apartment was demolished, the people [inside it] beaten." Once released, on 16th April 1940, the future leader of the underground Confederation of the Nation [*Konfederacja Narodu*] remained in hiding.

As for any cooperation with the Germans, the stance of the National Party (Stronnictwo Narodowe), which operated as a conspiratorial organisation from autumn 1939, was no different from the position expressed by the *Biuletyn Informacyjny* editorial team. In the article "*Linia generalna i jej konsekwencje*" ("The general line and its consequences"), published in *Walka* magazine's issue of 9th August 1940, we read: "Any political or military 'understanding' with the occupiers is disqualified. This would mean a capitulation. The general line is straight, and arouses no doubt. There is no pro-German party that has emerged in Poland; moreover, there is no room whatsoever for a 'legion', which could be fighting side by side with the Germans against the Bolsheviks. Such ideas could only be fancied in the minds of people who represent no-one and nothing, save for their own stupidity. [...] The Germans will never manage to proactively cooperate against the Jews, as this is clearly our own business, which we can, under appropriate conditions, sort out by ourselves." Stanisław Piasecki, the editor-in-chief of *Walka*, was quite probably the author; arrested by the Germans on 4th December 1940, he was executed by a firing squad in Palmiry on 12th June 1941.[85]

Let us however resume the main thread of our considerations, the anti-Jewish riots in Warsaw of the spring of 1940. We have focused so far on their presumed organisers among the Poles; now, let us see who actually participated in these occurrences. Probably all the sources contain mentions of "gangs" of juveniles, that is, children and youth, taking part in these incidents.

At the same time, we can learn that there was somebody controlling them, mobilising them to act, and, as it turns out, remunerating them. To try and answer the question who it was, let us use the conspiratorial press coverage and

---

[85] Cf. a biography of Stanisław Piasecki by Jerzy J. Terej, *Polski Słownik Biograficzny*, vol. XXV, Wroclaw 1980, pp. 792–794.

witness accounts. The article *"Wyrostki na służbie Gestapo"* ("Striplings at the Gestapo's service"), published in *Biuletyn Informacyjny* of 19th July 1940, tells us that during the first winter of the occupation in Warsaw, there was a lieutenant named Wiśniewski at Fort Bema who ran a course for boys aged 13 and above. Their assignment was to collect information in the town and to denounce people. The course of another group, of thirty, was reportedly held three times a week. For their participation in anti-Jewish riots, the boys were paid "royalties", in bars, of 5 zlotys per day. The matter was raised also in an article titled *"Szkoła zbrodniarzy"* ("School for criminals") published in *Polska Żyje!* on 27th July 1940. According to the article, the Germans apparently began to recruit children from *Volksdeutsch* families in February 1940. From all accounts, a troop of some thirty such young people "made a pogrom" during Easter, which probably is to mean that they initiated it.

In his book published in 1947, *Organizowanie wściekłości*, Michał M. Borwicz quotes an account of Antoni Bartnicki: "I was buying some books at one of the second-hand bookshops. Suddenly, a group of striplings, aged fifteen to nineteen, rushed from Marszałkowska St. onto Świętokrzyska St., armed with walking-sticks and stones. Exclaiming 'Down with Jews!', running, they began breaking all the store-fronts featuring the Star. There was a truck moving forward right behind the running huddle, uncovered, out of which two individuals in civilian dress were doing the camerawork. [...] A truck was waiting for the heroes at Krasińskich Sq., a covered one, where each of the striplings received his prize for the work fulfilled: a chunk of sausage, half a loaf of bread, and ½ litre of vodka."[86]

The anti-Jewish riots that took place in Krakow on 11th August 1945 evoked in the memory of Jerzy Zagórski the images of the events from a few years earlier. In the article *"Żydzi, Polacy i zaminowane dusze"* ("Jews, Poles, and mined souls"), published by *Tygodnik Powszechny*, the Krakow-based leading Catholic periodical, he wrote: "On 11th August, I recollected the day of the year 1940 when the only pogrom of Jews committed by Polish hands during the occupation occurred in Warsaw. It was announced to the ten- and twelve-year-old striplings that the Jews had killed a Polish boy. A small group of boys, mainly from the suburbs, ran to the district where the Jews lived, not yet enclosed by a wall, and lunged on them with their bare fists. German reporters, brought there right on time, filmed the incident and then in turn filmed the gendarmes pacifying those

---

86 M.B. Borwicz, *Organizowanie wściekłości*, with an introduction by Zofia Nałkowska, Warsaw 1974, p. 49.

boys. The lorry carrying away the corpses of the boys shot by the gendarmes was probably not filmed."[87]

A few words regarding this message are in order. It confirms that there were rumours about the Jews having killed a Polish Christian child. It could have been that initially the Jews were pounced upon with bare fists indeed, but later on, as it is known, the attackers were armed with rods, crowbars, and stones. Zagórski, characteristically, clearly talks about a single incident, using the singular; he must have not been aware that the scene he described had recurred over several days.

The following note, made by Emanuel Ringelblum in his diary on 27th March 1940, deserves our attention: "They say that the Polish youngsters received from those ones 2 zlotys each, and more, per day. They were brought by cars and let out into the Jewish quarter; however, I did not receive this piece of information from a reliable source." It is without a shadow of a doubt that that the reference to "those ones" means the Germans. Their active participation in the riots, apart from photographing and filming the excesses, is also attested by the vehicles appearing on a regular basis, although none of the witnesses to those events took an effort to note down their registration numbers.

Bernard Goldstein, whom I have already quoted, recollects that students of the "Polish Handcraft School at 72 Leszno Street" took an active part in Warsaw's anti-Jewish incidents. It is easy to guess what school this was. The "Stanisław Konarski" Municipal Vocational (Mechanical and Electrical) School No. 1 was located at that time at 72 Leszno Street; a few months later, the Germans ousted it from its host edifice. The headmaster, Wincenty Czerwiński, Eng., proudly described it years afterwards as "Warsaw's largest, excellently equipped" school.[88] As may be presumed, the students mainly came from petty-bourgeois families, where anti-Semitism was strongly rooted. It turns out that the students did not limit their hostility toward Jews to the incidents of March 1940. In a note on the school published on 8th November by *Biuletyn Informacyjny*, "*Szkoła im. Konarskiego*", we read: "On Leszno St., Karmelicka St., and Nowolipie St., rather frequent incidents are taking place with the Jews being beaten by school youth from the 'S. Konarski' school of crafts. We request and appeal to the colleagues of this school's students to think the matter over. Besides the ethical considerations, we find that only German propaganda benefits from such actions. It would be

---

87 *Tygodnik Powszechny*, no. 26 of 16th September 1945. I have found no confirmation of the information that the Germans were shooting at those taking part in the incidents.
88 Cf. W. Czerwiński, C. Sitarz, "Szkolnictwo zawodowe", [in:] S. Dobraniecki, S. Pokora, eds., *Walka o oświatę, naukę i kulturę w latach okupacji. Materiały z terenu m. st. Warszawy i woj. warszawskiego*, Warsaw 1967, pp. 227, 244.

interesting to investigate whether there are any German contract agents amongst those inspiring these riots."

As is therefore evident, albeit their scale was incomparably smaller compared to the Easter riots, anti-Jewish incidents were occurring in Warsaw all the same. *Biuletyn Informacyjny* of 12th July 1940 quoted the following piece of news: "Beginning with the 5th of July, a few anti-Jewish actions were observed in Warsaw that were organised by German agents under the slogans 'Away with Judeocommies and Stalin!' – 'Long live Hitler!' Some people were wounded, in a few cases (Żelaznej-Bramy Square)." Who of the Poles had a finger in the pie this time, we regrettably do not know – and probably never will.

The accounts on the participants of the 1940 street incidents in Warsaw oftentimes mention gangs of hooligans and urban rabble. I have already quoted a mention from the reminiscences of Zygmunt Przetakiewicz about Andrzej Świetlicki forming his own "storming parties" "composed of the lumpenproletariat, among others." Elsewhere, Mr. Przetakiewicz quotes an utterance made by Bolesław Piasecki in the post-war years: "The *Falanga* was an organisation of students and lumpenproletariat, that is, a very dangerous component, as a combination of the two factors, since students plus lumpenproletariat make a terribly explosive power."[89] I am confident that this apt statement also refers to the militias mobilised by Świetlicki for the action in March 1940.

The conduct and attitudes of Varsovians

A note regarding the activities of the anti-Semitic organisation "*Atak*" published early by *Biuletyn Informacyjny*, the organ of the ZWZ, in its 19th January 1940 issue contains a very telling declaration from the editorial board: "Our statement is that any direct or indirect collaboration with the Germans in persecuting Jews is a diversionary act, like any other cooperation with the deadly enemy of Poland." This stance was not changed when it came to assessing the anti-Jewish occurrences in the Easter 1940 period. The article "*Prowokowanie pogromów*" ("Instigating pogroms"), published in *Biuletyn Informacyjny* of 29th March 1940 found that: "Neither the 'action' in itself nor the child and youth 'sections' call for any broader discussion from the standpoint of morality or the Polish *raison d'état*. What we recommend to our readers is: (i) to shed light on the issue in the most extensive spheres of the society; (ii) to respond in the streets to the excesses

---

89 Przetakiewicz, op. cit., pp. 34–35.

of children and youth." Whether the Varsovians complied with these recommendations – especially, the second of them – is a legitimate question.

When trying to answer this question, if we only referred to the opinion of Szymon Huberband, the answer would be unambiguously negative. Although Huberband was aware that the anti-Jewish riots were designed and conceived by the Germans, he opined that

> It is saddening that there are Poles who allow themselves to be used as a tool of the Germans for their own interests. It is even more saddening that there are no Poles to persuade the Jew-beaters to stop their dirty work.[90]

Indeed, the various attempts to eliminate the Warsaw unrest by persuasion failed. It did happen that passers-by expressed their disfavour aloud, condemning the acts of violence, vandalism, and pillage. As Ludwik Landau observed on 23rd February 1940, "there also occur incidents of resolute response in defence of the Jews from non-Jewish passers-by." In an account submitted on 12th May 1940 in Jerusalem by a witness of the Easter incidents, we read: "The attitude of the Polish intellectuals toward the Jews was clearly a friendly one, and against the pogrom. It is a known fact that at the corner of Nowogrodzka Street and Marszałkowska [St.], a Catholic priest attacked the youngsters participating in the pogrom, beat them and disappeared."[91] Emanuel Ringelblum wrote in his diary on 30th March 1940: "I have heard about the indignation of many a Christian. 'They are disgracing Poland, they're attacking the Jews today, and, tomorrow…'. A conductor halted the tram and shouted, 'Do you know who is using you as their tool?'. […] In many cases, Christians warned Jews against going in a given direction, for the hooligans would be there, [waiting]. A Christian woman gave the hooligans a severe beating in Bankowy Square. […] The hooligans were calling the Polish police 'Jewish flunkeys.'" We therefore learn that there had been interventions of the Polish police, opposing the participants of the incidents.

This same chronicler, however, while hiding on the "Aryan" side and working in autumn 1943 on a study on Polish-Jewish relations, gave a much more critical assessment of the attitudes and behaviours of the Poles during the Easter incidents. As he observed:

> The Warsaw Jews were deeply pained that no reaction against these things came from the Polish community. It did sometimes happen that an elderly Christian would stop a Jew in the street and warn him that they were beating up Jews on such and such street. But it never happened that passers-by dared to actively oppose the excesses of the hooligans.

---

90   Huberband, op. cit., p. 56.
91   Cf. footnote 16.

I witnessed pogroms on many streets. I would take off my badge and follow the raging mob. Only once did I see someone stop the rowdies, an elderly woman on Bankowy Square, who reproached them for profaning the good name of Poland and for aiding and abetting the Germans. Sneering laughter was the ruffians' only answer to this Polish woman's noble words. [...] No one will accuse the Polish nation of committing these constant pogroms and excesses against the Jewish population. The significant majority of the nation, its enlightened working-class and the working intelligentsia, undoubtedly condemned these excesses, seeing in them a German instrument for weakening the unity of the Polish community and a lever to bring about collaboration with the Germans. We do, however, reproach the Polish community with not having tried to dissociate itself, either in words – sermons in the churches, etc., – or in writing, from the anti-Semitic beasts that cooperated with the Germans, and for not having actively opposed the constant excesses, for not having done anything whatsoever to weaken the impression that the whole Polish population of all classes approved of the performances of the Polish anti-Semites. The Polish Underground's passivity in face of the filthy tide of anti-Semitism was the great mistake in the period preceding the creation of the Ghetto, a mistake which was to take its revenge in the later stages of the war.[92]

These accusations targeted at *Polska Walcząca* (Fighting Poland) are not completely legitimate. Emanuel Ringelblum never had access to the full array of the conspiratorial press, and probably did not know of the publications fiercely condemning the anti-Jewish excesses. The clandestine organisations were too weak in the spring of 1940 to actively stand in defence of the persecuted Jews; moreover, as we know, at that very time there were fears of a German provocation to prematurely draw out the Underground.[93]

Ringelblum did not know at all about certain actions devised to condemn the anti-Jewish riots – or, he simply did not remember them when writing his treatise in the absence of any available sources. We can learn of some of these activities from a "Note from the conference with Artur Śliwiński, Chairman of the Capital-City Social Self-Help Committee [*Stołeczny Komitet Samopomocy Społecznej*, abbreviated below as 'S.K.S.S.'], of 11th April 1940", compiled by Michał Weichert, who represented the Jewish Social Self-Help. As we read, "Mr. Śliwiński read

---

92 Ringelblum, *Polish-Jewish Relations* ..., pp. 52–53.
93 *Wiadomości Polskie*, the organ of the Union of Armed Struggle (ZWZ), published an article on 10th March 1940 titled "*Uwaga! Prowokacje trwają!*" ("Attention! Provocation continues!"), warning: "The Germans are spreading rumours about an armed rising that will soon break out in Poland. One has to take into account the possibility that the Gestapo will arrange a comedy of an alleged armed struggle, which would serve as a pretext for continued mass executions by shooting. Let us remain cautious and vigilant; a rising, given the present situation, would bring about no benefit. The entire Nation will be called to take arms in due time."

out to me a copy of the letter sent by the S.K.S.S. in connection with the anti-Jewish incidents to Mr. Julian Kulski, the Lord Mayor, and a circular issued by the S.K.S.S. to the District Committees and regional, district, and domestic S.K.S.S. patrons. I requested copies of the letter and the circular; having received them, I hereby attach them hereto [unfortunately, these copies have been lost – T.S.]. Mr. Śliwiński also mentioned an intervention by Archbishop Gall and an appeal made to the clergy for condemnation of the anti-Jewish incidents."[94]

The mention of the intervention of Archbishop Stanisław Gall, possibly with Ludwig Fischer, Governor of the District of Warsaw, as well as of his appeal to the clergy to condemn the incidents – in the sermons, I should suppose – may be deemed sensational. However, we do not have access to the content of the Archbishop's letter to the German authorities or of his letter to the clergy. Nor do we know whether any such sermons were actually delivered. This would have to be explained based on relevant documentation kept at Church archives. Here I would like to indicate the following record from Ringelblum's diary from late March: "In the course of the incidents, as they say, there was a delegation of Jews paying a visit to Archbishop Gall, who expressed his indignation, but issued no proclamation to the Polish people." Had such a proclamation existed, it would have been quoted at a number of occasions, I should suppose.

There is, for a change, a confirmation of the steps taken by the S.K.S.S. authorities. In its note entitled *"Echo zajść antyżydowskich"* ("Echo of anti-Jewish incidents"), *Biuletyn Informacyjny* brought the following news, on 5th April 1940: "The Capital-City Social Self-help Committee has assumed an official position denouncing the anti-Jewish incidents, [and] has requested the municipal authorities to take measures that would prevent excesses of the like in the future. At the same time, field agencies reporting to the SKSS received instructions aiming at this objective."

I have already mentioned Bernard Goldstein's message concerning Jewish self-defence organised on initiative of the Bund. This author mentions one thing Ringelblum might have been unaware of, namely: "a small group of Polish socialists, whom we had requested for assistance, went out together with our comrades. They endeavoured to calm down the gamins, making an appeal to [their] human sentiments, and tried to defy the pogrom. They shouted 'You Jewish minions!'

---

94 This note is in the collection of the Jewish Historical Institute; a photocopy was made available to me by Ruta Sakowska, PhD, who quotes it in her book *Ludzie z dzielnicy zamkniętej*, 2nd ed., Warsaw 1993, p. 236.

and threw stones at them. Yet, some of the Christian passers-by reacted resolutely and strongly, insulting the scoundrels."[95]

As it turns out, the Jewish incidents in Warsaw were not condemned only by socialists and people with liberal-democratic views, like those who set the tone among the editorial teams of such conspiratorial magazines as *Biuletyn Informacyjny* or *Wiadomości Polskie*. Jerzy Zagórski recalls a meeting at the time of the riots with Stanisław Piasecki, who before the war edited *Prosto z Mostu*, a periodical clearly anti-Semitic in its tendency, and at the time of their meeting was an editor with the conspiratorial *Walka* magazine (which has been quoted in this text). "He had done all he could," Zagórski wrote of him, "to urge the youth who still respected his authority to counteract the excesses and offer help to the Jews in need. All the leaders across the entire Polish political spectrum who were in communication with one another acted in a manner similar to his. It is to their influence, and their care for the nation's moral dignity, that we owe thanks in no small measure, that the event described [i.e., the anti-Jewish incidents in Warsaw of March 1940] proved to be the only and the last victory of the provocateurs during the occupation."[96]

As it appears, even when the conspiratorial press unambiguously condemned the riots, displaying overt indignation at the disgraceful actions of their participants, the language of some of their enunciations still bore a resemblance for the Jews to the anti-Semitic manner of expression they otherwise were well familiar with.

The time has come look back at the already-quoted article *"Nie naśladować Niemców"*,[97] published in *Polska Żyje!* in March 1940. A further passage reads as follows:

> German photographers would stop by, in order to photograph and film the incidents. (Edited appropriately, these pictures will doubtlessly be circulating in the very nearest days across diverse screens and in neutral newspapers.)[98] The German soldiers were

---

95 This fragment is missing from the U.S. edition (cf. footnote 18); quoted after the French version of these memoirs, i.e. *Cinq années dans le ghetto de Varsovie*, Brussels 1962, p. 25.
96 Cf. footnote 74.
97 Cf. footnote 10, where I quote the date 27th March 1940, based on my own calculation, as there are dates specified in the subsequent issued. Ringelblum (see further on) confirms the said date.
98 I have not had an opportunity to trace whether the German press and, possibly, the press of the neutral countries, published any photographs concerning Warsaw's anti-Jewish incidents of March 1940. Arguably, similarly as the pictures showing the results of the German bombings of Warsaw in September 1939, or the outcome of the actions

encouraging the infuriated crowd: take it, go on take it. What use is it for the *"Juden"* to have the stuff? (It is said that the Germans pay 5 zloty per capita for starting a brawl.) And this stance of the occupiers, these words of kind-hearted encouragement, ought to, like a stream of cold water, immediately bring round and sober up the manifesters. These things should be nothing of the doable sort! *Any and all pogroms should be explicitly condemned by the entire Polish society.* Incidents of this kind are detrimental from the standpoint of both Christian ethics and the national interest. The crime was horrible and the severest punishment ought to have accordingly been claimed – this being a right punishment, though, afflicting the substantial evildoers, rather than a lynch-law combined with loot. *Plunder can never be an instrument of justice.* Lynching is a blind act, and therefore is always an instance of Evil. Mob-rule never concludes an affair, but instead, it opens up a long chain of avenge and lawlessness. And, first and foremost, *the Germans must not be imitated!* There is nothing for us to do that wins their support and assistance. One must not accept their principles, methods, and ideas. We do not close our eyes to *the Jewish peril*. We know what stance the Jews assumed with respect to the Poles under the Soviet occupation.[99] We know it, and remember it. *Once rebuilt, one free ancestral home shall offer no room for these occupiers, either.* We know how to free ourselves from them. But, never shall we resort to the German system of cruelty and plunder. We shall not become murderers or thieves. We shall punish in a fair fashion. We shall fight as humans do, and not as criminals do. *Off with the German methods!*

The condemnation of the anti-Jewish occurrences, which, to the mind of the author of the article, was an instance of mob rule, is completely unambiguous in this article. In addition, no doubt is expressed in this text as to whether the riots were sparked by the killing of a Christian child by the Jews. Yet, the phraseology referring to the "Jewish peril" and Poland to be freed after the war from "these occupiers" is significant. For Emanuel Ringelblum, at that time – and for us today too, I daresay – it smells of anti-Semitism. As Ringelblum would put it in his diary, "In the National-Democratic paper *Wiadomości Polskie* of 27th March, there was an editorial article on the pogrom in Warsaw. A Polish boy took something from a Jew by the Żelazna-Brama, and incidents broke out after that." The editorial Ringelblum refers to was obviously published in *Polska Żyje!*, rather

---

of a team of German propagandists in the Warsaw Ghetto in May 1942, such photographs have never been shown to public.

99 This is a clear allusion to the attitudes and behaviours of those members of the Jewish populace who received the fall of "lordly Poland" with satisfaction, and gave a joyful welcome to the "Soviet liberators". There is no afterthought about the disillusionment following soon afterwards, or that the Jews in the region were not immune to the repressive measures applied.

than in *Wiadomości Polskie*, the ZWZ organ, whose tendency was clearly liberal-democratic, and whose subsequent issues were published, around that time, on 10th and 20th of March and on 1st April. It is the article's content, though, that induced Ringelblum to name the periodical "National-Democratic" [orig., colloq., *endecki*]. In the same note, dated 27th March, somewhat further on, he at the end makes the correct reference to *Polska Żyje!*, slightly distorting the article's title into *Nie idźmy śladami tamtych* (Let's not follow their tracks) and quoting its conclusive passage not-too-accurately.

Dr. Michał Weichert, who headed the Jewish Social Self-Help, expressed an even more strongly-worded assessment of the article in his already-quoted talk with Artur Śliwiński. To his mind, "the content and form" of this text placed it among "the worst of the pogrom literature." This is doubtless a wrongful and unjust assessment, but it has to be borne in mind that the editorial team of the clandestine newsletter did their best to reach and stir the consciences of people in whose minds there still inhered prejudices and anti-Jewish phobias. These phobias and prejudices were reinforced by the hard-to-verify news about the behaviour of a part of the Jewish community after the Red Army's invasion in the Eastern borderlands of the Republic of Poland and the subsequent Soviet occupation of that territory.

In concluding our considerations on the lamentable events that took place in the streets of Warsaw in March 1940, the question may be asked whether the Varsovians could have more vigorously and resolutely opposed the riffraff. The answer is not so simple: can one expect a casual passer-by to tackle a bunch of armed cutthroats with his or her bare hands? It is, I should think, fear that prevails in any such situation, dictating passivity and discouraging active resistance. A person is left, however, with a sense of shame for this lack of courage and the cowardice displayed. Who knows? – this might be one of the reasons these events seem to have been erased, as it were, from our memory.

It is hard not to agree with Israel Gutman, who assesses the consequences of the attitudes and behaviours of Varsovians during the March incidents as follows:

> The Polish police looked the other way, the then-infant Polish resistance movement did not react – and the hooligans must have come the conclusion that the pogroms were accepted by not only the Germans but also by most Poles. It can be assumed that the lack of energetic counteraction on the part of Polish society at that stage helped the stratum of extortionists and *szmalcownik*s to get crystallised, one which would grow, with time, to become a serious threat to the Jews in hiding.[100]

---

100   I. Gutman, *Żydzi warszawscy 1939–1943. Getto – podziemie – walka*, transl. from the Hebrew by Zofia Perelmuter, Warsaw 1993, p. 55.

The role of the Germans: Instigators, or organisers and active participants of the incidents?

In an attempt to reply to the above question, I will regrettably have to deal with suppositions and my own hypotheses: such is the condition of the German file documentation concerning the Polish lands under occupation. An additional hindrance is that the published Polish memoirist accounts rarely contain the names of the German partners of their talks. Since such conversations were – quite rightly – treated by the public opinion as manifestations of collaboration with the enemy and invader, there is no wonder that any interlocutors who survived the war preferred to remain silent on the matter.

As some individuals associated with the NOR plainly appeared among the organisers of the anti-Jewish incidents in Warsaw, we first need in these considerations to try and determine who on the German side patronised the undertaking in the autumn of 1939. One thing seems certain: the consent for setting up a Polish equivalent of the NSDAP was strictly connected with the idea to establish some residual Polish state (a *Reststaat*). The concept was soon relinquished, in the end: it ceased being topical when the United Kingdom rejected Hitler's peace offering, Stalin took a resolute stance against it, and several Polish politicians, Wincenty Witos being one of them, decidedly refused to cooperate.

Assuming that the idea to create NOR was conceived in the mind of Bolesław Piasecki, then, the contacts with the Germans – or more specifically, with a few officers, probably of lower rank – were established thanks to Marian Reutt, to whom they, known to him from before the war, "proposed to enter into talks," as W. Sznarbachowski writes. Around 10th November 1939, Władysław Studnicki talked to Karl-Ulrich Neumann-Neurode, the German military commander of Warsaw – whether as an envoy of NOR or as a private person, we do not know.[101] Adam Roniker mentions a visit paid at Neumann-Neurode's on 8th October 1939 by a certain Lieutenant-Colonel Heltz, who – as an emissary of Harry von Craushaar, head of the civil administration with the commanding staff of 8th German Army, who still officiated in Łódź – inquired him about the local sentiments and offered him to come to Łódź in order to hold political talks.[102] It can be presumed that for those Germans who held consultations with representatives of NOR, Professor Zygmunt Cybichowski was the one who probably enjoyed their trust and reinforced the prestige of the emerging organisation.

---

101   For some unknown reason, he refers to him as 'von Nesselrode'; see: *Tragiczne manowce* ..., pp. 52–3.
102   A. Roniker, *Pamiętnik 1939–1945*, Krakow 2001, pp. 21–22.

The authors who write about NOR usually have no doubt that the organisation's life was very short, and was put an end to by the establishment of the Generalgouvernement (from 26th October 1939 onwards), which marked the takeover of the authority of that part of the Polish occupied territory from the military administration by a civil administration. What it supposedly meant in practice was that the rule of a police formation – referred to, most imprecisely, as the Gestapo – thereby commenced. Włodzimierz Sznarbachowski, a witness to those events, has proposed such a depiction. Following him, but not referring to the account received from him, Lucjan Blit first repeated it in his biography of Piasecki, published in London;[103] it was subsequently taken over by Jacek M. Majchrowski[104] as well as by A. Dudek and G. Pytel. Let me draw the reader's attention to the fact that accepting as axiom NOR's early demise has done much to help us lose sight of its contributions to the anti-Jewish incidents described herein.

In my opinion, the moment the Germans abandoned the concept of creating some substitute of Polish statehood, they quit the idea of taking political advantage of the milieus which had declared the will to cooperate with them to this end. As for NOR, such a decision was all the more legitimate since, following the detention (on 13th December 1939) of a few leaders of the former *Falanga*, the fact was probably revealed that a conspiratorial organisation meant to struggle with the Germans in the future was being created alongside the overt NOR. There was an additional factor which spoke in favour of quitting the political use of NOR: it was, namely, its ostentatiously declared anticommunism and anti-Soviet position, which could be troublesome to the Germans, given the overall circumstances. This, again, did not mean that they would reject the idea of using the organisation, once it existed, for their own purposes – more specifically, for the actions aimed at solving "the Jewish question". The anti-Semitism of that milieu patently made it more attractive in the occupiers' perception, while the Germans realised that this partner was not quite trustworthy. I am confident that, just like Bolesław Piasecki, who entered the game with the Germans believing that he could outsmart them, the Germans, by allowing NOR to further exist, also entered a game whose aim was to overreach the Poles.

Studies concerning German policies in occupied Poland generally tend to overlook the fact that the Germans followed the development of the Polish resistance movement with considerable concern. They would not conceal their

---

103   L. Blit, *The Eastern Pretender. Boleslaw Piasecki: His Life and Times*, London 1965, pp. 84–86.
104   J. Majchrowski, *Geneza politycznych ugrupowań katolickich. Stronnictwo Pracy i grupa „Dziś i Jutro"*, Paris 1984, p. 124.

anxiety that it might become a pressing threat, the moment military action was commenced in the West. Let us refer to an utterance, quite symptomatic in this respect, of SS-Standartenführer Josef Meisinger, commander of the police and the Security Service, who held office in Warsaw at the time. He delivered a speech during a police meeting held in the city, in the presence of General Governor Hans Frank, on 2nd March 1940. I will start with a fragment which is missing in the German edition of Frank's diary (which has remained unnoticed so far): "Poles are, overall, born-and-bred organisers of illegal operations and underhand dealings. They can perfectly pretend to be friendly, of this we all have become persuaded, and a moment later, stand against us in one way or another." Is the mention of "pretended friendship" alluding to the contacts with NOR? Meisinger also uses other phrases: "One of the most threatening perils is the fantastic belief among the Poles that Poland would regain independence. [...] We have at present more than 2,000 names and addresses of people being members of specified organisations." In conclusion of his argument, he said, "Here, in the District of Warsaw, we are sitting on a barrel of gunpowder. A single spark would suffice for all to be turned into pieces; what can only rescue us is an order to gradually liquidate the individual organisations." General Erwin Jaenecke, who attended that same meeting, added: "When the fighting begins in the West, one would have to take the option of insurgent movement into account."[105]

In the spring of 1940, there admittedly existed in the occupied Poland at least several dozen conspiratorial organisations, most of them formed spontaneously and not related with one another. There was, apparently, no agenda in place for any common "insurgent" actions in view of aiding Poland's Western allies. It was, however, the fear of the Germans that some anti-German occurrences could soon take place that underlay the decision to undertake an "extraordinary pacification action" (*AB-Aktion*) aimed at liquidation of the Polish Underground. Hans Frank said about it, on 8th March 1940, in Krakow: "It has to be presumed, and this ought to be taken into consideration, that we will be more and more frequently encountering manifestations of resistance on the part of the intelligentsia, the clergy, and former military officers. Organisations targeted against our rule in this country have already been formed. [...] The slightest attempt at any forward action undertaken by the Poles will entail a tremendous liquidation action taken against them. [...] In order to ensure peace there for the coming

---

105 *Okupacja i ruch oporu w dzienniku Hansa Franka*, vol. I: 1939–1942, Editorial Team Leader: Andrzej Janowski, p. 159 (fragment missing in the German edition), pp. 160, 163; cf. *Das Diensttagebuch des deutschen Generalgouverneurs in Polen 1939–1945*, ed. by Werner Präg and Wolfgang Jacobmeyer, Stuttgart 1975, pp. 132–135.

days, I have commanded that several hundreds of members of such organisations be arrested for three months." At the end of his speech, Frank forwarded to a group of his associates an instruction he had personally received from Hitler at a Berlin audience in 29th February 1940: "Spare no efforts, sir, to make it completely calm and quiet there. Any manoeuvre disturbing the quietness in the East will not suit me."[106] The delivery of Action "AB", which was thus announced, began on 30th March 1940. The day before, apparently not incidentally, the anti-Jewish brawls in Warsaw came to a sudden end. Further toleration, to say nothing of support, would mean to oppose the Führer's will.

There is no surviving document, or none such is known to us, based on which we could determine, with all certainty, that the anti-Jewish riots occurred in Warsaw in March 1940 at the initiative or on the order of the German occupational authorities: civil, military, or, possibly – and most probably – police authorities. It is quite possible that the idea had originally been conceived among Polish anti-Semites and collaborationists, with the Germans just approving of it and providing support to the action, as they decided to make use of it for their own propagandist purposes.

Both the chroniclers' records and the articles dealing with the events in the conspiratorial press emphasise the behaviour and conduct of the Germans, with the conclusion drawn that the anti-Jewish incidents did not surprise them at all. On the contrary, the Germans contributed to their preparation and, afterwards, took part in them and oversaw their unfolding events. The point is not that individual officers or even soldiers joined the excesses, encouraging the mob to pillage the Jewish shops. What is essential is that the actions were planned beforehand, executed on command, and managed from some instruction centre. What I have in mind is the youngsters transported by vehicles to the rioting area, the incidents being filmed and photographed, doubtlessly, by special crews, and the participants of the disturbances receiving gratuities in kind or in money – to point out to the most prominent elements.

In the course of these disturbances, a dominant trend was to see propaganda objectives behind the action as a whole, the goal to discredit and bring shame to the Poles, on the one hand, and to present the Germans as guarantors of law and order, on the other. An article titled *"Przejawy wściekłości czy prowokacja"* ["Manifestations of rage or a provocation?"] is an excellent case in point. Published on 1st April 1940 by *Wiadomości Polskie*, it observed: "It was found in the course of the brawls that German agents in civilian dress were the fomenters.

---

106   *Okupacja i ruch oporu ...*, p. 172; *Das Diensttagebuch ...*, p. 151.

When the disturbances were 'on', the Gestapo, in uniforms, would intervene – well, calming the crowd down. The whole thing was filmed (what a brilliant propaganda idea to show to America: the Gestapo defending Jews oppressed by the Polish doggery!)."

We can find penetrating remarks and extremely close conclusions on this subject in the 1943 study by Emanuel Ringelblum, which has been quoted several times already. We read:

> The Germans realized what excellent propaganda material was provided by their role as protectors against Polish aggression. This was a remarkably effective psychological propaganda trick. The Jews, the Germans claimed, are a harmful, destructive, unproductive element. They are hated by the Polish population, as is proved by the frequent attacks on the Jews. The Germans are instrumental in restoring law and order. They defend the Jews and put them to productive work. Photographs depicting Germans in their role of protectors against attacks by Poles, pictures sometimes authentic and sometimes faked, and staged for this purpose, were proof of the fact that the Germans were *Kulturträger* in the "Wild East", where they were introducing elements of civilization and culture. The photographs of Germans saving Jews from the aggression of the Poles would from then on be repeated with every possible variation. A very important propaganda success was thus achieved. News was reaching the outside world of German atrocities in the occupied Polish cities, of mass murders of the civilian population and especially of Jews, of the burning down of towns, etc. By reproducing pictures of the Germans as defenders of the Jews, evidence would be given of the Germans' humanitarianism.[107]

This argument is convincing; such were, probably, the intents and purposes of the propaganda sections operating in the territory of the *Generalgouvernement*, both civil and military ones. Someone must have ordered the photographing and filming of the incidents. But, as I have already said, these materials were eventually not used in public. Probably, the intention was not to provoke the public opinion in the West of Europe; another reason was, perhaps, that the concept to form in Warsaw a Jewish district enclosed with walling was temporarily quit.

Rumours of a ghetto in Warsaw formed by the Germans first appeared in the autumn of 1939. These rumours intensified a few weeks later, as plaques were fixed in the Jewish quarter warning against potential epidemic within the area. Rumours that the area had been enclosed arose from time to time. On 18th March 1940, four days before the anti-Jewish turmoil broke out, A. Czerniaków noted down: "A demand that the Community ring the 'ghetto' with wire, put in fenceposts, etc., and later guard it all." This time, the decision was made, then; the question is, who made it? As it seems, the decision was not taken at the office

---

107   *Polish-Jewish relations* ..., pp. 45–46.

of the Head of the District of Warsaw, that is, Governor Ludwig Fischer. After all, the Jewish Council Chairman writes, clearly enough: "In the morning at the SS" – and it was there that the move was decided. And it was there, I should suppose, that it was decided to make the Jews aware what threats were implied in case there is no enclosed ghetto area in Warsaw. It cannot be determined, unfortunately, whether the concept of provoked anti-Jewish incidents was conceived at the Warsaw Gestapo headquarters on Szucha Avenue. – or, the initiative of Polish fascists was accepted there with delight, and backed with a promise of cooperation, support and, possibly, impunity to the participants.

As is known, the execution of the plan to build in Warsaw an enclosed ghetto had eventually to be postponed for a couple of months, albeit fragments of the walling-under-construction began emerging in spring 1940 at various spots in the city. There is much indication that the initiative to enclose the Jewish district, pushed by the police media, met with resistance from the occupation administration authorities. As Ringelblum noted on 27th March 1940, "They say that the Mayor of the City and the military authorities are against erecting the walls. Those ones [Ringelblum's description of the Gestapo – T.S.] as well as the sanitary authorities vote yea, however." As for the sanitary authorities, they put forward the argument of epidemic. Mentioning a Mayor, the author might have had Governor Ludwig Fischer in mind, who, after the dismissal of Oskar Dengel the day before, assumed the post of *Stadtpräsident*, appointing Ludwig Leist his plenipotentiary for the City of Warsaw.[108]

On reconstructing the course of the anti-Jewish riots in Warsaw, I have already mentioned that during their course, on 26th March 1940, Adam Czerniaków travelled to Krakow, leading a Judenrat delegation. The trip had been planned earlier on and its main goal was to discuss the living problems of the Jewish populace with the German authorities, including its share in the assistance that had been provided by U.S. charity organisations. Due to the ongoing situation, intervention in response to the Warsaw incidents had become an urgent question. Regrettably,

---

108 Fischer must obviously have known about the anti-Jewish incidents in Warsaw; he might arguably have not approved of these developments but, perhaps, did not dare oppose the doings of the Police. In any case, his report as for 11th March to 10th April 1940 contains no such mention; see: Raporty Ludwiga Fischera, gubernatora dystryktu warszawskiego 1939–1944, transl. from the German by M. Borkowicz, J. Czepulis, J. Kosim; ed. by K. Dunin-Wąsowicz et al., Warsaw 1987, pp. 168–184. Let me remind that A. Czerniaków was ordered, apparently not accidentally, to get in touch, once back in Warsaw, with Ludwig Leist, who as from 26th March 1940 exercised the occupational power over the city, on behalf of Fischer.

we have neither a shorthand report nor any minute notes from these talks, which could have possibly helped unveil some of the behind-the-scenes developments or, in any case, facilitate an answer to the question which of the German authorities supported them, and for which did the events come as a surprise. It should be regretted that the information Czerniaków provides is so enigmatic. The day after he arrived in Krakow, he noted down: "In the afternoon, received by Dr. Artl and his colleague Heinrich. I spoke on the topic of the security of life and property. [...] I described the present pogroms in Warsaw, the like of which has not been seen since 1880." Let us explain that Adam's interlocutors were Fritz Artl, who managed the Central Department of Population and Social Care within the so-called "Government" of the *Generalgouvernment*, and Dr Herbert Heinrich, who acted, under F. Artl, as an officer for Jewish affairs.

In Czerniaków's note of 28th March, we can not only find much more information but also learn about certain decisions of enormous importance which were taken in Krakow. In the morning of that day, Isaac Bornstein, a delegate of the American charity Joint (JDS) who resided in Warsaw, joined the delegation together with his associate. The arrivals shared the recent news of the Warsaw incidents. The delegates visited Mr. Artl again. As Czerniaków noted, "Artl received us and made a call to Dr. Gauweiler who reported that the appropriate steps had already been taken." Let us explain that Otto Gauweiler was manager of the Internal Affairs Section with the office of the Head of the Warsaw District, Governor Fischer. Czerniaków goes on to write: "At our request he agreed to call Meisinger. (He did in fact get in touch with the SS-Krüger and – I suppose with Meisinger.). He told us to leave today for Warsaw and get in touch with Leist, Meisinger, and Gauweiler on arrival." We already know who Meisinger was. It was probably Meisinger who, together with his deputy (and, a year later, successor) Joachim Müller, played the whole "game" with NOR and organised the course of the anti-Jewish incidents in Warsaw. In turn, the said Friedrich-Wilhelm Krüger, SS-Gruppenführer, Higher Commander of the Generalgouvernment's SS and the Police, was, along with Hans Frank, a pretty central figure in the German elite ruling occupied Poland. In the afternoon of that same day, 28th March, Czerniaków, together with his colleagues, was called to see Artl once again. As he put down in his diary, "We were received by Heinrich and one after another reported what we have observed in Warsaw. Those statements were being taken down. I again mentioned the matter of the beatings."

Before his return to Warsaw, Czerniaków learned the most important thing, which meant a great success of the delegation. He was namely informed that a written instruction issued by SS-Standartenführer Friedrich-Wilhelm Siebert, head of the Central Office of Internal Affairs with the Generalgouvernment's

"Government", whereby all the matters regarding Jewish people were meant to thenceforth be made part of the exclusive competence of the local authorities of the occupational civil administration. Probably, after receiving detailed information on anti-Jewish incidents in Warsaw, the Germans realised that the actions taken by the local police "media" had not been agreed with, nor accepted by, any supreme authority residing in the Generalgouvernment's "capital town". The aforesaid instruction was meant to bring an end to the excesses, and indeed, from 29th March 1940 onwards the Warsaw streets were calm.

The already-quoted account of a witness to the Warsaw incidents, written down in Jerusalem on 12th May 1940, explains the reason behind the decision taken in Krakow in a different way: "The reason why the pogrom was stopped was perhaps this: an official of the Joint (American Jewish Joint Distribution Committee) who was called to Krakow to discuss the organization of social relief, told the official of the Governor General Artl, that so long as pogroms continued it was out of question to arrange for any organized social relief. Probably because of this the Germans ordered the ruffians to be sent away and the pogrom was stopped."[109] Taking into account that Artl, who was responsible for social care issues in the Generalgouvernment, was indeed the highest-ranking figure the delegates talked to in Krakow, the monetary argument put forth by Bornstein certainly could not be neglected by the Germans.

In Ringelblum's diary (erroneously dated 2nd March; the correct date is 2nd April), we can read: "There is complete peace prevailing in the streets. The Jewish people, who were hiding in their flats last week, are coming out of their houses. [...] They say that action has been taken against the saddening events. [...] Intervention was undertaken with SS commander Krüger, and the excesses were consequently subdued. A certain Puławski was arrested, who apparently had something to do with the incidents." Thus, we have received a confirmation of the information concerning Mr. Puławski and, in parallel, a piece of news on the start of *AB-Aktion*.

During this Action (which came to an end only on 10th July 1940), Bruno Streckenbach, SS-Brigadenführer and commander of the Generalgouvernment's Security Police and Security Service, said at a conference in Krakow: "Paralysing the resistance movement by removing its leaders called for toilsome anterior preparation. The action was commenced, all of a sudden, on 30th March. [...] Resulting from the action of 30th March, approximately 1,000 people have been arrested, which is even more than was expected. There were 2,200–2,400 resistance

---

109   Cf. footnote 16.

movement members listed in the Police records, and hiding under false names; some 1,200 of them have been completely identified. About 1,000 persons were arrested out of these latter mentioned, including 700 more outstanding activists of the Polish resistance movement." *Biuletyn Informacyjny* of 5th April 1940 so commented on the Action: "The Gestapo are sensing the pulsation of the independence-oriented life; however, incapable, so far, of concretely grasping its manifestations, they are striking in a boorish manner, at haphazard, in line with the 'collective responsibility' method. They are striking the stratum that might potentially be the inspirer and supervisor of every independence action." This is a completely correct assessment, as among those arrested and then killed during the "extraordinary pacification action" were representatives of individual professional groups typical of intelligentsia, who oftentimes had no contacts with the Polish Underground whatsoever.

In conclusion, I will briefly describe the how the anti-Jewish incidents in Warsaw were presented to the Germans themselves, and what was the image that the Hitlerite propaganda intended to transmit to other countries. One finds coverage in the article *"Polen verprügeln jüdische Wucherer. Wachsende Erkenntnis der wahren Schuldigen. Auf jüdische Händler gestürzt"* ["Poles batter the Jewish profiteers. A growing cognisance of the true culprits. Jewish tradesmen toppled"], published in *Warschauer Zeitung* of 3rd April 1940. As we can learn, it is the Jews that are the reason for the poverty suffered by wide strata of Polish society. It is they who push up the prices of goods, hoard supplies, deal with illegal trading. The assaults on Jews from the Poles is an attempt to straighten this, getting even with the "Jewish parasites". It was found, on that occasion, that the pre-war Polish Government was a "tool of international Jewry", the Jews in Poland "enjoying the largest patronage that enabled them to exploit the Polish nation." Apparently, the German civil authorities eventually extended their efficient care to the Polish populace.

Chapter 2 Paris

Anti-Semitic propaganda and first anti-Jewish incidents at the threshold of the occupation

The German army entered Paris on 14th June 1940. The French capital surrendered without struggle, but the town was depopulated. Out of its almost three million pre-war inhabitants (within the limits of the city's twenty arrondissements), only a few hundred thousand remained. Aware of how the German occupiers were treating the people in Poland, the French were escaping as they expected a barbarian invasion, as well as retaliation for Germany's defeat in World War One. But the victors behaved in Paris quite appropriately, sometimes even cordially and with sophisticated kindness. All the sources concerning the beginnings of the occupation are unanimous in this respect. One thing definitely stood out: their never-saturated will to shop. The shop owners, who thus found the way to sell off their slower-moving commodities and trashier goods, were naturally delighted; unlike the local clientele, as attested by the nickname they bestowed on the Germans – *les doryphores* ("potato beetles").

As was the case with Poland, the occupiers' propaganda was targeted primarily against the English. Posters put up in Warsaw and in Paris laid the blame on them for the military defeat of the Poles and the French and for the devastations and human sufferings.[110] These posters were designed by the same artist, Theo Matejko, which is not a well-known fact. No anti-Semitic accents appeared during the first two weeks of the occupation in Paris. No public assaults of Jews, or instances of their mistreatment or abuse were recorded, either, as opposed to the daily routine in the streets of Warsaw. Moments after Paris was seized, however, German crews began looting Jewish property, beginning with collections of art.[111]

One comes across signs of anti-Semitic propaganda in the legal press in the early days of July 1940. The campaign was launched by *La France au Travail*

---

110 In Warsaw, the drawing was subtitled "*Anglio! Twoje dzieło!*" ["That's your work, England!"], while in Paris, "*C'est l'Anglais qui nous a fait ça!*"; both posters are reproduced in my book *Życie codzienne w stolicach okupowanej Europy*, Warsaw 1995, following p. 16.

111 Cf. "Zum nationalsozialistischen Kunstraub in Frankreich. Der 'Bargatzky-Bericht'", ed. by W. Treue, [in:] *Vierteljahrshefte für Zeitgeschichte*, 1965, fasc. 3, pp. 285–337; also, J. Cassou (ed.), *Le pillage par les Allemands des œuvres d'art et des bibliothèques appartenant à des Juifs en France: recueil de documents*, Paris 1947.

[*France at Work*], a newspaper created on the initiative of Otto Abetz's team, first issued on 30th June 1940. (Abetz and his associates will be mentioned several times in this chapter.) The daily's title as well as the subtitle (*Grand quotidien d'informaiton au serivce du peuple français*) were indicative of its target reading public – the common strata, the working class. In his memoirs, written down in 1950, when serving time in French prisons, Abetz wrote: "In order to provide an authoritative press to the working class, the newspaper *La France au Travail* was created, with support from the embassy."[112] This was of course not about providing the workers with a tribune but about a measured political game which aimed, on the one hand, to pursue the group's own populist propaganda and, on the other, to draw political clientele away from the communists. Let me point out that the newspaper was set up when talks were underway between Abetz and representatives of the Communist Party of France; the latter had proposed to the Germans that their press organ, *L'Humanité*, be legally published. By all indications, both parties to the bargaining expected to outsmart their partner.[113]

The Germans ultimately did not consent to the use of the name *L'Humanité* but permitted *Ce Soir* instead (the galley proof of the magazine's first issue bears the date 8th July 1940, but it never came to publication). In connection with the ongoing talks concerning a legal communist periodical, an anonymous note was compiled, dated 7th July and titled "*Aufzeichnung über die französische kommunistische Partei*". Its author, probably Otto Abetz himself, stated: "The editors appointed by the communist movement to run the publication of this newspaper expressed their readiness not only to submit the typeset texts for inspection but also to strictly adhere to the policy of the newspaper, *La France au Travail, as edited by us* [emphasis – T.S.], in the planning of individual articles and discussing all the political issues."[114]

---

112 O. Abetz, *Das offene Problem: Ein Rückblick auf zwei Jahrzehnte deutscher Frankreichpolitik*, Köln, 1951, p. 136.

113 These talks are continually evoked as evidence to CPF's collaboration with the German occupiers, whereas the former's striving for cunningly outwitting the counterparty is rarely recognised. Among the important publications on this topic are: D. Peschanski, *La demande de parution légale de L'*Humanité *(17 juin 1940–27 août 1940)*, 'Le mounvement sociale', no. 113, October–December 1983, pp. 67–89. The text of the galley proof of *Ce Soir* newspaper was published in 1983 by R. Bourderon and G. Willard, *Cahiers d'histoire de l'institut de recherches marxistes*, no. 14, pp. 168–172; for the most comprehensive take of the matter, see: S. Courtois, *Un été 1940. Les négociations entre le PCF et l'occupant allemand à la lumière des archives de l'Internationale communiste*, in: 'Communisme', nos. 32–33, 1992–3, pp. 85–127.

114 Centre de Documentation Juive Contemporaine (hereinafter, CDJC), ref. no. LXXa.

The signal to kick off an anti-Semitic propaganda campaign in occupied Paris was given by George Montandon's article "*Les juifs démasqés*", published in *La France au Travail* on 2nd July 1940. The author, soon to become an expert in racial issues in the Germans' service, was introduced as a professor of ethnology with the Ecole d'Antropologie of Paris, with renowned achievements to his credit.[115] "It would be a crime against France," he wrote, "not to resume the anti-Jewish action and bring it to an end. The purpose ought to be: (1) strip the Jewish citizens of their French nationality; (2) expropriate them; (3) remove them to an autonomous country that would be assigned for them."

Two days later, this same newspaper published on its front page a framed slogan reading: "The lesson learned from the war: Throw the Jew out, and you shall win. Breed and tend him, and you shall be conquered." Montandon's text was probably commissioned by the Germans but was concordant with the author's own views; the slogan was coined by the French anti-Semite, rather than forced on him by the editorial board. It nonetheless happened that the legal Paris press published texts supplied directly by the occupiers. Such was the case, for instance, with an article printed by *Les Dernières Nouvelles* of 11th July 1940 demanding that all Jews naturalised after 1900 be expelled, in stages, from the territory of France. The writer Paul Léautaud reported in his diary a conversation he had had about that particular article with a journalist working for the paper; as it turns out, the article had been "delivered to the journal for publication" – quite obviously, by the Germans.[116]

Anti-Jewish texts appeared in the legal Paris press from mid-July 1940 onwards in increasing numbers. On 17th July, the daily *Le Matin*, with a circulation of several hundred thousand, published an item titled "*Interdit aux Juifs*", featuring a photograph of a plate fixed on a Paris grocer's shop, with an inscription reading: in German, "*In diesem Lokal Juden unerwünscht. Rein Arischer Betrieb*",

---

[115] The figure of George Montandon (1879–1944), a scientist and intellectual, a collaborator who was killed by the Résistance in July 1944, doubtlessly deserves a serious scholarly biography. Perhaps Marc Knobel, who has written several important contributions (among others, "L'ethnologue a la dérive: George Montandon et l'ethnoracisme", *L'Ethnologie française*, 18 (1988), pp. 107–113) might write one. Also, cf. Birnbaum, P., "*La France aux Français*": *Histoire des haines nationalistes*, Paris, 1993, pp. 187–198 (chapter "George Montandon: l'anthropologue vichyste au service du nazisme"). It is rather odd that the authors writing on Montandon have not become acquainted with the sizeable file of materials gathered by the German authorities regarding this man that is presently kept at the Archives Nationales in Paris (hereinafter, "AN"), in the *Militärbefehlshaber in Frankreich* collection (hereinafter, "AJ40"), box 567, dossier 9.

[116] P. Léautaud, *Journal littéraire*, vol. III, Paris 1986, p. 127.

and in French, "*Les Juifs ne sont pas admis ici*" (see Fig. 3). The following day saw the publication in *La France au Travail* of an article by Prof. G. Montandon, "*A quoi reconnaît-on les Juifs?*", briefing the reader on how to recognise the Jewish physiognomy (as part of a cycle titled "Scholarly chats"). In two Paris newspapers of 4th August 1940, we can find texts on the capital city's district of Marais, populated to a significant extent by Jewish people. Martin Dubois's article in *La France au Travail* was entitled "*Au coeur du vieux Paris. Le Ghetto. Quartier réservé et bastion avancé de la Juiverie française*" ("In the heart of the old Paris. The Ghetto. A reserved district and an advanced bastion of French Jewry"). The report in *Le Matin* titled "*Tache au coeur de Paris. Le ghetto doit disparaître. Un dédale de voies étroites et sordides dans le quartier du Marais*" ("A blemish at the heart of Paris. The ghetto ought to disappear. A maze of narrow and sordid bystreets in the district of Marais") is much more extensive. The reader is reassured that "Every single thing is Jewish there: the things, the people, the inscriptions. […] Almost everyone is dealing in something in this quarter. […] It is strange that in a time when fighting microbes is the topic of the day, that detestable blemish in the very heart of Paris, the ghetto, is allowed to continue to exist."

Whereas the journals mentioned so far published their anti-Semitic texts rather sporadically, the weekly *Au Pilori* (*At the Pillory*), first issued on 12th July 1940, was a different case in point. Its subtitle, reading *Hebdomadaire de combat contre la judeo-maçonnerie*, left no doubt as to the guiding purpose of its editors. As they proudly declared, their magazine was "one-hundred-percent French"; in issue no. 2 of 19th July, they claimed that one of their purposes was goal of putting the Jews, recognised as foreigners, in labour camps. The following issue, dated 26th July, published an article claiming that "the Jews of France ought to pay for the war, or die." Issue no. 5 of 9th August announced a six-item programme of actions meant to lead to a solution to the Jewish issue", demanding that: "(1) Masonic lodges and their branches be dissolved; (2) Jews be barred from holding any post in the judiciary, the press, the radio, and public administration, with '*numerus clausus*' being introduced for Jewish physicians and barristers; (3) Jews be registered in order to be deprived of French nationality and civil rights; (4) special passports be launched for the Israelites as well as all foreigners; (5) all Jews, instigators of disturbances, profiteers, exploiters, and embezzlers be concentrated in labour camps, so that they may be employed in the redevelopment of the regions affected by the war; (6) Jewish property be registered, so that all the appropriate measures be undertaken, for the good of the masses, to gradually eliminate the Jews from the national economy which is being destroyed by the international Jewish capital." Let it be noted that the Germans carried out most of these postulates by the summer of 1942.

Au Pilori was no doubt the most abhorrent magazine of those published in German-occupied Paris. Even when the German authorities restricted the allotment of printing paper for other periodicals, this particular weekly always enjoyed special care and could afford a circulation of several dozen thousand. *Au Pilori* was created and run by Henry-Robert Petit, a Paris attorney, who was its editor-in-chief till about 20th September 1940.[117] Before the war, he was known as the author of many anti-Jewish and anti-Masonic lampoons as well as editor of the monthly *Le Pilori*, which was suspended by the censorship authorities in 1939.[118] As Henri Amoroux aptly points out, the magazine, re-established by Petit under a slightly modified title, was essentially not collaborationist, as one would find in it no commendations of Hitler or the German army, or of the occupational system. As perceived by the journalists contributing to *Au Pilori*, the occupation worked as a sort of "shield behind which they could seek refuge, to keep pursuing their own goals with impunity."[119] I should think that something of the sort might be said about the Warsaw periodical *Atak* and the milieu gathered around Andrzej Świetlicki.

Now that we have an idea of the anti-Semitic propaganda that was circulating in the legal press, it is time to move to the topic of the anti-Jewish disturbances for which Paris set the scene in the first weeks of the occupation. We know quite a lot about these occurrences from two primary sources: the regular police intelligence reports (*Rapports de quinzaine des Renseignements Généraux*; hereinafter, "RG"), stored today at the Police Prefecture Archive in Paris, and the published diary of the French police prefect Roger Langeron (1882–1966).[120]

---

117 According to a Propaganda-Abteilung report of 4th November 1940, the circulation of *Au Pilori* was 60,000 in mid-August and as much as 110,000 by early November; AN, fund AJ40, box 1001, dossier 4, c. 20. As of December 1941, the number of copies fell back to 60,000 (of which 24% did not sell); still, *Au Pilori* was categorised as one of periodicals that "have to be published in any case"; ibidem, box 1013.

118 During my stay in Paris, I read copies of *Au Pilori* at the Bibliothèque Naitonale, but missed the opportunity to take a look of the editor's other publications. The U.S. Congress Library Catalogue mentions seven pre-war and two occupation-period items by Petit; cf. *The National Union Catalog. Pre-1956 Imprints*, vol. 453, Mansell, 1976, pp. 154–5.

119 H. Amoroux, *La grande histoire des Français sous l'occupation*, vol. V: *Les passions et les haines*, Paris 1981, p. 249.

120 RG reports, titled *Situation à Paris*, covering the city's political, cultural, and economic life, form one of the most important sources for researchers of the history of occupied Paris (in spite of the description "*de quinzaine*", the reports were issued on a weekly basis). Prefect Langeron's diary, published in Paris in 1946, encompasses – in

It is in Langeron's diary that we can find the first mention of actions taken against the Jews. Thus reads the note dated 18th June 1940: "The anti-Semitic propaganda now specialises in obstructing the entrances to Israelite shops. Young people gather in front of the doors, forbidding the customers to go inside, until the police arrives to enable unrestrained passage again and arrest those who brought about the disorder." The first preserved RG report, of 22nd July, in its column headed *Antisémitisme*, reads: "Clearly manifesting itself in the press, the anti-Semitic propaganda has clearly jelled in an attempt at opposing the customers entering certain shops whose owners are considered to be Israelites. These actions have not occurred on a large scale, for the time being." Let us add that *Au Pilori* first announced a slogan calling for the boycott Jewish shops on 19th July.

A note in Langeron's diary of 29th July 1940 tells us that a new means of fight became used: "Butterflies of anti-Jewish propaganda posted on the walls. The police immediately cause them to disappear." As we learn from the RG report for the same day, these stickers with anti-Semitic slogans were produced by an organisation called *Les Gardes Françaises*, which had developed under the patronage of Henry-Robert Petit and *Au Pilori*. We will encounter this organisation again later on; now, let me point out that the "butterflies" were posted in the streets of Paris mostly by young men who also dealt with the distribution of *Au Pilori*. Frankly speaking, I never thought I would ever see original copies of these stickers, as they were not attached to the RG report. By a stroke of luck I came across them, rather coincidentally, in an archival collection (ref. no. AJ40) of the German occupational authorities kept at the Archives Nationales in Paris. What I found there was a report on a police-station interrogation of a certain André Vieillevigne who was detained on 18th August 1940. An eighteen-year-old mechanic, jobless at the time, Vieillevigne was caught by a policeman on that day posting some of those "butterflies". Eighteen such gummed stickers were attached to the report, featuring eight various texts or drawings, as evidence. Some of them read: "*Ici maison juive*" ("Jewish house here"; see Fig. 4); "*La fortune des Juifs est la propriété de la communauté française*" ("The property of the Jews is property of the French community"); "*Abbatez la féodalité Judéo-maçonnique et la France sera sauveé*" ("Overthrow the Jewish-Masonic autocracy, and France shall be saved"); "*Acheter chez les Juifs, c'est ruiner le commerce français*" ("Purchasing from Jews means destroying French trade");

---

spite of its title: *Paris juin 40* – the period of 14th June 1940 to 20th January 1941; four days after the latter date, Langeron was arrested by the Gestapo. See his biographical note in: *Dictionnaire biographique des préfets septembre 1870–mai 1982*, Paris 1994, pp. 329–330.

"*Les Juifs sont des étrangers* ("The Jews are foreigners"); "*Faites payer les Juifs*" ("Let the Jews pay!").[121]

The already quoted RG report of 29th July 1940 described two incidents from the preceding week. The first occurred on 26th July in the evening when "300 young Israelites" gathered in rue du Pas-de-la-Mule, which led toward Place des Vosges, to manifest their protest in front of the Gardes Françaises office which was housed at a café located in the said square. A brawl occurred; the police eventually suppressed the protest. The following day, early in the afternoon, an incident took place in the Place de la République. The clash involved sellers of *Au Pilori* on the one hand and some "*soi-disant israélites*", that is, "alleged Israelites", as the report described them. Thus, the report unambiguously insinuated a provocation. Prefect Langeron had no doubt about it, as he noted in his diary, on 31st July 1940: "A few brawls occurred between sellers of *Au Pilori* and so-called Israelites whom we have very quickly debunked as provocateurs on the Boches' military pay." What this tells us is that some German institution very much wanted to have street riots occurring in Paris, with anti-Semitic sentiments heightened, to create a climate of support for the soon to come orders discriminating against the Jews. It seems that these actions did not produce the expected effect. Jacques Biélinky, a Jewish journalist, noted down with satisfaction in his diary on 24th July 1940: "Animated talks in the queues (for milk, or meat) – not a trace of anti-Semitism."[122]

The anti-Jewish incidents intensified in August. As Langeron observed on 3rd August 1940: "Are some anti-Semitic acts of violence just about to begin? A window of a certain shop has been plundered by a raging group of protesters. Many of them were arrested, a result of my efforts." The RG report tells us that it was on the same day that the police dispersed a crowd gathered around *Au Pilori* sellers on Boulevard de Ménilmontant. We cannot tell in this case whether the occurrence was a matter of provocation again or whether it was a Jewish protest against the anti-Jewish propaganda. An incident was also seen in Boulevard Hausmann when a man in front of the "Bouchara" shop began shouting, "*A bas les Juifs!*" ("Down with the Jews!"). On Sunday, 4th August 1940, as we read in the RG report, the flea market by Porte de Saint-Ouen became the scene of a struggle between *Au Pilori* sellers and Jews. The report does not refer to "so-called Israelites", nor does it use inverted commas for the expression. My presumption

---

121 AN, fund AJ40, box 878, dossier 2, cc. 254–265.
122 J. Bélinky, *Journal 1940–1942. Un journaliste juif à Paris sous l'Occupation*, ed. by R. Poznanski, Paris 1992, p. 38.

is that this was a manifestation of Jewish self-defence, spontaneous rather than organised.

On that same Sunday, one more occurrence of essential importance took place, also described in an RG report. The Cirque d'Hiver in Pasdeloup square, not far from Place de la République, witnessed the first anti-Semitic rally in occupied Paris. The main speaker was a certain René Saint-George, member of the editorial team of *La France au Travail*, the newspaper published by the Germans (a fact worth stressing). Among the few other attendees who took the floor, the report mentions a "former activist with Rassemblement antijuif de France", apparently named "Cezille". The spelling of this name was erroneous, awkwardly enough. A year later, we see Captain Paul Sézille, then a director of the Institut d'étude des questions juives, controlled by the Security Service and the German Embassy, acting as the organiser of the notorious exhibition "Je Juif et la France". The first anti-Jewish rally, convened probably on the inspiration of the Germans, attracted no crowds – with a mere fifty people attending.

The next RG report is dated 12th August 1940 and describes the events of the preceding week, including new anti-Jewish incidents. As it turns out, 6th August saw *Au Pilori* sellers along with other Les Gardes Françaises members break into two Jewish shops on rue Lecourbe, devastating them, knocking over the counters and shelves with goods. The following day, prefect Langeron wrote that the police arrested four of these attackers. On 8th August, another group of fascist-inclined youth, members of the Union Populaire de la Jeunesse Française, associated with Doriot's Parti Populaire Français, made a commotion in front of the "Bouchara" shop on Boulevard Hausmann. A sticker with the inscription "*Maison juive*" was placed outside the shop, and those gathered exclaimed "A bas les Juifs!" – with no echo from the crowd, though, as the police report remarked. Jacques Biélinky noted down in his diary a different incident from that same day: in the passage at Barreau du Temple, a brawl broke out between *Au Pilori* sellers and a group of Jewish merchants, former combatants. The police report does not mention this particular incident.

The fifth issue of *Au Pilori* published on 9th August 1940 comprised an open letter from Henry-Robert Petit, Editor-in-Chief, to the Prefects of the Seine and the Police, which reads as follows: "In view of ensuring health and public safety, we demand from you, Sirs, that you deign to issue a regulation to be binding for the Seine Department that would summon all the owners of shops to place in a visible manner outside their premises their own family surname and first name. Such a regulation would enable the French people to recognise one another and disclose those Israelite merchants who are hiding under pseudonyms, which is misleading to those buying goods from them in good faith. We are awaiting your decision, Sirs, so that we can judge your own national sentiments." A noteworthy *Avertissement* – which was both an announcement and warning – was placed below the letter. "Our comrades, reviled by the Jews, have always briskly responded to the provocations coming from the Jews. It is disgraceful to see a police force which is called French take the side of the Jews against the French. We demand that exemplary sanctions be imposed on the policemen, regardless of their rank, who have perpetrated any such impermissible chicanery. These gentlemen ought to well know that neither the lodge nor the consistory is in power here anymore." The last sentence quite clearly alludes to Roger Langeron, Prefect of the Paris Police.

The same issue of the magazine published an article titled *En Pologne*, which described the legislation introduced for the Generalgouvernement as exemplary. The marking of local Jews with the Star of David, the creation of the ghettos, and obligatory coerced labour imposed on the Jews was received with satisfaction. Let me remark that almost in parallel, on 10th August, *Le Matin* published an article titled *Le sort des Juifs est fixé en Roumanie*, which informed about the bans introduced in Romania on Jews – such as getting married with Romanians of either sex and holding public functions.

A police report observed that on the 10th of August twenty members of the previously mentioned Union Populaire de la Jeunesse Française gathered in front of the "Levitan" retail outlet in Boulevard Magenta. The delegation announced to the owner, "We want France to be for the French, not for Jews." When he declared that he also employed demobilised soldiers at his place, the attackers went away. On the following day, Sunday 11th August, a second rally of Parisian anti-Semites was held at the Cirque d'Hiver. The RG report clearly states that the gathering was held by René Saint-George, editor of *La France au Travail*, under the authorisation of the German authorities. "*Capitaine* Cezille" chaired the assembly; one of the speakers was Monsieur Lefebvre (of whom more is to come) of the Gardes Françaises, who has "uncovered the disastrous effect exerted by Judeo-Masonry on our economic, political, and social life." The rally lasted some ninety minutes and was attended by as many as a hundred people. The following RG report, dated 19th August 1940, speaks about a third rally of anti-Semites, held the day before (on Sunday) at the same place, the Cirque d'Hiver, involving some 200 attendees. "The numerous speakers," the report tells us, "recommended that a government be formed with the help from the Gardes Françaises, as the Vichy Government, in their view, was nonexistent." Clearly enough, the ambitions of the Parisian anti-Semites reached very far. They felt supported by people influential with the occupational authorities, but probably remained unaware that they were pawns in a complicated game whose basic objective was to agitate and divide French society and to crush it politically in order to ensure the country's internal weakness against Germany's domination.

The following message was announced in the *Le Matin* daily of Monday, 19th August 1940: "*Manifestations contre les Juifs. Et contre les francs-maçons. À Vichy, à Toulouse et à Lyon*". This piece of information was said to have come from Geneva the previous day. In Vichy, the parade was joined by members of Parti Populaire Français, run by Jacques Doriot. The crowd exclaimed "*A bas les Juifs et les francs-maçons!*" and "*A bas l'Angleterre!*" A release published on the same day by *La France au Travail* was similar, but not identical; the title read: "*Nouvelles de Vichy. Aux cris de: 'A bas les Juifs! A bas les maçons!'. La foule manifeste à Vichy et à Toulouse. Des mouvements analogues ont déjà signalés à Nice et à Lyon*". The short note stated: "Geneva, 19th August [*sic!*]. As we have learned, Vichy was the scene for demonstrations against the Jews and Masons. The protesters formed a parade that marched through a park full of people, from the casino to the therapeutic waters pavilion. They carried a bust of the founder of the city's Masonic lodge which they hanged from a tree shouting, 'Down with Jews and Masons!', 'Down with England!'. Similar demonstrations were carried out in Toulouse where they were primarily aimed against the former Interior Minister Sarraut and his brother, who was the owner of the newspaper *La Dépêche de Toulouse*." Remarkably enough, Doriot, a politician towards whom ambassador Otto Abetz was disposed very negatively, was not mentioned at all. The time has come to deal with this figure in more detail, highlighting the role he played in Paris during the first few months of the occupation.

French anti-Semites and their German counterparts

While probably all the countries conquered by the Third Reich witnessed jurisdictional disputes between the various bodies, authorities, institutions, and "duty stations" (*Dienststellen*) of the occupational authorities, it was probably in France that the phenomenon occurred with particular clarity. This reflected to a significant extent the situation at the top of the Nazi hierarchy, with the accompanying struggle for influence amongst its members at the time, involving the supreme military command, the Reich Security Main Office, the Abwehr (the military intelligence organisation), the Goebbels-run Ministry of Propaganda, and the Ministry of Foreign Affairs, headed by Ribbentrop. It must have been due to several factors that an envoy of Ribbentrop played a completely unique role in France, at least in the course of the first months of the country's occupation. Crucial to this end was the fact that the brutal actions of the SS, Sipo (Security Police), and SD (Security Service) in Poland, which had met with severe criticism from even some of the generals, became an argument for restricting the responsibilities of this "department" – all the more so, as far as creating a certain image of the occupation was concerned, which in the West European countries was allegedly meant to conform to the rules of international law. On the other hand, although Hitler had resolved to introduce a military management system within the occupied French territory, he was afraid of entrusting his generals with the delivery of political goals which he had not yet made precise for himself; he apparently did not think highly of the intellectual advantages of these men. He needed someone who knew the country and had established contacts, someone who could act as a counsellor, propose certain solutions, and facilitate reaching those who saw the future of France in Europe under German hegemony and win them over for cooperation.

Otto Abetz (1903–1958), who was proposed to Hitler by Ribbentrop, seemingly fulfilled all these conditions.[123] This modest drawing teacher in a school for girls in Karlsruhe had attended meetings of German and French youth since the early thirties. In 1932, he joined the NSDAP and married Suzanne de Bryuker, a Frenchwoman and secretary to Jean Luchaire, an influential journalist who after the war was sentenced to death for collaboration. Two years later, Abetz assumed a post dealing with French affairs with the *Reichsjugendführung*. From 1935 on, he was employed with the office of Ribbentrop, who was advisor to Hitler on international policies. Thanks to Abetz's efforts, the same year saw the establishment in France of Comité France-Allemagne, an organisation that facilitated the influence of German culture and Nazi ideology on the French intellectual elite.

---

123 For more on O. Abetz and the role he played in occupied France, mainly in 1940–1941, see, in the first place: E. Jäckel, *La France dans l'Europe de Hitler*, transl. from German by D. Meunier, Paris 1968, pp. 99–104; R. Thalmann, *La mise, au pas. Idéologie et stratégie sécuritaire dans la France occupée*, Paris 1999, pp. 34–43; P. Burrin, *La France à l'heure allemande*, Paris, 1995, pp. 60–63 and 98–104. Abetz's activities in the 1930s have attracted increased attention among researchers – cf.: B. Unteutsch, *Vom Sohlbergkreis zur Gruppe Collaboration. Ein Beitrag zur Geschichte der deutsch-französischen Beziehungen ahnand der "Cahiers Franco-Allemands/Deutsch-Französische Monatshefte" 1931–1944* (a doctoral thesis defended in 1990 in Münster); M. Grunewald, "Le 'couple France-Allemagne' vu par les nazis: L'idéologie du 'rapprochement franco-allemand' dans les 'Deutsch-Französiche Monatshefte/Cahiers Franco-Allemands' (1934–1939)", [in:] Bock, H.M., Meyer-Kalkus, R., and Treibitsch, M. (eds.), *Entre Locarno and Vichy. Les relations culturelles franco-allemandes dans les années 1930*, Paris 1993, pp. 131–146. The book by B. Lambauer, *Otto Abetz et les Français ou l'envers de la Collaboration*, Paris 2001, offers no new findings with respect to Abetz's contacts with the Paris-based anti-Semitic formations.

The incentives behind the participation of various individuals in the work of this committee varied, so the team included Germanophiles, pacifists, adherents of the Nazi regime, anticommunists, and anti-Semites. Some of the latter did not officially contribute to the organisation's activities while receiving financial support all the same; such was the case of, for instance, the leader of the Parti Français National-Communiste, established in 1934.

In the summer of 1939, the magazine *L'Epoque* published an article by Henri de Kérillis charging Abetz with financing National Socialist propaganda in France; as a result, Daladier's Government considered Abetz *persona non grata* and had him expelled from the country. In September, we find him in a group of trusted men travelling across Poland in Hitler's saloon-carriage. In March 1940, we see Abetz recruited for the Third Reich's diplomatic service. The day after Paris fell to the Nazis, he would appear, heading a team of a few men, thus "representing the Ministry of Foreign Affairs affiliated to the military administrator in Paris, until the military administrator for France (*Militärbefehlhaber in Frankreich*) was appointed." It was only on 3rd August 1940 that Abetz was granted the title of ambassador; later in the same year, on 20th November, Hitler decided that the institution run by Abetz be named "the German Embassy in Paris".

Initially, among the closest associates of Abetz were Prof. Friedrich Grimm, the known expert in French affairs; Dr Karl Epting, a long-term manager of the Paris branch of DAAD, a German organisation dealing with exchanges of student youth; Dr Ernst Achenbach, a professional diplomat already accredited to the Paris-based embassy before the war; Friedrich Sieburg, a former correspondent of *Frankfurter Zeitung* and author of the book *Gott in Frankreich?* (*Dieu est-il français?*); and, Rudolf Schleier, who managed the NSDAP unit in France. The team was tasked mainly with supervising the cultural life of occupied France, eliminating the political and ideological opponents of the Third Reich from it, and taking actions aimed at breaking the unity of French society and preventing the emergence of a strong national faction or party, thus ensuring the internal weakness of the subdued country. This programme was, to a considerable extent, compliant with the directives for the press provided by Goebbels on 9th July 1940, whereby: "In the future, France shall play in Europe the role of an 'augmented Switzerland' and will become a country of tourism, one that is simultaneously capable of ensuring for itself the manufacture of certain goods in the area of fashion. Therefore, to maintain the efforts of the French Government toward creating an authoritarian regime would make no sense whatsoever."[124]

---

124 Quoted after: Thalmann, op. cit., p. 15.

Neither before his arrival in Paris, nor afterwards, when Hitler spoke with him at Obersalzberg on 3rd August 1940, did Abetz receive any detailed instructions, nor did he have an assigned scope of responsibilities. Reading Franz Halder's wartime diary, we find it apparent that the German military authorities in France simply feared Abetz, realising that he enjoyed the "support of the highest figures".[125] On his part, talking to his French interlocutors, Abetz spoke openly of his contempt for military-men, even if holding high ranks. When Pierre Laval once mentioned to him proudly that he had invited General Alfred von Streccius, Head of the Military Administration, to pay him a visit, Abetz responded, "Neither a general, nor a *von*," and referred to the man as "councillor Streccius", which was the post of advisor Streccius had held for a number of years in China.[126]

The surviving documentation tells us that once he arrived in Paris, Abetz resolved to begin by dealing with two issues: first, win influence in the leftist milieus and take away the political clientele from the communist party; and second, mobilise the mutually contending extreme-Right factions, which was meant to eventually stir up discord among French society whilst also helping "solve the Jewish question" with the hands of the French themselves.

In my opinion, the aforesaid Professor Grimm, a lawyer, was initially the main political advisor to Abetz. A sort of memorandum he prepared for the military authorities, entitled *Eindrücke und Anregungen* ("Impressions and initiatives"), is dated 19th June 1940. Grimm wrote it after four days spent in Paris, based on a series of talks with French people, probably his acquaintances from before the war. He quotes some of their utterances: "What you have to do is to found your actions upon the simple people, rather than the bourgeoisie: the latter are Judaised and instigated"; "Freedom and social justice, as well as liberation from Jewry, international capitalism, masonry, and corruption should be your guiding motto"; "Before the war, there were five million voters supporting the communists. Persecuting the communists, the way it was done, has proved to be the Government's

---

125 F. Halder, *Kriegstagebuch*, record dated 4th August 1940. There is an English version of Halder's diary that I know of (*The Halder Diaries: The Private War Journals of Colonel General Franz Halder*, 2 vols., Colorado 1976, with an introduction by T.N. Dupuy), but since it is unavailable to me, I follow the Polish edition (i.e., F. Halder, *Dziennik wojenny*, transl. by W. Kozaczuk, vol. II, Warsaw 1973, p. 75).
126 This anecdote is quoted by R. Langeron, op. cit., p. 144 (record of 7th August 1940). The said General Streccius, to whom Abetz (in any case) reported, scorned him as a civilian, and in turn advised French general de La Laurencie to settle all the matters with him, "as the German Embassy is not empowered to this end"; see Amoroux, op. cit., vol. 3, *Les beaux jours de collabos*, Paris 1978, p. 56.

severe error" and as a result, the communists have been forged into martyrs; "You have to win the communists over. It is feasible today. The communists will become anti-Semites and anti-Marxists. Then, the step toward National Socialism is not so far. Allow a communist newspaper but protect yourselves against its misuse." Grimm himself considered the Catholic and Protestant clergy to have been the primary enemies of the German occupiers, followed by the Jews and representatives of the upper stratum of bourgeoisie, including attorneys-at-law and police heads. We moreover find there a denunciation of Langeron, Prefect of the Police, and of Seine Prefect Villey: "neither of them deserving trust, for they are masons and both were followers of the People's Front."[127] Let me remark that no such memorandum is to be found in the collection *Frankreichberichte*, edited and published in Germany in 1972 by a circle of Grimm's friends.

As for Abetz's own intentions, he made a clear account of them in a memorandum of 30th July 1940, addressed to Hitler and titled *Politische Arbeit in Frankreich*. He considered it advisable to permit of a broad array of political options and views polemicising against one another in the press, radio, and propaganda, thereby preventing the emergence of a unity front of the French nation while "leaving them an illusion for the option of some future agreement with the Germans." He considered ensuring the cultural influence of Germany in France through interactions with French publishing houses, theatres, the distribution of movies, organisers of artistic exhibitions or lectures, to be his task. His other objective was to "limit French cultural influence abroad," proposing specifically such steps as: (i) relocating institutions and scientific congresses from Paris to the Reich; (ii) destroying the instruments of the French cultural propaganda, Alliance Française being the first to go; (iii) the oversight and control of exports of French literature and cultural goods to third-party countries.[128] Again, it is worth emphasising that we will not find this text in post-war publications – particularly, in Otto Abetz's already mentioned memoirs, available also in French.[129]

---

[127] AN, fund AJ40, box 539, dossier 2, cc. 8–21. Dismissed on 25th June, Langeron resumed his office on 16th July.

[128] For the text of this memorandum, cf. CDJC, ref. no. LXXI-28 (I thank Ms. Karen Taieb, manager of the Archive, for sending me a photocopy of this enormously important document).

[129] O. Abetz, *Mémoires d'un ambassadeur. Histoire d'une politique franco-allemande*, Paris 1953. These memoirs are mendacious, which is not quite surprising when one realises that they were written by a man who was soon to appear before a French court-of-law. In 1949, Abetz was sentenced to twenty years of imprisonment but left prison in as early as 1954. He was killed in a car crash.

There is a document indicating that it was Abetz who sent directives to the military occupational authorities in France – namely, a letter from Dr Werner Best, head of the administrative military staff, dated 19th August 1940, which contains the *Grundsätzliche Richtlinien für die politische Behandlung des besetzten Gebietes* ("The primary political guidelines for handling the occupied territories"). He had received these guidelines two days earlier from Abetz. In the text of these guidelines, which were agreed upon with Hitler, we read: "The Reich is interested in having France remain internally weak, on the one hand, and in having it kept far from powers hostile to the Reich, on the other." In order to ensure discord among the French, those who speak against national unity ought to be supported; hence, "there is no benefit from supporting genuine people's or national political forces in France." The instructions also contained a significant fragment concerning the attitude toward communists, which was inserted there in the context of supporting the efforts of the multifarious opposition groups: "From this standpoint, the communists should not be destroyed, either"; yet, one had to ensure the possibility "to render them harmless with a determinative blow."[130]

Another document, also dated 19th August 1940, tells us that in the course of the talks held two days earlier, "Ambassador Abetz suggested that the military administration in France: (a) ordain, with immediate effect, that no Jews would be let into the occupied territory anymore; (b) prepare the expulsion of all the Jews from the occupied territory; (c) investigate whether the Jewish property in the occupied territory could be expropriated."[131] The first item was carried out a few weeks later; the second was delivered by the Germans with help from the French; German lawyers' opinions with respect to the expropriation of French Jews were negative.[132]

In his letter to Ribbentrop of 20th August 1940, Abetz not only restated his idea to impose a ban on Jews against return to the occupied zone but also proposed that Jewish shops be recognisable through special signage, that obligatory registration be imposed on Jews, and that temporary wardens of the property of those Jews who were outside the occupied zone be appointed. He suggested that appropriate action should be taken by the French authorities and considered it desirable that preparations for the expulsion of all the Jews from occupied French territory

---

130 AN, fund AJ40, box 539, dossier 2, c. 4.
131 Ibidem, box 548, dossier 1, c. 2.
132 As above, cc. 7–11. Walter Bagratzky, who wrote a volume of valuable memoirs *Hotel Majestic. Ein Deutsche rim besetzen Frankreich* (publ. 1987), warned that expropriating the Jews would be in contradiction to Article 46 of The Hague Convention.

be commenced straight away.[133] Abetz would write in his memoirs after the war that he was never an anti-Semite.[134] The conclusion proposed by Ulrich Herbert, a young but quite outstanding researcher, in his biography of Werner Best, is apt in every respect: "On the German side, it was the Embassy and the military administration staff that took the initiative [in occupied France – T.S.] with respect to the policy concerning Jews – rather than the BdS [*Befehlshaber der Sicherheitspolizei und des Sicherheitsdienstes* – i.e., SS-Sturmbannführer Helmut Knochen – T.S.], who initially acted without a clear influence."[135] Perhaps it should be stated even more precisely that the military authorities were receiving instructions in this respect, after all, from Ambassador Abetz.

By all indications, Abetz's anti-Jewish activities were not limited to his participation in the pillaging of works of art belonging to Jews or to giving advice and guidelines to the military authorities with respect to discriminatory regulations. His activities were extended to supporting the doings of French anti-Semites. This is what Henri Michel, no doubt one of the leading experts in the history of the occupied France, had to say about the subject:

> French political life in Paris completely faded away: the President, the National Assembly holding its sessions, the Government and the ministers were not there anymore. [...] Into the gap thus created, which seemed a long-lasting one, some new people muscled in, realising that there were posts to assume and places to take in the realm of public opinion. To emerge, what they needed was merely a permit received from the German Embassy, together with certain subsidies. This was precisely in line with Abetz's mission to create a pretence of political life existing in occupied France, preferably making the impression of diversity. What mattered was to have an office or meeting venue, someplace to make phone calls from – the apartments deserted by their former Jewish owners had seemingly been provided right for the purpose. Then, you would headhunt a few of your friends, school or military service mates, people with whom

---

133   Cf. S. Klarsfeld, *Le Calendier de la persécution des Juifs en France, 1940–1944*, Paris 1993, p. 18.
134   Abetz, *Das offene Problem* ..., p. 319: "Numerous French and German witnesses, including Jewish ones, have confirmed that the Embassy interceded in innumerable individual cases to the benefit of the persecuted Jews as well; and, that I have personally never been an anti-Semite." In all probability, he did not perceive himself an anti-Semite – also when he proposed, in a letter of 6th December 1940 to Gen. Otto von Stülpnagel after the Paris tertiary schools were closed down, that they might be reopened once all the Jewish professors and docents were expelled from these schools; cf. AN, fund AJ40, box 565, dossier 4 (no page numbering).
135   U. Herbert, *Best. Biographische Studien über Radikalismus, Weltanschauung und Vernuft*, Bonn 1996, p. 262.

you happened to fight together or sympathised with sometime in the past, jobless ones included. They would be provided with uniforms; their first task was to post up posters and disseminate leaflets. Once this first step was made, distribution of a magazine published on a regular basis came next. Then, they were told to parade, most preferably on a Sunday afternoon, along the Champs-Elysées or down one of the grand boulevards. They shout so loudly as they are so scarce and no-one cares about them; to prove their intrepidity, they would abuse some passersby who weren't quick enough to give them way. Throwing stones at Jewish shops was the climax of their "courageous" action.[136]

As we already know, the anti-Semitic weekly *Au Pilori* was first published in Paris on 12th July 1940, and its sellers perpetrated the first anti-Jewish incidents in the city under the German occupation.[137] The magazine's third issue of 26th July 1940 contained an article titled *"Les Gardes Françaises"* ("The French Guards") which read:

> Considering the remarkable successes of our action, particularly among the youth and the workers, and in order to coordinate the struggle against the Jews and the Masons, we are forming and organising the "French Guards". In order to become a member of this elite corporation, one should not be a Jew or a Mason, ought to have been born of French parents, and be a minimum of sixteen years of age. Every "French Guardsman" is obliged to swear an oath to the standard of service for the cause of the Homeland. Enrolments are accepted at the movement's headquarters at 33, rue Vivienne, Paris (2e). May our organisation be joined by those who want France cleansed, so that we can be liberated from the Judeo-Masonic influences. We shall build our country anew, to be freed forever from politicasters, profiteers, and international capitalism. Young French people, move forward! Tomorrow belongs to you!

The address of the "movement's headquarters" coincided with that of the *Au Pilori* editorial office. Hit squads – and such was the character of the Gardes Françaises – were thus formed under the weekly's patronage. As Prefect Langeron noted down in his diary on 31st July 1940, the magazine "has founded a youth organisation called 'Gardes Françaises', devised for coordinating the combat against Jews and Masons."

---

136 H. Michel, *Paris allemand*, Paris 1981, p. 99.
137 The money to launch the magazine (more than 150,000 francs) was put up by Jean Lestandi de Villani, who acted as a guarantor for the German authorities – specifically, the Propaganda-Staffel which operated from 28th June 1940 at no. 52, avenue des Champs-Elysées. In March 1941, *Au Pilori* received a subsidy of 100,000 francs from this source. Significantly, Lestandi, an ardent anti-Semite, was before the war a member of the Comité France-Allemande set up by Abetz; cf. P.-M. Doiudonnat, *L'argent nazi à la conquête de la presse française, 1940–1944*, Paris 1981, pp. 141, 227.

Based on a release published in *Au Pilori* on 16th August 1940, we can learn that apart from the Gardes Françaises, which were now to be joined by young people aged eighteen or older, an organisation called Jeune Front, targeted at those aged fourteen to eighteen, had been formed. The office of the Gardes Françaises was moved to 20, rue de l'Arcade. We also read there that the Movement's Propaganda Centre was housed at 28, Champs-Elysées. The Gardes Françaises were led by Charles Lefebvre, born 1901, a Paris building administrator, who was soon to be ousted by competitors. The hit squads of younger boys, members of the Jeune Front, were run by Robert Hersant (1920–1996), who years after the war was to become one of France's greatest press magnates. Before this happened, Hersant had been sentenced to ten years in prison for national indignity; in 1952, he was released under the general amnesty and was elected a member of the National Assembly four years later. While in the Parliament he was reminded of his past during the occupation. Jean Legendre, a parliamentary deputy, stated that on 16th August 1940, Hersant appeared at the building at 28, Champs-Elysées and offered the following memo to a certain Mme Bodê, the concierge: "On order of the German military authority, upon receipt of this letter, you are supposed, Madame, to make available the keys to the respective rooms," this concerned the premises of a British tourist office, the rooms of "Lang" (a Jewish enterprise), and the private apartments of Mr. and Mrs. Rosenthal. The memo ended with a warning: "In case you refuse to follow this instruction, we shall be forced to arrest you immediately." Although the original copy of this letter apparently survived, Hersant categorically denied that it had ever existed.[138] It is strange, in any case, that on the day Hersant expected to receive the keys from the concierge, *Au Pilori* informed the readers of the movement's propaganda centre functioning at that very address. On the other hand, it is known that the same building housed the headquarters of the Jeune Front led by Hersant.

The 26th of August 1940 saw the Parisian daily *Le Matin* publish a release titled *"Le Jeune Front a inauguré son centre national de propaganda"*, which read: "The Jeune Front, the Gardes Françaises, and the Parti Français National-Collectiviste have inaugurated their national centre for propaganda at a friendly meeting yesterday, during which the leaders, Pierre Clémenti, Charles Lefebvre, and Robert Hersant, delivered brief speeches in order to precisely formulate the objectives behind their movement, which is foremost anti-Jewish

---

138   For more details on R. Hersant's career, see: N. Brimo and A. Guérin, *Le dossier Hersant*, Paris, 1977; H. Rousso, *Le syndrome de Vichy (1944–198…)*, Paris 1987, pp. 74–6; E. Coquart and P. Huet, *Le monde selon Hersant*, Paris, 1997.

and anti-Masonic." The Parti Français National-Collectiviste and the name of its leader, Pierre Clémenti, are new to us here.

Pierre Clémenti (1910–1982), earlier a young editor in the sports section of *La République*, decided in 1934 to join the struggle for the healing of the nation, opting for the extreme Right. In 1936, we see him found *Le Pays Libre*, an irregularly published review; Clémenti was taken to prison on three occasions during that period. As I have already mentioned, the Parti Français National-Communiste, an organisation formed by Clémenti, operated thanks to German financial support.[139] After the German troops invaded Paris, Clémenti requested the German authorities to permit him to resume the party's activity. Objections were raised by the last segment in the organisation's name: replacing the adjective "*communiste*" with "*collectiviste*" allowed it to keep the abbreviation PFNC.

I have found no proof that Clémenti had enjoyed Otto Abetz's patronage and backing from the start. The gentlemen certainly knew each other from before the war. It is known that when Clémenti was arrested on 4th December 1940, he was released on the German Ambassador's intervention (this thread will be resumed as the story evolves). During a conference with Abetz on 7th January 1941, he described Clémenti as follows: "This man ought to be assessed in positive terms. He is ready to act, albeit at times he would seem to be a madcap."[140] When a rally was held in Paris on 18th July 1941 which proclaimed the formation of the Légion des volontaires français contre le bolchévisme, Clémenti was one of the seven speakers, along with Déat, Doriot, and Deloncle; however, his speech "was received with whistles [of disapproval] and shouts of '*Pfui*'."[141] To determine the mutual interdependencies between the editorial team of *Au Pilori*, the hit squads

---

139 For the most exhaustive source of information on Clémenti and his party, see: H. Coston, *Partis, journaux et homes politiques d'hier et d'aujourd'hui*, Paris, 1960, pp. 90–91 (the author had been a collaborator himself, and so was excellently versed in the matter); P.P. Lambert, and G. Le Marec, *Partis et mouvements de la collaboration*, Paris, 1993, pp. 111–8. Also, cf. P. Ory, *Les collaborateurs 1940–1945*, Paris 1976, p. 94.

140 AN, fund AJ40, box 551, dossier 3 (no page numbering). Abetz said that the numerical force of the organisations subordinated to Clémenti is not too considerable (500–1,000 members), but as for himself, he "*ist persönlich positiv zu beurteilen. Er ist einsatzbereit, obwohl er gelegentlich als Wirkopf erscheint.*" In March 1941, when the French submitted a list of their proposed candidates for the Commissariat général aux Questions Juives to Abetz, he recommended, in addition, a few persons on his part, Clémenti among them. Cf. Amoroux, *Les beaux jours ...*, p. 175.

141 Report on a rally at the Vélodrome d'Hiver, attended by some 15,000 Parisians: AN, fund AJ40, box 552, dossier 3, cc. 107–112.

of the Gardes Françaises and Jeune Front, and Pierre Clémenti as the head of PFNC is not an easy task. The probable initiator of the movement, Henry-Robert Petit, head editor of *Au Pilori*, was quickly waning in importance and eventually, on 19th September 1940, ceased managing the periodical. A contributing factor might have been the unambiguously negative opinion of him which was expressed in a report of Helmut Knochen, the BdS, who accused him of breaking his word, participation in forgery, trafficking in cocaine, and moreover, the fact that he had once been a secretary to a freemason.[142] In contrast, Clémenti's role was growing, especially once he got rid of his competitor – Charles Lefebvre, head of Gardes Françaises.

A preserved photograph of the edifice at 28, Champs-Elysées taken in summer 1940 features uniformed guards keeping watch in front of the movement's propaganda centre, and the three-colour flag blowing in the breeze.[143] The appearance of the members of Gardes Françaises and Jeune Front was detailed in a report of the German military authorities for August 1940. They wore blue shirts and trousers, forage caps, and Sam Browne belts adapted for carrying weapons, as well as red armbands with a white circle in the centre, inside of which was a cross made of four arrows with their heads pointing to the centre. They greeted one another in a Nazi-like, raising the right hand.[144] There is some resemblance, let me remark, of this symbol to the *Topokrzyż* sign used in Warsaw by members of "*Atak*" organisation. It has to be remarked that certain patterns of the attire described above – such as the forage cap or the sign of the cross of arrows within a circle – were later taken over by Les Jeunesse Populaires Françaises, a youth extension of Doriot's Parti Populaire Française (though the cross's lower arrow was pointed outwards in that version). By 1942, some PPF leaflets clearly featured a *Topokrzyż* sign in their seal.

What was the attitude of the organisers and supervisors of the anti-Jewish action toward the German occupiers? Are there any bases for concluding that the German authorities were treated purely instrumentally, their support used for implementation of the rioters' own goals? In other words, did the boyish Robert Hersant act from drives similar to those characteristic of Andrzej Świetlicki? The meetings held at the latter's place concluded with singing the *Rota* or the Polish national anthem. The files of the German Police of Paris (*Geheime Feldpolizei*, Gruppe 540) preserve quite a thought-provoking document, a denunciation from

---

142   H. Knochen's report to W. Best of 28th August 1940, CDJC, ref. no. LXXIXa-1.
143   The photograph has been published by Lambert and Le Marec, op. cit., p. 113.
144   Gen. Streccius's report as for August 1940: AN, fund AJ40, box 444 (no file marking or page numbering).

a certain Robert Patte, in whose opinion "an anti-German spirit is masked within the Jeune Front." It quotes an utterance of Pierre Clémenti from 11th August 1940: "I make use of the Germans but I reject them," and then, the words Hersant uttered on 1st September 1940: "I don't want any Germans or Krauts in my place. I am using them but I hate them."[145] Andrzej Świetlicki would probably have said the same thing.

Let us now try and answer the question, what was it that the members of the occupational authorities who supported, or even perhaps inspired, certain actions of the Parisian anti-Semites were actually after? A propaganda effect was definitely an incentive: the desire to demonstrate that not only the Germans but also the French were hostile toward Jews and demanded that they be thrown out of their country. Another important aim, which I have already mentioned, was to cause a feud within the society and to break the political spectrum in order to prevent the consolidation of the nation. But there was one more factor, which tends to be completely neglected in these considerations: the Vichy regime were namely blackmailed by the possibility for the Germans to create a competitive government that would be more promising in terms of efficient and productive collaboration. Franz Halder made a note in his diary on 10th August 1940 on a conference of the occupational military authorities with Ambassador Abetz where we can read: "The decision was finally made regarding the removal of the French Government to Paris. The relocation is due in the end of September, October. [...] Abetz is to establish contacts with the French communists so that the extreme left can be caused to assume power, if need be. He ought to carefully feel his way! A dangerous game!"[146]

Let us note that Abetz had commenced talks with the communists a month earlier, apparently without notifying the military. In the same diary we can find a note dated 22nd August 1940 concerning the Ambassador's actions: "Abetz is also holding other negotiations than those of which he informs us." This statement might allude to his contacts with anti-Semitic extreme-Right groups or factions. It is a fact that the paper *La France au Travail* – brought into being by Abetz, we can recall – published some very critical opinions with respect to the Vichy Government. Another fact is that during a rally of Parisian anti-Semites on 18th August 1940, demonstrators called on the members of the Gardes Françaises to form a new government. In order to present those pretenders for the legacy of

---

145   AN, fund AJ40, box 888, dossier 12, cc. 69–70 (this document is cited in P. Burrin's book, *La France à l'heure allemande 1940–1944*, 2nd ed., Paris 1995, pp. 379 and 532).
146   Halder, op. cit., p. 82.

Vichy to the broader public, it was decided that some spectacular action would be carried out in the centre of Paris.

The incidents on Champs-Elysées of 20th August 1940

Although the events that took place on 20th August 1940 in the Champs-Elysées area are mentioned in almost every book concerning Paris under the German occupation, they have never been the subject of reliable research that would produce a study using all the available sources. There is a considerable number of such sources, as historians today have access to police reports, official memos or notes of the German authorities, eyewitness accounts, records made in personal diaries, and finally, echoes resounding in the official as well as conspiratorial press. Although the Paris occurrences are not quite comparable to the German *Kristallnacht* of November 1938, the glass of the broken windows of Jewish shops on Champs-Elysées allows us to coin the phrase "crystal day". The purpose of both actions was similar: they were meant to show the anger of the common people who, purportedly in a spontaneous spurt, would demand that the Jews be removed from their country.

To explain the origins and immediate reason behind the incidents on Champs-Elysées, emphasis should necessarily be placed on a certain incident that took place on Sunday, 11th August 1940. At 4:30 p.m. on that day, a group of some twenty members of Gardes Françaises burst into the office of the Centre laique des Auberges de la Jeunesse (a centre for youth hostels) with the intention to take it over, as the police report has it,[147] or to enter their own people in the lists, as the leader of the "movement", Charles Lefebvre, maintained.[148] In his opinion, the management of this the organisation, which had 36,000 members, was controlled by Jews or their supporters. He remarked that they had been received at the office by a "Polish half-Jew" and a mademoiselle "Abraham, said to have been born in Auvergne." They did not agree to listing any new members, and finally called the police as the aggressors did not want to leave the premises. On that same day, police guards were posted in front of the building at 15, rue de Valois. Noting this incident in his diary, Prefect Langeron stated, "I will not tolerate these assaults, despite the German support they are enjoying."

---

147 Archives de la Préfecture de Police, Paris: *Rapports de quinziane des Rensiegnements Généraux* (hereinafter, 'RG'), repport of 12th August 1940.
148 Lefebvre offers his own version of these events in: *Lettre ouverte à M. Lafaille Représentant du Minstère de la Famille, Au Pilori*, no. 7, 23rd August 1940.

Lefebvre nowise intended to quit the idea of taking over head office of the youth hostels, which would enable him to win a new office space for the organisation in the central area of Paris and also offer the opportunity to seize a network of youth hostels across France. The game was worth the candle. Three days later, he managed to get to the office of a certain Lafaille, a high-ranking official with the Ministry of Family, who agreed to arbitrate in the dispute. The decision was to be taken within forty-eight hours but, in fact, came a few days later. On Monday, 19th August, Lefebvre learned that the decision proved unfavourable for him and, moreover, that fire had broken out at the head office, devouring the archive and documentation, while the police took down their guards from in front of the building. On the same day, Gardes Françaises and Jeune Front members, who were gathered at the movement's headquarters, at rue de l'Arcade, were instructed to turn up there at 8:00 a.m. on the following day in order to join an action which was to demonstrate that, "having received no satisfaction of its demands in the legal way," they would forthwith resort to other measures to this end.

The morning of Tuesday, 20th August 1940 saw several dozen people gathering in rue de l'Arcade; they were divided into a few groups, each assigned a task. Thus, some of them were to go to rue de Valois and forcefully seize there the central office of the youth hostels; some sixty militants went to Champs-Elysées: they were given the addresses of specified Jewish shops where they were supposed to break the windows.[149] As we are told based on the testimonies of the action's participants collected afterwards, before they set off, they were told not to steal merchandise and – probably, most importantly – that they did not have to fear the consequences of their deeds, since "the German authorities have consented to this action" (*"die deutschen Behörden seien damit einverstanden"*).[150] This phrase regrettably does specify which authorities were meant in particular; in other words, we are not told who gave permission for the action to be carried out, and who assured the participants' impunity. In a written declaration submitted on 23rd August 1940 Charles Lefebvre stated that no-one had recommended to him to carry out anti-Jewish incidents in Champs-Elysées, and he had done this "out of his own free will."[151] He explained his reasons in an open letter to Monsieur Lafaille, which was published on that same day in *Au Pilori* – a text I have already

---

149 RG report of 26th August 1940; the most detailed report was submitted by Monsieur Marchand, Directeur général de la Police Municipal: AN, fund AJ 40, box 890, dossier 2, cc. 114–7. Ibidem, c. 66.
150 Memo in German: AN, fund AJ40, box 879, dossier 10, cc. 63–4.
151 Ibidem, c. 66.

referred to. That the Germans cared about proving that they had not taken part in preparing these incidents is evidenced by a declaration collected from a certain Theo Perschbacher, a journalist employed with the Propagandaministerium, who was present at Champs-Elysées when the action was on. He categorically stated he had had nothing to do whatsoever with those incidents; he explained that although he had been interested in the anti-Semitic movement, "he had not deemed its methods proper."[152]

One of the most important documents concerning "crystal day" on Champs-Elysées is the report drawn up immediately after the occurrence by Marchand, Director-General of the Municipal Police, for Prefect Langeron and, in a German translation, for the military occupational authorities.[153] The time the riots started is quoted as 11:45 a.m., and a list detailing the names and addresses of the nine shops where the windows were broken, along with – quite important an item – the full names of and birth dates of thirteen rioters who were detained by the police. Of these thirteen men, as many as ten were young people, aged between sixteen and twenty, all identified as members of Robert Hersant's Jeune Front. The leader himself was absent from the list, as was Lefebvre, who had participated in the "conquest" of the youth hostels head office. He was arrested there but was released after consultation with the German authorities. Again, who interceded for him is not known; my presumption is that it was Ambassador Otto Abetz. An RG report dated 26th August 1940 finds that "the police quickly put an end to these incidents," although as we can learn from elsewhere, the Champs-Elysées incidents lasted about two hours.

One witness to these events was Madeleine Gex Le Verrier, who in the spring of 1941 moved to London and, once there, published her memoirs from occupied Paris in the following year. It is significant that she had no doubt about who was behind the anti-Jewish incidents. As she writes, "The officials from Abetz's circle confided to the French industrialists, the moment they arrived in Paris: 'We will free you from your Jews.' Before the whole political action began, the Germans run their propaganda; you could read in the press and hear in the Radio-Paris that the Israelites were to blame for the defeat. Later on, no doubt entertaining a hope that they would create a movement that would enjoy support from the street, they sent their hit squads to break the Israelite shop windows. I watched with my own eyes the demonstration in Champs-Elysées, which the

---

152 Ibidem, c. 65.
153 Cf. footnote 40, German transl., cc. 118–9, duplicate: CDJC, ref. no. LXXIX-5.

crowd observed not understanding anything, the passers-by asking themselves why the Germans had taken off to breaking the windows."[154]

In a diary of the Russian journalist, *Pravda* daily correspondent Vasyl Sukomlin, who was in Paris at the time, we can read the following note, dated 21st August 1940: "Yesterday, a gang of uniformed youth, members of the Jeune Front, organised a real pogrom on Champs-Elysées. In the course of two hours, shouting 'Down with Jews!', they were methodically breaking shop windows in fashion stores and textile shops that has just been opened by the staff, while their owners had not yet turned up. The shop assistants, terrorised, cried. The passers-by were openly displeased, but did not intervene. The German officers, in the company of their ladies, enjoying fresh air in café terraces – on that wonderful summer evening – remained indifferent."[155] The erroneous information as to the time of the day is somewhat astonishing, as we otherwise know that the riot took place around noon.

It was probably before the incident began that police prefect Langeron was called to the Bourbon Palace by Dr Franz Albrecht Medicus who represented the German military occupational authorities. Langeron was requested to take his closest associates with him. "He wants to have witnesses," Langeron noted in his diary, "and so do I." The same source so describes the course of this very important talk: "He declared to us that the German authorities condem the anti-Jewish demonstrations of recent days and have no problem with us opposing such developments most sternly. I pointed out that we had intervened severely *but the other German authorities* [emphasis – T.S.] demanded that the individuals we had detained be released. And this is not a very good method for suppressing a demonstration, or for preventing its reoccurrence. He assured me that this had been the last time a thing like this would happen, and that from now on we would have a free hand. But he did not explain his reasons for such a stupendous policy or for the divergent points-of-view. Wouldn't he have known that the latest violent acts were organised with support from his own compatriots? Would he be willing to leave the responsibility for the repressions against Jews over to other Germans? Or perhaps, his intention is to offer apparent peace to the Israelites?" Further on in the Prefect's diary's entry (of 20th August 1940) we can read about the Gardes Françaises' assault on the youth hostels central office and the breaking of shop windows on Champs-Elysées. Thus, the conference at the Burbon Palace concerned the riots of the preceding days. The Prefect was given at that

---

154 M. Gex Le Verrier, *Une Française dans la tourmente*, Paris 1945, pp. 60–61.
155 V. Soukhomline, *Les hitleriens à Paris*, Paris 1967, pp. 82–82.

point a clear consent for applying repressive measures, which the police used as they arrested thirteen anti-Jewish protesters in the action of that same day. As we will soon see, a few days afterwards they will have to be released! It is not known whether Langeron made it clear in his talk with Dr Medicus who those "other German authorities" were that extorted the earlier release of the troublemakers who had been detained by the French police; and in any case, his diary makes no specific mention of it.

Taking into account that the Security Service played a crucial role in organising anti-Jewish actions in other countries – as well as in Paris itself, in the night of 2nd/3rd October 1941, to which developments we will return – it might be presumed that this formation backed the participants of the incidents under discussion in the summer of 1940 as well. As I mentioned earlier, however, SS-Sturmbannführer Dr Helmut Knochen, acting as Head of the Security Police and Security Service in occupied Belgium and France, and simultaneously managing the Dienststelle and Sonderkommando in Paris, did not yet have the significant position in Paris that he would develop with time.

A letter survives, written by Knochen on 21st August 1940 to Dr Werner Best, the key figure in the military administration in France under the occupation, which reports on an organisational meeting of the "Gardes de France" (this proves that he was not even aware of the formation's actual name) held in the afternoon on 19th August: "It was emphasised at the meeting that as far as foreign policy is concerned, a position against England should be assumed, whereas in the internal policy, the Jews ought to be targeted in the first place." Next, he informs about a telephone conversation between Lefebvre and Lafaille in which the movement's leader threatened that "if the youth hostel archives cannot be found, a hundred Jewish shops in Champs-Elysées will have their windows broken tomorrow." Knochen concludes as follows: "As it follows from the anti-Semitic declaration [made] at the meeting, this is a purely French anti-Jewish action of the 'Gardes de France' movement."[156] In a report written on the same day, Knochen informed that the Champs-Elysées incidents made an appalling impression on the American diplomats; the only diplomats that remained in occupied Paris at the time would probably send a cable message to Washington about what had occurred. A photographer was reportedly seen on the spot, thought to be a German (this could have been the aforementioned journalist Perschbacher). Emphasising that only young people took part in the Champs-Elysées incidents, Knochen offers the following viewpoint: "If there really existed a great anti-Semitic movement which could present

---

156 CDJC, ref. no. LXXV-181.

its position in a powerful manifestation, forming parades full of dignity, then nobody would have anything against it."[157] In my opinion, this is a completely frank personal opinion, which seems to confirm that neither Sipo nor SD took part in the preparation and/or sponsoring of the Parisian anti-Semitic riots in the summer of 1940.

By all indications, the military occupational authorities in Paris were completely astonished by the anti-Semitic incidents taking place on Champs Elysées, and offered no support to such developments. Langeron noted on 21st August 1940 that when riots took place again on Champs-Elysées and rue de Valois, they were "condemned in an official German statement" (unfortunately, I have not found a trace of this document). Two days later, ministerial counsellor Kiessel, appointed as the military authorities' special liaison officer to the Prefecture of the Police, was introduced to Langeron. "He declared to me," the Prefect writes in his diary, "that he does not trust the Gestapo or the Military Gendarmerie, and that he will endeavour to take care of everything, should there be a conflict, in the interest of good relations between the Germans and the French. I remained somewhat cool, for I have mastered the skill of recognising the extraordinary German hypocrisy."

During the incidents of 20th August, the police found a cover of some lampoon directed against Hitler on one of the arrested participants. It was for this reason that an August 1940 report of General Alfred Streccius, head of the military administration in occupied France, finds that "the political stance taken by the 'Garde Française' has not yet been clarified."[158] Another document, a memo prepared on the day the riot took place (the one I have already referred to), mentions that the lampoon cover was found along with an anti-Hitler leaflet, and as a result, "it has not been ascertained beyond a doubt whether a purely anti-Semitic action has been the case here, or perhaps some simulated action aimed at worsening the people's attitude towards the occupation."[159]

Probably the most important document concerning the Champs-Elysées incident is a memo of 1st September 1940, which was probably prepared on the order of Dr Best; I have found its original copy at the Centre de Documentation Juive Contemporaine in Paris. Its most important fragments are as follows: "Based on the specified findings, it has turned out that the trusted people [*Vertauensmänner* – that is, simply put, agents – T.S.] of the German authorities did know about

---

157 AN, fund AJ40, box 550, dossier 3, cc. 14–15.
158 Cf. footnote 144.
159 Cf. footnote 150; duplicate: CDJC, ref. no. LXXV-144.

it, though they did not take part in the action itself. One of the German duty stations provided the youth group with official premises, among other things. This was the reason why, after a discussion attended by *Ministerialdirektor* Dr Best, *Staatsrat* Dr Turner, *Ministerialdirigent* Dr Medicus, and KVR [i.e. *Kriegsverwaldungsrat* – T.S.] Dr Kiessel, it was resolved to refrain from taking further steps regarding the case. A trial before some French court of law might possibly generate an undesirable picture [of the developments – T.S.], which the accused French would, naturally, use in an attempt to shift the blame to the German side."

The same document also mentions Dr Kiessel's conference with Langeron on 23rd August 1940, the one the Prefect described in his diary. Now, we are told a couple of things that were missing in the diary. Langeron, namely, does not mention that members of the Field Police also participated in the talk, nor does he mention the orders received from the Germans on that occasion. The memo makes it clear, however, that "Police Prefect Langeron was told to take care that neither the investigating magistrate nor the French police carry out any further enquiry until a new order is issued by German party."

Finally, we learn about a decision taken by Dr Best, who was – we may recall – one of the central figures in France's occupational authorities: "The prisoners are to be released and told that if something like this ever happens again, they will be judged by a German military court, and that the present proceedings are not continued only because it can be believed that the accused were not aware of the regulations of the German law, while the motives behind their deeds were justifiable." In conclusion, it was mentioned that on Sunday, 25th August 1940, the participants of the Champs-Elysées and rue de Valois incidents, arrested five days earlier, had been released from detention. They were also notified that the type of activities they had been pursuing was forbidden.[160]

Significantly enough, this particular document also did not make clear which German representatives had been in contact with those who formed the fighting squads of French anti-Semites. Instead, we only have the enigmatic remark that the premises at 28, Champs-Elysées had been provided for the use of Gardes Françaises by *"eine deutsche Dienststelle"* – that is, a certain German duty station.

Let us recall, at this point, the reports of the anti-Jewish riots on Champs-Elysées which appeared in the press. Let us start with *Au Pilori*, the periodical directly associated with the rioters. In its issue no. 7 of 23rd August 1940, a framed article by the Editor-in-Chief titled *"Ceux qui ont faim"* was published on the front page. Henry-Robert Petit laid the blame for the incidents with the

---

160   CDJC, ref. no. LXXV-144.

Police Prefecture of the Seine Department, as they had permitted the Jews to set up their shops whereas "non-associated" French merchants were encountering obstacles. The riots expressed, he continued, "the people's anger," a "spontaneous act of the outraged crowd." Petit urged that workers' cooperatives should be formed by French personnel employed in shops and called for the "elimination of Jewish parasites." To his mind, the perpetrators of the Champs-Elysées incidents were starving youths who know "that if they are suffering, dying of hunger, are denied their right to live, then that which constricts them and starves them is called the international Jewish capital!"

The same issue published the *Lettre ouverte à M. Lafaille* in which Charles Lefebvre, as I have already said, explains the reason behind the riots without using all this phraseology. The following issue of 30th August 1940 published a short notice which is easily overlooked and which initially did not catch my attention at all. Titled "*Au livre d'or*", it quoted the surnames (no first names) of twelve persons entered in the "Golden Book" of the Guardes Françaises. When I decided to compare this list with the names of those specified in the police report as arrested on 20th August 1940, I discovered that they were almost identical! Two names mentioned by the police are missing in the release, which, in turn, mentions a name that is not specified in the police list. Thus have the anti-Semites made a record of their heroes and martyrs.

An item titled "*Manifestations antijuives aux Champs-Elysées et rue de Valois*" that was published in *Le Matin* (with a circulation of several hundred thousand) of 21st August 1940 is worthy of note. Let us quote an excerpt:

> Utterly deplorable incidents took place yesterday on the Champs-Elysées. The marchers, members of more or less defined organisations, broke the windows in many shops under the pretext that they were owned by Jewish merchants. Although we fully support the combating of Jewish influence, we would not think that breaking windows is a good remedy of the situation. There are too many ruins awaiting reconstruction in France to add new ones to them. Paris has been experiencing order and peace so far, and the capital city's good reputation would be exposed to harm if such excesses are repeated. It is essential that the police put an end to these lamentable disturbances which have nothing to do whatsoever with the benign measures that readily prove themselves quite fit. To be frank, these disorders seem to be the work of agents and provocateurs.

The item, moreover, mentions a certain Portal Spada, a leader of the group that operated on Champs-Elysées, who was detained. He is mentioned in the police report as well, as one of two men aged forty-seven, while his name is not listed among those from the movement's "Golden Book". The commentary of the editors of this Paris "rag" is quite characteristic – and quite possibly in agreement with the stance shared by a considerable fraction of the public opinion. Taking on the struggle with Jewish influence meets approval, while street brawling is not seen as a commendable method.

It is a strange coincidence that the response of the Résistance movement, which in August 1940 was only beginning to take shape and remained in a seminal state, can only be found in the illegal communist press. Two days before the Champs-Elysées riots, issue no. 70 of the underground *L'Humanité* published an article, "*Les bandes de décerveleurs s'organisent*" ("Gangs of the brainwashed are getting organised"), informing about meetings of "*cagoulard* hit squads"[161] taking place at the Cirque d'Hiver (mentioned earlier) and finding that, "The authorities have given them *carte blanche* and they take satisfaction in hunting communists." No description such as "German" or "occupational" appears here; the phrase "*les autorités*" was apparently clearly understood by the readers. The next issue of *L'Humanité* (no. 71, 22nd August 1940) contained a note on the incidents from two days earlier entitled "*Les bandes de décerveleurs*", again implying that the actions were taken by unstable or lame-brained people. The note goes as follows: "In Paris, the anti-Semites from the *Au Pilori* magazine, which insults communists, are forming gangs of fanatics whose organisational office is open day and night, whereas staying in the street is forbidden after 11 p.m. It is against the workers, against human rights, against the freedom and independence of France that these groups are getting organised, funded by capital and *protected by the authorities* [emphasis – T.S.]. Against these gangs, capable as they are of any provocation, the communist party summons the people's masses of France to consolidate and unite."

A third text entitled "*Qui les paye?*" was published in *L'Humanité* no. 72 of 26th August 1940. It reads thus: "The gangs of fanatics collected by the periodical *Au Pilori* with the complicity of the authorities [*avec la complicité des autorités*], have organised an anti-Semitic manifestation in Paris, while Doriot operates in Vichy and elsewhere. Who pays them? Who are they working for?"

The anti-Jewish excesses were also condemned in no. 1 of a periodical of the French Trotskyites issued in Paris. The article "*A bas l'antisémitisme*" was published by *La Vérité* of 31st August 1940. A description of the incidents on

---

161 *Cagoulard* was the name of a clandestine, mafia terrorist organisation called Comité Secrète d'Action Revolutionnaire, established in France in 1935 (the reason for the name was the hood worn by its members at their meetings). One of its founders was Eugène Deloncle, who, by odd coincidence, appeared on 20th August 1940 in the company of Charles Lefebvre, the organiser of the riots, and made a statement to the police on this subject two days later; AN, fund AJ40, box 879, dossier 10, c. 69.

Champs-Elysées and some examples of anti-Semitic propaganda were followed by an appeal to organise "workers' defence groups," which were to stand up to the disgraceful incidents.

Excesses continue. Competition amongst anti-Semitic organisations. Anti-Jewish legislation

The Parisians' attitude

The day the juvenile hooligans on Champs-Elysées were breaking the windows of Jewish shops, 20th August 1940, Jacques Biélinky noted in his diary: "In the fourth arrondissement [i.e., the district Saint-Paul and Marais], a few boys, dowdy and dirty, walked down the Jewish quarter's streets shouting, 'Read *Au Pilori*, the anti-Semitic magazine!' The passers-by cast brutal invectives at them, but the fomenters refrained from any violent acts. The speed with which they moved makes one suppose that they were afraid of getting beaten, as it happened in the area of Belleville and Carreau du Temple." Two days later, Biélinky records an incident that happened while German soldiers were dispensing soup for the most indigent. Someone noticed some Jews in the queue and started insulting them, demanding that they go away. The German soldiers stood up for them. The diarist also cites another example where a German police patrol, called by the owner of a café who wanted to have a Jew thrown out, took the side of the Jew, explaining that no ban on using cafés by Jews had been issued by the German authorities. A note in Biélinky's diary of 25th August 1940 tells us that for the purpose of defence of the Jewish people against aggressive attacks, police patrols began coursing across the 4th arrondissement, including rue des Rosiers. A day later, Prefect Langeron noted that anti-Jewish "butterflies" and leaflets reappeared, which the police tried to catch around the area; anti-Jewish incidents occurred as well. "I have ordered," Langeron wrote, "that they be very firm and frustrate or suppress any such manifestation."

This was the kind of action that the prefect was urged to take by the German military authorities, for whom the anti-Jewish street brawls simply constituted a breach of law and order. I presume that Dr Helmut Knochen, the Paris plenipotentiary of the Head of Sipo and SD, still took a similar position at the time. As he wrote in a report of 13th September 1940: "The Gardes Françaises and the Jeunesse Française again took part in anti-Semitic actions, smashing the windows in Jewish shops. Actions of this sort will be observed with anxiety by certain figures from the Paris Chamber of Commerce, since, presumably, settlement of the Jewish question in the French economy is expected there only as part of a planned cooperation with the German authorities. Any isolated action may, in their opinion, merely be taken advantage of by the communists."[162]

A few days after the Champs-Elysées incidents, the military occupational authorities issued an ordinance regarding associations and public meetings. The establishment of new associations or societies was barred unless permitted by the German authorities; street manifestations, demonstrations, and rallies were prohibited, as was the wearing of uniforms or battledresses, or the posting of national flags or standards.[163] This was meant, it was presumed, to prevent anti-German activities as well as any actions not agreed upon or approved by the military occupational authorities. These authorities, however, were not the only factor exerting an impact on the course of events and pursuing a policy within the occupied territory. We are already aware of the part Ambassador Abetz and his people played in that arrangement, but the activities of the Abwehr as well as the Propaganda-Staffel team sent to Paris by Goebbels should also be considered. This latter institution often regarded the steps taken by Abetz as encroaching on their authority.[164] When anti-Jewish riots reoccurred on Champs-Elysées and rue de Valois on 21st August 1940, Prefect Langeron thus commented: "An argument must have certainly arisen between the Germans from the Embassy, who support [Pierre] Laval, and the Germans of the Propaganda-Staffel, who support Doriot and hope to influence Laval and Pétain with his help."

The ordinance of 28th August 1940 nowise obstructed anti-Jewish incidents in Paris. Stones continued to be thrown at Jewish shops, Jews were accosted in the streets, anti-Semitic cries resounded here and there, "butterflies" were posted around the area, and leaflets with anti-Semitic content were distributed. Clémenti's party, Gardes Françaises, and Jeune Front no longer monopolised the anti-Semitic front. New parties and hit squads appeared alongside them, as if jousting with one another. The military occupational authorities, as well as the French and German police, took efforts to keep such actions in check, but other German "duty stations" continued to support them. Anti-Jewish incidents more and more frequently aroused the objections of passers-by on the street, or even

---

162 CDJC, ref. no. LXXIXa–1a.
163 *Verordnungsblatt für die besetzten französischen Gebiete*, no. 7, 16th September 1940.
164 It needs to be added that the Propaganda-Abteilung operated from 18th August 1940 within the military administration, with its offices at the Hôtel Majestic (28, rue La Perouse, not far from the Etoile). Run by Major Schmiedtke, this institution was competitive with respect to Propaganda-Staffel as well as the Embassy.

triggered reactions aimed against their organisers and deliverers. On 1st September 1940, Jacques Biélinky recorded the fact that the notices banning entry to Jews that had been placed a few weeks earlier at a grand restaurant on rue Chateaudun suddenly disappeared. The diary entry for the 5th September 1940 brings us a completely astonishing piece of information: it was permitted that the shop windows of the Jewish shops in Champs-Elysées which had been destroyed in the course of the recent riot feature notices stating "This window/showcase has been smashed by anti-Semites."

On the same day of the 5th September, Prefect Langeron noted down in his diary: "Yesterday and today, in the grand boulevards, violent anti-Jewish demonstrations of P[arti] P[opulaire] F[rançais] under the slogan 'France for the French!' Doriot is persevering. So are his German friends." Two days later, we find the following piece of information in this diary: "It is to Déat that reportedly the Marshal at Vichy has entrusted the mission to organise a 'Unity Party'. Resulting from his friends' insistences, Déat consented to collaborate with Jacques Doriot. [...] Doriot was twice received at the German Embassy by Abetz and by the NSDAP representative for France. The programme of the new party has been, in broad outline, accepted by the German dignitaries." This does not seem to be precise. Abetz, let us recall, was quite reluctantly disposed toward Doriot;[165] instead, he very much favoured Déat and placed his bets on him. Pétain certainly cherished the idea of forming one mass-scale national party that would offer him support, but such a concept would be completely contrary to Hitler's directives. The establishment, with the Germans' consent, of an organisation amassing various collaborationist groups or formations was enabled a few months later. The formation of the Rassemblement National Populaire, with Marcel Déat and Eugène Deloncle playing leading roles, was completed by early February 1941.

However, let us resume the core subject-matter of these considerations, the anti-Jewish incidents and riots in the streets of Paris under occupation. As we learn from the list of events featured in the French police reports, on 1st September 1940, anti-Semitic aspersions were cast at "presumed Israelites" from the terrace of a café on avenue Wagram. The evening of 5th September witnessed two incidents. Around twenty members of the Gardes Françaises screamed "Down with Jews!" in front of the "Tourtel" café at place de la République. One of the customers protested and got beaten. Thirty minutes later, someone broke the windows at the nearby Gardes Françaises office situated at boulevard des

---

165 Cf. Ory, op. cit., p. 38 ("*il deteste Doriot*").

Filles-du-Calvaire. In the evening of 10th September 1940, in an area with a significant concentration of Jewish people in the 11th arrondissement, as many as sixteen shops whose owners were "probably" Jewish (as the report put it) had their windows smashed. The following day saw similar occurrences in various points of the city. Again, on 11th September, after a meeting at the aforesaid office of the Gardes Françaises at 4 boulevard Filles-du-Calvaire, there was a brawl between two Frenchmen and one "Israelite".[166]

Referring again to Prefect Langeron's diary, we find a note of 23rd September 1940: "Yesterday and today the 'National Council of P[arti] P[opulaire] F[rançais]'. Doriot gave a great speech. Batter the English, the Jews, the Masons, and the communists. All that 'to deliver the unity of the French nation-at-large'. [...] To illustrate the speech, a large number of 'butterflies' were posted across the 10th arrondissement [in the area of Gare du Nord and Gare de l'Est – T.S.], specifically, on the buildings' windows. The 'butterflies' feature the following handwritten captions" – and now the prefect quotes the content of as many as twenty stickers, of which I will quote just a handful: "One, two, three – boom! And your store's blown up!"; "You are nothing other than an alien Jewish swine, worthy of nothing"; "Do you want yourself destroyed? Just let me know, as you will, my old chap"; "Jews benefit from the war. A Jew is here. Frenchman, don't step in"; "Be a good player, Jew. You've lost. Give your seat up to someone else – to a Frenchman"; "If you happen to be a Jew, you can go to Palestine or flee"; "Jews live on the exploitation of the proletariat"; "This is a Jewish building. Close down your store. It might be blown up soon." The prefect unambiguously condemned such "creativity"; he called it *Ignoble literature*, considering it vile and boorish. As to whether the "butterflies" were produced by Doriot's party members, as Langeron suggests, there is absolutely no certainty – anyone could have easily made them.

Let us, then, take a closer look now at the potential competitors – beginning with the movement that was the first to commence anti-Jewish operations. A note contained in *Paris-soir* of 31st August 1940 tells us that the two existing youth organisations attached to the Parti Français National-Collectiviste, led by Clémenti, were followed by Femmes Françaises, a women's organisation. As we are told by the report of the Renseignements Généraux of 9th September 1940, the organisation was led by a certain Mlle Camille Dietz; assisting the families

---

166   AN, fund AJ40, box 884, dossier 5; and, RG report of 9th Sept. 1940.

of French POWs was part of its responsibility. The same report describes an incident that occurred on 7th September 1940: Jean Lestandi de Villani, the owner of *Au Pilori*, together with about a dozen members of the Gardes Françaises, attacked the periodical's editorial office at rue du Vivienne in order to remove the officiating chief editor, Henry-Robert Petit. He was accused of using the periodical to blackmail people. The police interviewed the attackers at a police station and sealed up the editorial office. Later Police reports tell us that H.-R. Petit resumed his function as chief editor of *Au Pilori* four days afterwards, but he was eventually sacked for good on 19th September 1940. The editorial office was now housed at 55, avenue George V; Robert Pierret, a friend of E. Deloncle who was half-German, assumed the responsibilities of Editor-in-Chief.[167]

Figure 3: Signs on a Paris establishment inform potential customers in German and French that Jews are "undesirable" and not allowed – summer 1940

---

167   RG reports of 19th September 1940 and 23rd September 1940.

Figure 4: A *"butterfly"* reading "Ici maison juive. N'achetez pas" (*"A Jewish house here. Don't buy"*) posted by Parisian anti-Semites in the summer and autumn of 1940

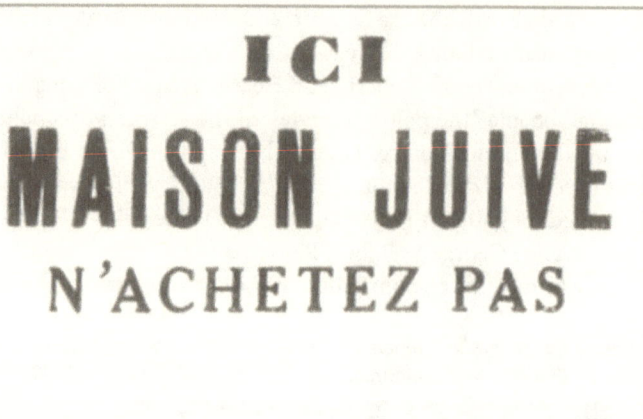

Figure 5: Below the obligatory notice marking a *"Jewish store"* the owner has placed a notice stating: "Veteran ID no. 409150. Wounded in the War. Ancestors are exclusively French since the 17th century" (Autumn 1940)

Figure 6: A Paris-soir *release reporting the "attacks at the synagogues" perpetrated in the night of 2nd/3rd October 1941*

SAMEDI 4 OCTOBRE 1941

Paris

Deuxième Année. — N° 447

CETTE NUIT A PARIS

DES ATTENTATS
ont été commis
CONTRE
des synagogues

Des attentats ont été commis la nuit dernière contre des synagogues dans divers quartiers de Paris. Quelques dégâts matériels ont été enregistrés.

Figure 7: The demolished entrance of the synagogue on rue Sainte-Isaure

As it turns out, an attempt was made to take over the power in PFNC at about the same time. The usurper was Robert Hersant, then a very young man, who led his followers on 17th September 1940 to take possession of the party's main offices and the propaganda centre located on Champs Elysées. The attempt failed and Hersant was forced to leave the Jeune Front leadership; a certain Claude Viriot was appointed by Clémenti as his replacement.[168] The struggle for power within PFNC did not disturb their continuation of anti-Jewish activities. The police reports mention several instances of Gardes Françaises and Jeune Front members throwing stones at the windows of Jewish shops in various Paris districts (arrondissements 1, 18, and 20 in September; arrondissements 8, 10, 11, 13, and 20 in the first half of October). An RG report dated 21st October 1940 describes a meeting of PFNC members held two days earlier. The attendees were informed that the structure of the Jeune Front would consist of a "phalange" of 1,000 members, divided into ten "troops", each such troop to comprise ten "patrols". It was announced that Charles Lefebvre, the head of Gardes Françaises, was to resign "for personal reasons" (and replaced by someone named Damaze). A particularly important point was that the movement's leadership had ordered the youth hit squads to discontinue smashing the windows and storefronts in Jewish cafés, restaurants, and similar premises. The group's further activities were to consist in the distribution of *Au Pilori*, posting "butterflies", and disseminating leaflets. The RG report of 4th November 1940 confirms that at that time their activities were indeed limited as declared. A report from the following week tells us about two meetings of the PFNC (held on 5th and 6th November, respectively) at which a new field for action was set: the Jews were to be forced to remove the descriptions such as "veteran" or "French merchant" from the plaques they were otherwise obliged to place outside their establishments (more on this requirement will be said in a moment).

At a meeting with the military authorities on 5th November 1940, Prefect Langeron still mentioned Clémenti's organisation among the four parties enjoying support from the Germans, yet its importance was undoubtedly declining.[169] As per the ordinance of 18th November 1940, PFNC was listed as a tolerated party.[170] On 4th December, having been notified of weapons kept at the party's office in

---

168 RG report of 23rd September 1940; a study titled *Französische National-Kollektivistische Partei*, AN, fund AJ 40, box 889, dossier 6, cc. 24–5.
169 AN, fund AJ 40, box 889, dossier 1, cc. 9–10.
170 A letter of 21st November 1940 to the occupational military authorities implies that listing a political party or faction as "tolerated" meant that its political activity was barred; as above, c. 20.

Champs Elysées, the German police searched the site and arrested Pierre Clémenti and his secretary Labat. The homes of both detained men were searched as well. Since some arms and ammunition were found (of the six pistols found, three were useless), Clémenti and Labat were brought before a military court. They were eventually released as was "explicitly wished by Ambassador Abetz," due to "political considerations."[171] This seems to be clear evidence of the connections between the organisers of the anti-Semitic riots on Champs Elysées with this particular German "duty station".

On 13th December 1940, Clémenti was called to the Police Prefecture together with the leaders of two competing anti-Semitic parties, Parti National-Socialiste Français and Volonté Française (about which more will be said shortly), where they were told: "1. that 'friendly' meetings will be allowed in the future only if no political issues are debated at them; 2. that no political assemblies are allowed in the future, in whatever form; 3. that they were not supposed to wear any uniforms or armbands; 4. that they will be arrested in case of violation of these regulations."[172] When a list of "fascist formations" was drawn up at a conference on 7th January 1941 at Ambassador Abetz's residence, Clémenti's party was listed second after Doriot's Parti Populaire Français, with the following note: "Supervision conducted by Dr Sonnenhol."[173] It is worth adding that Deloncle's Mouvement Social Révolutionnaire (hereinafter, MSR) was the only other group noted with a German "liaison" (a certain Col. Faber).[174]

While the *Au Pilori* weekly was not completely PFNC's own press organ, the party was finally granted one: *Le Pays Libre* functioned as such from 7th February 1941. The journal soon joined the campaign pursued by the so-called "Paris Fronde"[175] which consisted of collaborationist formations in opposition to the Vichy regime. Let us recall that these developments occurred after the dismissal of Laval by Pétain (13th December 1940), the release of the former Prime Minister from detention by Abetz, and after the latter drew Déat out of a Paris prison. On 22nd February 1941, Clémenti published an article in his periodical entitled

---

171 *Geheime Feldpolizei*'s letter of 5th December 1940 to the military authorities; AN, fund AJ 40, box 889, dossier 5, cc. 21–22.
172 RG report of 16th December 1940.
173 AN, fund AJ40, box 551, dossier 3 (no page numbering).
174 Ibidem. A note made by the German authorities regarding right-wing parties mentions that the name "Mouvement Social Révolutionnaire" was coined on 20th August 1940, the day anti-Jewish riots took place on Champs Elysées; the party had its office at 80, rue Saint-Lazare; AN, AJ 40, box 889, dossier 6, c. 20.
175 This being the title of a chapter in P. Burrin's brilliant work (see fn. 36), pp. 378–390.

"*Il faut purger Vichy*" ("Vichy should be purged"), criticising the "Jewish statute" issued in Vichy on 3rd October 1940, which he found overly liberal. He demanded that radical steps be taken in order to "free the country from the Jews," threatening that otherwise, "if the Government in Vichy keeps on mocking us, we shall disperse them." On a list of political parties prepared four days later by the military occupational authorities, Clémenti's PFNC was listed as merely "tolerated" (*geduldet*);[176] on another list, dated 30th April 1941, it is mentioned among the parties with pending admission status (surprisingly enough, another one of them was Doriot's party).[177]

The decline of PFNC is best testified by police denunciations and reports. One can learn that a meeting of 28th May 1941 was attended by only twenty people; in turn, "The meeting that had been announced for 31st May at the party's office at 4, boulevard des Filles-du-Calvaire, was cancelled due to lack of attendees."[178] A breakdown of 15th March 1942 shows as many as eight formations permitted to practice political activity, while PFNC and – importantly – Deloncle's party MSR were classed as "tolerated". It was also found that Clémenti's organisation, "as far as the number of its members is concerned, is of little importance," and "there is no remarkable interest from the German side."[179]

As I have already mentioned, several formations appeared in occupied Paris in the aftermath of the Champs Elysées incidents whose goal was to fight "Jewish influence." It might have seemed for a while that Parti Français National-Socialiste (hereinafter, "PFNS") would play the first fiddle. Established in 1938, referring in its name to the Nazi NSDAP, the organisation was led by Christian Message (b. 1905), who before the war had been imprisoned seven times for his political activities.[180] This banned party was revived in August 1940 and obtained office space from the Propaganda-Staffel in a building located at 21, rue Casimir Perrier, but was expelled by a competing formation supported by Ambassador Abetz: La Croisade Française du National-Socialisme (which was initially run by a certain Luckaus, and subsequently by Maurice-Bernard de la Gatinais). PFNS

---

176 AN, fund AJ40, box 551, dossier 3 (no page numbering).
177 Ibidem.
178 RG report of 3rd June 1941.
179 Cf. footnote 176.
180 As we learn from H. Coston (cf. footnote 139), Message had once attended a theological seminary and then was active as a trade union activist and editor of the periodical *La Défense Passive*, p. 91–92.

officially commenced its activity on 20th October 1940, at its new office at 19, rue Saint-Georges.[181]

The relevant police reports do not tell us much about PFNS's activities; in contrast, the movement's typical "fighter" can be described in detail, as the party had its own task force – the "Black Guard", commanded by Georges Rubino. The militants wore black uniforms with red shirts featuring a skull on the collar and red ties. They also wore armbands: a very characteristic red band with a white circle in the centre of which was a blue Gallic rooster, referring to the French national colours and symbols.[182]

It was PFNS that Prefect Langeron mentioned as first among the parties "supported by the Germans" at the meeting (already mentioned) with the military occupational authorities on 5th November 1940, adding that this particular formation caused him the most trouble. The 17th of November 1940 saw the merger of PFNS with the competing National Socialist Croisade.[183] During the night of 2nd/3rd December 1940, Message led his men to attack the headquarters of Clémenti's party at 28, avenue des Champs Elysées, assisted to this end – quite surprisingly – by German soldiers.[184] Given the fact that shortly afterwards, on 4th December, Clémenti was denounced and detained, it becomes clear that what we witness here is a struggle for leadership among the anti-Semites. Let us point out that in mid-November 1940, Message, during his interrogation by the German police, invoked his contacts with the "SS-Einsatzkommando, place Beauvau" and even mentioned the name of the responsible agent – Witaska, nom-de-guerre "Rudolf".[185] One thing is certain – the German military authorities and the French Police both had a negative opinion about the activities of Mr Message; I presume that Otto Abetz also opposed them. On 13th December 1940, a formal ban was placed on PFNS, but the party continued to convene meetings of its members. Their main meeting place became the beer-house "Le Tyrol" at 144, avenue des Champs Elysées, where at a meeting of 5th January 1941, as many

---

181 AN, fund AJ40, box 889, dossier 6 (no page numbering). H. Coston tells us that the Israelite Consistory had been previously housed at this address.
182 For more on PFNS, see: AN, fund AJ40, box 889, dossier 1, cc. 9–10; dossier 5, cc. 5–11 (incl. C. Message's own declarations, signed by "Chef Suprême du Parti National-Socialiste").
183 RG report of 18th November 1940.
184 RG report of 9th December 1940.
185 Report of the Geheime Feldpolizei of 16th November 1940; AN, fund AJ40, box 889, dossier 5, cc. 17–20.

as 400 people gathered.[186] Two days later, at the previously mentioned meeting at Ambassador Abetz's place, a statement was made that "no cooperation is possible" with Message's party; a representative of the military authorities demanded that the PFNS leader be arrested.

Christian Message, who called himself the "Chef Suprême", was indeed arrested on 12th January 1941, together with the commander of the Garde Noir. A letter from the German authorities dated 13th January regarded the further operation of their party "highly undesirable owing to political reasons."[187] A German military tribunal sentenced Rubino to one month and Message to two months of imprisonment. At the time, although the premises at 19, rue Saint-Georges had been closed down by the Police, the party's members assembled at 45, rue Orfila. Louis-Charles Julien, once a communist and an associate of Clémenti in the early days of the occupation, was now in charge; proud of his "revolutionary" leanings, he fought against the police and had contacts with workers.[188] Having sworn an oath claiming "that they are ready to die, or even kill, if this should be needed, for the final victory," members of the formally banned party limited themselves, for the time being, to posting anti-Jewish stickers around the town.

During the meeting between Prefect Langeron and the military occupational authorities on 5th November 1940, which I have referred to several times, the last of the four "parties supported by the Germans" that he mentioned was a formation named Volonté Française. Police reports say it had been established in September 1940, Guy Chevalier being its founder and leader.[189] Earlier on, he was among the political friends of Charles Lefebvre, the Gardes Françaises leader; the organisation Chevalier founded was a sort of fronde against Clémenti's PFNC. The RG's report of 7th October 1940 states that Volonté Française was housed at 21, rue Pont-au-Choux (3rd arrondissement). Members of this organisation took actions aimed at "intimidating the Jews"; they made efforts to demonstrate their patriotism by laying flowers at the Tomb of the Unknown Soldier, but were not permitted to do so. The group was not overly active. The RG's report of 30th December 1940 tells us that at a meeting held two days earlier, Guy Chevalier called

---

186 French Police's report to the German authorities, 11th January 1941, as above, cc. 26–27.
187 AN, fund AJ40, box 551, dossier 4 (no page numbering).
188 Report of SS-Hauptsturmführer Kurt Lischka, 5th February 1941; as in footnote 185, cc. 37–39.
189 For the German report on Volonté Française, cf. AN, fund AJ40, box 889, dossier 6, c. 14. No mention of Guy Chevalier is to be found in Pascal Ory's or Philippe Burrin's book.

to unite the effort and pursue joint combat against Jews and Masons. The appeal resulted in a "pact" signed by three organisations: Volonté Française, Le Francisme (led by Marcel Bucard), and Christan Message's PFNS. Although occupied Paris had at the threshold of 1941 become home to quite a number of organisations that announced "fighting Jewish influence" as part of their programme, they were, in fact, mutually competitive formations that fought against one another even though this prevented them from taking efficient anti-Jewish action. In any case, taking such action was becoming increasingly difficult due to changing moods and shifting public opinion.

There is no question that in the first weeks of the occupation, a part of the French population believed that the Jews were to blame for France's war disaster. In the already-quoted memorandum of 30th July 1940, Otto Abetz wrote: "Frenchmen are brave by nature. However, they have not been faring well during this war, as they have put credit in our propaganda which claimed that it was not all about some 'French' war but about the war of international Jewry as well as English imperialism and plutocracy against the Germany of Adolf Hitler, who seeks agreement with France." He concluded that the "Anti-Semitic attitude is so strong in the French nation that it does not call for support from us."[190] In reality, anti-British as well as anti-Semitic sentiments were stimulated, highlighting the responsibility of the Britons and Jews, respectively, for the situation defeated France suffered. The anti-Jewish incidents, which were most likely inspired by the Germans, were meant, on the one hand, to reinforce aversion with respect to the "alien strays" and "exploiters", whilst on the other, breaking down any eventual resistance to the elimination of Jews from political, economic, and cultural life. The preliminary stage in "solving the Jewish question" in France had to be the registration of the local Jews and taking steps to enable the seizure of their properties and livelihood.

On 30th August 1940, Ambassador Abetz passed on to the military occupation authorities Hitler's command to accelerate the following moves in the occupied French territory: (a) implement regulations preventing the Jews definitively and without exception from entering the area under occupation; (b) cause the French authorities to register the Jews and their residences in a "designated registry"; (c) cause the French authorities to label Jewish shops with notices in German and French; (d) cause the French authorities to appoint a trustee for all the shops, enterprises, residential buildings, and depots whose Jewish owners have

---

190   Cf. footnote 112.

fled.[191] Less than a month later (on 27th September 1940), the German – and not the French – authorities issued the first ordinance concerning the Jews, barring them from return to the occupied zone, imposing the obligation for Jews to register with the local police station by 20th October, and requiring the placement of signage reading *"Entreprise juive"* ("Jewish enterprise") outside commercial enterprises owned by them.[192]

In a letter of 1st October 1940, Abetz proposed to the military occupation authorities using a representative of the French Government to incite the Vichy government to have the Jews removed from all official posts within the occupied territory, and to have their identity cards (*cartes d'idéntité*) marked in a special way.[193] A "Jewish statute" issued two days later by the Vichy regime dismissed Jews holding public offices, which extended to jobs in the education sector. Another German decree of 18th October 1940 imposed on the Jews the obligation to report their enterprises by the end of the month, and to set the date for a trustee to assume the management of deserted Jewish property.

The occupational authorities probably expected that the regulations discriminating against the Jews would meet with common approval, if not applause from a majority of the French population. Yet this did not happen; in any case, the mood prevailing in Paris in the autumn of 1940 differed considerably from that of the summer. The yellow signboards reading *"Entreprises juives"* posted on Jewish shops had been meant to frighten clients away and bring the owners to financial ruin. The Jews decided to defend themselves by highlighting their patriotism and their merits for their country. "One merchant," Jacques Biélinky noted on 5th October 1940, "a former combatant and disabled soldier, posted alongside the notice another one which specified his battle honours and citations in the commanding staff's orders-of-the-day. This idea was followed by all the Jews, former combatants." A remarkable number of them did so indeed (see Fig. 5). The already mentioned anti-Semitic fight squads found now a new field for action – they tried to make the Jews remove the "additional notices"; nevertheless, the labelling of the

---

191 AN, fund AJ40, box 548, dossier 548, c. 14. Further correspondence in this matter tells us that in September the military occupational authorities received suggestions from their superior (Oberbefehlshabers des Heeres) for anti-Jewish measures very similar to those proposed by Abetz.
192 As published in the *Vorordnungsblatt für die besetzten Französischen Gebiete*, no. 9, 30th September 1940. This was the first *ordonnance* to impose discriminatory practices on the Jewish people. The eighth made the Jews wear the Star of David emblem, and the ninth, and last, banned the Jews from being in public places.
193 As in footnote 191, c. 38.

Jewish shops produced the opposite of what was intended or expected. Prefect Langeron was wrong when he predicted in a note of 2nd November 1940: "The windows of the Jewish shops are receiving yellow notices from the Germans. It sets them up as targets of attack. We will only have more trouble protecting them."

As it turned out, the expected wave of assaults did not occur at all. Attacks were prevented owing to the increasingly resolute steps taken by the police – as well as due to lack of public acceptance of actions of this sort. In autumn 1940, occupied Paris saw the appearance of the first Gaullist "butterflies", which called out – "People of France, join the movement for free France! Long live de Gaulle!" (note in Langeron's diary, 3rd October 1940). It is also not a coincidence that a dozen-or-so days later, on 20th October, a crowd of protesters opposing the anti-Semitic actions gathered in front of Message's fascist party office at 19, rue Saint-Georges where they shouted "Vive de Gaulle!"[194]

The Parisians began sympathising with the Jews, understanding the injustice they were dealt. Jacques Biélinky noted each manifestation of solidarity on the part of the Parisians with satisfaction. On 25th October 1940, he writes about the proprietor of a haberdashery shop on rue du Temple, who below the "*Entreprise juive*" notice had fixed a sheet of paper with information on the enterprise's founder who had died for France on the Douaumont battlefield in 1916, and whose son had been decorated for his part in the 1940 campaign. This resulted in an increase of customers, including Christians. Let us quote Biélinky's record dated 12th November 1940: "A Jewish merchant trading in clothes on rue Mouffetard, a man of Russian descent, claims that the yellow signboard has brought him new clients, all of them non-Jewish; however, he cannot meet all their wishes due to a shortage of goods. A furniture seller from avenue d'Orléans, a veteran of the 1914–1918 war, wounded three times, has told me that the yellow signboard has caused an inflow of new Catholic customers who come to his place solely to show their liking for him."

When the first patriotic demonstration took place in the streets of occupied Paris, attended mainly by school and university students, it was quite expectable that a clash would occur with the fascist formations whose members had participated in anti-Jewish incidents. A brawl flared up first in front of the "Le Tyrol" beer-house, then outside the offices of PFNC, Gardes Françaises, and Jeune Front,

---

194   AN, fund AJ40, box 550, dossier 3.

as well as on Champs Elysées.¹⁹⁵ There is little surprise that the demonstrators could not stand their compatriots' raising their hands in the Nazi salute.

Among the preserved documents of the German occupational authorities is an interesting notification from an anonymous agent, dated 6th January 1941, that describes the reasons for the altered change of mood in occupied France. The informer says that after the country's defeat, the French were hostile toward Britain and the Jews, while de Gaulle was regarded by them as alien, someone standing apart. "Today, the situation is quite the opposite," he states, with widespread "admiration for the resistance offered by the English, compassion for the Jews, and the conviction that de Gaulle could finally be the right person for France." There is also a characteristic mention of the protagonists of the anti-Semitic riots of summer 1940: "A formation such as the Jeune Front perhaps attracts busybodies who turn their backs on it a moment later with a pitiful smirk."¹⁹⁶

The observations of this German agent are very close to the opinion expressed in a *Study on the situation of the Jews in the occupied zone*, compiled in the underground by Léo Hamon in spring 1941. In his opinion, the anti-Semitic formations and hit squads who busied themselves smashing the windows of Jewish shops disappeared after a few weeks. Save for a few exceptions, he reports, the notices banning admittance to Jews disappeared from restaurants. As Hamon states, "As a matter of fact, public affection for the persecuted Jews is commonplace, which all the observers consistently state. Anti-Semitic inscriptions are very rarely seen, […] and moreover, people willingly buy at Jewish shops where the yellow signboard causes longer queues." The author, soon after to become one of the leaders of the armed communist resistance movement, clearly finds that anti-Semitism has been roundly "condemned" by the French people.¹⁹⁷

A *Kristallnacht* in the city on the Seine. Paris synagogues attacked in the night of 2nd/3rd October 1941

On Saturday, 4th October 1941, the front pages of the Paris dailies published the following brief notice: "Last night, attacks were made at the synagogues in

---

195 Cf. R. Josse, "La *naissance de la Résistance* à Paris et la manifestation du 11 novembre 1940", *Revue d'Histoire de la Deuxième Guerre Mondiale*, 1962, no. 2, pp. 1–31; relevant mentions on pp. 18–20.
196 AN, fund AJ40, box 539, dossier 2, c. 31.
197 The text in question was found, attributed, and published by Renée Poznanski in *Cahiers de l'Institut d'Histoire du Temps Présent*, no. 22, décembre 1992: L. Hamon, *Étude sur la situation des Juifs en zone occupée*, pp. 61, 91–92.

several quarters of Paris. Some material damages have been recorded."[198] In reality, the occurrence took place in the night of Thursday/Friday, causing quite severe material losses, as attested, for instance, by the surviving photographs.[199] As early as Friday, 3rd October, General Otto von Stülpnagel, the military governor (*Militärbefehlshaber*) of occupied France, received a report on this affair from SS-Obersturmbannführer Dr Helmut Knochen, who managed the Paris outpost of the Security Police and Security Service.[200] The document is worth quoting in its entirety:

> In the night of 2/3.10.1941, attacks were carried out at seven Paris synagogues with use of explosives. I hereby notify as follows with regards to the specified accidents, in chronological sequence:
> 1) At 2:05 a.m., an explosion occurred near the synagogue at 12, Av. Montespan. Material damage was caused within the building as well as in neighbouring buildings within a radius of 50 m.
> 2) At 2:45 a.m., an explosion outside the synagogue [at] 21 bis, rue des Tournelles.
> 3) At 3:00 a.m., a suspicious container was found in rue Pavée, which had been placed in front of the synagogue. Laboratory testing underway.
> 4) At 3:05 a.m., an explosion in front of the synagogue [at] 24, rue Copernic; damage caused on the ground-floor, as well as in neighbouring buildings within a radius of 80 m.
> 5) At 3:30 a.m., an explosion outside the synagogue [at] 15, rue Sainte Issure [sic – the correct name is "Isaure" – T.S.]; damage caused within the building as well as in neighbouring houses within a radius of 50 m.
> 6) At 3:40 a.m., an explosion outside the synagogue [at] 15, rue Notre-Dame-de-Nazareth; severe damage caused near the entrance gate, many window-panes in the neighbouring buildings shattered.
> 7) At 4:15 a.m., an explosion outside the largest Paris synagogue (the Israelite consortium), 44, rue de la Victoire; grave damage caused within the synagogue as well as in neighbouring buildings whose window-panes were destroyed. Two German soldiers who were in a nearby garage were slightly wounded.

---

198   Quoted after *Le Matin*, no. 20987 of 4th October 1941 ("*Attentats à Paris contre des synagogues*"); cf. *L'Œuvre* no. 9456, same issue date; *Paris-soir* no. 447, same issue date (see Fig. 6) – all publishing the same text.

199   Such photographs are published by Serge Klarsfeld in his book *1941. Les Juifs en France. Préludes à la Solution finale*, Paris 1991, pp. 78–79.

200   His official title was: Der Beauftragte des Chefs der Sicherheitspolizei und des SD für Belgien und Frankreich. Dienststelle Paris. Born in 1910, Knochen had a PhD in English Studies. Sentenced to death in France in 1954, he was eventually released in 1962. Knochen lived in Germany and died a free man in 2003; in 1990, he spoke with the historian Bernd Kasten.

There is no doubt that these attacks had no relation to those carried out before. One should rather be certain that the perpetrators are some radical French enemies of the Jews, who, just as with the recent blowing up of the synagogue in Marseilles, are now willing to act in a similar fashion in Paris.

Thus, this case is a purely French affair (*um eine rein französische Angelegenheit*), whose examination is the responsibility of the French Police. I shall report on the outcome of further investigations.[201]

Knochen draws a clear conclusion: the attack was carried out by French people; we, the Germans, have nothing to do with it. We may recall that his assessment of the incidents on Champs Elysées of August 1940 was almost identical.[202] At that time, I suppose – though am not completely positive about it – he might not have been be aware that the action had been planned; now, he simply lied and misinformed his superior. General Stülpnagel coincidentally came across evidence of Knochen's dishonesty and disloyalty the very day he received his report, or on the following day in the morning. This happened because a subordinate of Knochen's, SS-Obersturmführer Sommer, had blown the gaffe to two agents who dutifully supplied their reports to the Paris Abwehr, which immediately forwarded the sensational reports to Gen. Stülpnagel. He called for an investigation, ordered Sommer's arrest, and demanded Knochen's dismissal. An open conflict erupted between the top-level military and police authorities.

Based on the surviving reports of the said two agents, that is, Corvette Captain Meurer and a certain Egon Steinfeld-Clayton, Sommer's testimony, and the letters sent by Gen. Stülpnagel to the Oberkommando des Heeres (OKH), one can draw quite a detailed picture of what went on behind-the-scenes and the course of the action carried out in Paris during the night of $2^{nd}/3^{rd}$ October 1941.[203]

---

201 Translated based on a microfilm copy owned by Institut d'Histoire du Temps Présent (hereinafter, IHTP) in Cachan near Paris (ref. no. A. 106, frames 5424–5, cc. 263–264); the original copy is kept in the United States Alexandrian collection. The document has been published in German by Leon Poliakov, "A Conflict between the German Army and the Secret Police over the Bombing of Paris Synagogues", *Jewish Social Studies*, vol. 16, 1954, pp. 253–266; for the relevant fragment, p. 259.

202 On 20th July 1940, groups of Paris anti-Semites carried out an action of smashing the storefronts in Jewish shops in Champs Elysées. On the following day, Knochen reported that this particular incident was a "*rein französische Aktion der antijüdischen Bewegung*" (which did not reflect the truth as the organisers' connections with the Germans were evident). AN, fund AJ40, box 550, dossier 3, c. 19.

203 Most of these documents have been published by Leon Poliakov (attached as annexes to his article – cf. footnote 91); the complete set of these documents is stored in the U.S., a microfilm copy is kept at IHTP in Cachan, France.

The action was indirectly related to an occurrence that took place a few months earlier: namely, Paul Collette's attempt to assassinate Pierre Laval and Marcela Déat (the one who in 1939 would not "die for Gdansk") during the oath ceremony of the Legion of French Volunteers Against Bolshevism (LVF) held at Versailles on 27th August 1941. Eugène Deloncle was a witness to the attempt. Before the war, Deloncle had created the terrorist organisation La Cagoule and later the Mouvement Social Révolutionnaire, along with Déat, and was one of the leaders of the collaborationist Rassemblement National Populaire. Laval and Déat, who were slightly injured, believed that the attack had been organised by Deloncle. It is a fact that Deloncle's associate, Tania Masse, who is reported to have warned Déat that Deloncle was preparing his removal from the RPF leadership and who might have known something about Deloncle's connections with the assailant, was murdered; her body was pulled from the Seine in October 1941.[204]

No irrefutable proof confirming Deloncle's part in the Versailles attack has ever been found. What is certain, however, is that shortly afterwards he appeared at the Paris Sipo and SD office, probably to meet Knochen in person, offering to organise some anti-Jewish repressive action in retaliation for the attack in Versailles that had been "obviously" perpetrated by the Jews and requesting technical support for the purpose from the Germans. Knochen reported the matter to Reinhard Heydrich, the head of Sipo and SD, probably going over the head of his direct superior SS-Brigadeführer Thomas. After some delay, Heydrich consented for the action to be carried out. It was supervised by Sommer on behalf of Knochen, while Deloncle provided four men for the action (named Gaudot, Tremblay, Pedigrod, and Lehideux). The date was fixed at 2nd/3rd October 1941. The explosives were brought from Berlin. The Germans provided a truck for the plotters' use.

To insure himself an eventual alibi, SS-Obersturmführer Sommer designated the "Chantilly" cabaret at rue Fontaine for the action's headquarters. He intended to spend an "intoxicating" night there in the company of his colleague officers while simultaneously managing the action and receiving reports on the course of the commissioned task. As ill luck would have it (or perhaps it was no coincidence), the merry company was joined by the aforesaid Corvette Captain Meurer, an agent of the Brest-based Abwehr outpost who at the time was temporarily in Paris, and Egon Steinfeld-Clayton, probably an agent too, but, as may be

---

204 Cf. Philippe Bourdrel, *La Cagoule. 30 ans de complots*, Paris 1970, pp. 260–5.

inferred, in service of the Police.²⁰⁵ They witnessed how people entered and left the locale after communicating with Sommer during the night. Moreover, they met him at a private accommodation the following morning, and once their conversation turned to the bomb attacks on the synagogues, they heard from him a most sensational statement: "Excellent job, this time," he reportedly said, adding with a smile, "We've got a superb alibi for last night." Sommer told them also about the explosives that had this time been brought from Berlin much faster than previous dispatches.²⁰⁶ Meurer immediately reported on all this to the Paris Abwehr, as did Steinfeld-Clayton, in spite of Meurer's request to keep the matter secret. The contents of the two independent reports consistently agree each other.

Once General Otto von Stülpnagel became acquainted with the reports, he commanded that Sommer be arrested; the relevant order was signed on 4ᵗʰ October 1941 by General Ernest von Schaumburg, the military commander of Paris, proposing the charge of "having posed threat to property, health, and life."²⁰⁷ The case was referred to the Military Tribunal in Paris, which interrogated Sommer in the night of 4ᵗʰ/5ᵗʰ October. The extant record tells us that the investigating officer was SS-Sturmbannführer Kurt Lischka, and that another SS member and representatives of the Field Police and of the headquarters were also present. Sommer basically confirmed the description contained in the reports delivered by the two agents, adding to the story the antecedents of the matter, that is, his contacts with Deloncle. However, Sommer tried to cast a different light on the talk about the attacks. He ascribed the remark that the attackers "have found a very nice alibi for themselves" to someone else; as for himself, he said he only added that "at least, it all ended up in success, with a magnificent result." It is rather significant that the protocol signed by Lischka does not mention Dr Knochen, his superior.²⁰⁸ It is

---

205 The two probably joined Sommer's company completely incidentally. It cannot be precluded, however, that Deloncle had some connections with the Abwehr at the time and had notified the military intelligence of the action that was being prepared by SD – that is, a competitive formation. The Abwehr, perhaps, used the opportunity to discredit SD before General Stülpnagel. I should like to mention at this point that Deloncle travelled to Spain in 1943 on a commission of the Abwehr; in January 1944, he was shot dead in his own apartment by Gestapo agents.
206 It can therefore be concluded that the German Security Service operating in Paris had participated in organising earlier bomb attacks which were subsequently ascribed to the Résistance and meant to justify repressions against the French people.
207 IHTP, microfilm A 106, frame 5434, sheet 276.
208 L. Poliakov, op. cit., pp. 261–2.

only in the record of Sommer's testimony, compiled by Dr Eggers, a representative of the headquarters and member of the judicial committee, that we find the following passage: "The order to offer the immoral support for the bomb attacks was given to him by Dr Knochen, the head of his duty station. He is not aware whether Dr Knochen was acting on instructions received from his superiors."[209]

After he received the report, it became clear for Gen. Stülpnagel that everything had been going on behind his back, with nobody notifying him of anything before then. He was all the more angry because on the day preceding the attacks he had had a long conference with Knochen on combating the resistance movement, which would have given the latter an opportunity to tell his superior about the action being prepared for the coming night. What is more, Knochen dared to provide Stülpnagel, on 4th October 1941, with another report which referred to the repercussions of the attacks and an opinion regarding their possible perpetrators, without a single mention of the role of his own "station". On that same day, possibly having learned about Sommer's detention, Knochen went to Berlin, possibly summoned by Heydrich.

On Monday, 6th October, General von Stülpnagel sent to OKH, personally to General Eduard Wagner, the Head Quartermaster, a comprehensive letter describing the course of the events and explaining the adverse consequences of the Security Service's and Police's actions, which had been taken on their own account. To his mind, the blowing up of the Paris synagogues could cause recurring unrest, with ominous political consequences. To his letter, which was made in eight copies (one sent to Admiral Canaris), Stülpnagel attached as many as five appendices, including Meurer's report, the first and second report by Knochen, as well as Lischka's and Eggers's records of the investigation of Sommer.[210] As a result, this documentation was included in the Wehrmacht files which fell into the hands of the Americans – and it was on its basis that Roger Berg of the Centre

---

209 IHTP, microfilm A 106, frame 5422–3, sheets 262–263. Interrogated by Henri Monneray as a witness at the Nuremberg Trial, Knochen reported that Sommer acted behind his back, on direct command from Berlin. Otherwise, there would have been no need to import the explosives from Berlin; cf. H. Monneray (ed.), *La persécution des Juifs en France et dans les autres pays de l'Ouest presentée par la France à Nuremberg. Recueil de documents*, Paris 1947, pp. 324–6. (I am indebted to Ms. Karen Taieb of the Centre de Documentation Juive Contemporaine, Paris, for providing me with a photocopy of the interrogation record.).

210 L. Poliakov annexed to his article both reports by Knochen, the report by E. Steinfeld-Clayton, and the record of Sommer's interrogation signed by Lischka (omitting the Stülpnagel report; cf. IHTP A 106, frames 5412–15, sheets 253–256).

de Documentation Juive Contemporaine published in 1946 an article entitled "*Les attentats contre les synagogues en 1941. Comment et par qui ils furent perpétrés*" ["The attacks on the synagogues in 1941: How they were perpetrated, and by whom"].[211] As I have mentioned, most of these documents were published in 1954 by Léon Poliakov. It is worth noting that Stülpnagel's letter mentioned the detonation of some charges (contained in two canisters) that had not exploded in front of the synagogue at 10, rue Pavée, and which reportedly could only be neutralised in this way. "The material losses," Stülpnagel added, "were consequently inevitable, but they were basically limited to the synagogue." Jacques Biélinky noted on 10th August 1940 that the losses were in fact severe.

Two days later Stülpnagel sent another letter to OKH, informing that Sommer (released by then, as he was not subordinate to military jurisdiction) had been called by SS-Obergruppenführer Heydrich to Berlin, where Knochen had been since 4th October. The General demanded that Knochen be recalled from Paris, as he found further cooperation with him impossible – especially since Knochen provided him the "knowlingly false reports".[212]

A letter was subsequently sent to R. Heydrich, head of Sipo and SD, dated 21st October 1941 and signed by Field Marshal Walther von Brauchitsch, concerning the incidents in Paris of the night of 2nd/3rd October and his subordinates' participation in them. The letter pointed out that Knochen operated behind the back of his military superior, and that the actions and repressive measures taken by General Stülpnagel – which meant the executions of hostages – had brought the Résistance's attacks to an end after attempts of the 15th of September. The organisers of the attacks on the synagogues must have been aware that the newly menacing repressions could affect completely innocent people, implying grave political consequences – all the more so since the French would certainly be aware of who had given authorisation for the attacks. Brauchitsch demanded that SS-Brigadeführer Max Thomas be dismissed, and Sommer and Knochen completely removed from the occupational area in the West.[213]

Heydrich sent his reply of 6th November 1941 to Head Quartermaster Wagner, rather than to Brauchitsch. Significantly, the letter he had received was annotated *Geheime Kommandosache* ("Top Secret"), whereas his response was marked *Geheime Reichssache* ("State Secret"). For a number of reasons, this is an extremely important document. Heydrich nowise denies that the attacks against the Paris

---

211 *Le monde juif*, no. 1, août 1946, pp. 7–9. Since Léon Poliakov does not quote this article anywhere, I suppose that he may not have known it or known of it.
212 IHTP, microfilm A 106, frame 5411, sheet 252.
213 L. Poliakov, op. cit., pp. 262–3.

synagogues were carried out with the knowledge of his subordinate Dr Knochen. He goes even further by stating that Knochen "acted in line with the orders he had received." The reason why the action had been kept secret from Gen. Stülpnagel was, as Knochen explained to Heydrich, "the previous experience in cooperation with the Military Commander, from whom one could not in the least have expected the required understanding for the necessity of taking such steps when engaging an ideological opponent." Heydrich, moreover, explains the underlying reason why the action had been carried out. It all begins with the certitude that the perpetrators of attacks on industrial establishments, acts of railway sabotage, attempts at German soldiers and French politicians (which is to say, collaborationists) are traceable to "Jewish-and-communist circles." This was confirmed by "police findings, and pointed out by the press." Given the situation, Heydrich came to the conclusion that "it should be demonstrated to the French and international public opinion that there are forces within the French nation that are ready not only to fight bolshevism but also to attack the Jewry, so mighty in Paris in bygone days." His argument continues: "In the efforts directed against international Jewry, my outpost [in Paris – T.S.] has also made contact with organised French anti-Semites. The anti-Semitic group around Deloncle had already been known as the most active one, Deloncle himself – despite the objections related to his political unclarity – offered the greatest guarantee for uncompromised combat against Jewry. Deloncle personally declared his readiness to carry out retaliatory actions against Jewry as the perpetrators of the schemed attacks." The next sentence contains information that according to the Swiss historian Philippe Burrin is highly significant: "I accepted his offer only at that moment when also from the highest level (*von höchster Stelle*) Jewry, with full severity, was deemed the responsible incendiary of Europe, which definitively has to disappear from Europe."

Burrin has no doubt that the "top position" meant Hitler himself, and sees Heydrich's statement as evidence that the *Endlösung* decision had been made, including with regard to the Jews in the Western European countries. In line with this reasoning, which I completely share, the attacks against the Paris synagogues gave the signal, as it were, to begin the actions aimed at annihilating French Jewry.[214] Heydrich added: "I was fully aware of the political weight of the ordained actions, especially since for years I have been tasked with preparing a final solution to the Jewish question in Europe. I bear full responsibility for this." Concluding, he reported that SS-Brigadeführer Thomas had officially been

---

214 P. Burrin, *Hitler et les Juifs. Genèse d'un génocide*, Paris 1989, pp. 140–141, 194.

transferred to the East at an earlier date, i.e., 29th September 1941; Sommer had been called by him to Berlin; and, he sees no reason why Dr Knochen should be dismissed since he had been "operating under the received orders and his work so far has been irreproachable."[215]

Leon Poliakov, who published the document showing the reaction of the military circles to Heydrich's letter, has managed to read the manual annotation it contains, signed "H" (perhaps, made in General Halder's hand?):

> As long as the instruction regarding the military administration of France issued by the Führer to the High Command of the Army [OKH] remains valid, it is unbearable that any outpost initiate, by its own authority, some undertakings that necessarily disturb the Military Governor's [that is, Gen. Stülpnagel's – T.S.] scheduled work. The excuse that one would not have expected coming to an agreement with the Military Governor is worthless. If it is to be acknowledged, then it will become a safe-conduct pass given to anyone, for any instance of lawlessness.[216]

The military did not concede. A reply to Heydrich's letter was sent on 2nd December 1941 reminding the receiver of an agreement concluded on 4th January 1941 between OKH and the Head of the Sipo and SD, whereby the plenipotentiary of the latter acted as a clerk with the Military Governor, subordinate to his guidelines. Heydrich was also reminded about OKW's order of 4th October 1940 determining the competencies of the plenipotentiary of the Sipo and SD head and of the *Sonderkommandos*. Gen. Stülpnagel was namely to be informed on an ongoing basis about the activities of Dr Knochen, head of the Paris *Sonderkommando*, and about the results of his actions. Since Knochen did not comply with this, the request to dismiss him was renewed.[217]

The collection of documents published by Poliakov includes a memorandum by Otto Abetz, dated 2nd February 1942, in which the Ambassador opposes the idea to have Knochen removed from Paris as he considered him a "politically experienced and very active man." Abetz brings up Knochen's meritable service with respect to the Venlo incident for which Knochen was decorated with the Iron Cross 1st Class.[218] Abetz's advice was that Knochen simply apologise to General Stülpnagel for his error, and undertake to share with him all relevant

---

215 L. Poliakov, op. cit., pp. 263–264.
216 Ibidem, p. 263.
217 Ibidem, pp. 264–265.
218 In November 1939, two agents of the British Intelligence Service, Captain Sigismund Payne-Best and Major Richard Stevens, were arrested in Venlo, the Netherlands, by agents of the German Security Service and subsequently detained till the end of the war at the Sachsenhausen camp's *Zellenbau*. It was an act of provocation aimed at

information he might possess in future. Abetz, moreover, stands up for Deloncle who was forbidden by Stülpnagel to go to the front together with LVF troops owing to his alleged participation in a murder. To his mind, it would be recommendable, for political reasons, that Deloncle assume the command, especially since he had recruited most of the volunteers and "has a great moral influence."[219]

I find it rather odd that none of the scholars who have made use of the extant documentation concerning the destruction of the Paris synagogues and the conflict between the military and the Police has paid attention to Gen. Stülpnagel's dispatch sent to OKH on 5th February 1942 which makes it clear that the military governor of occupied France had visited Berlin and had a conference there with Field Marshal Wilhelm Keitel. It may be presumed that Keitel told Stülpnagel to reach an understanding with Knochen. Stülpnagel is reports that he has had a long conversation with him (referring to Knochen as *"Führer des SD in Frankreich"*), during which Knochen "declared his readiness to meet all my wishes with respect to full information and cooperation." Stülpnagel concludes, "Consequently, my earlier request for the dismissal of Dr Knochen has been dropped."[220]

In that same month, General Stülpnagel submitted his resignation and left Paris before the end of February. Heydrich's protégé retained his post until the summer of 1944.[221] There might be some probability that the unambiguous support for the position assumed by the *Militärbefehlshaber* contributed to the recall of Field Marshal Brauchitsch, which took place on 19th December 1941.[222]

Let us, however, return to the city on the Seine and resume the thread of the developments taking place in the night of 2nd/3rd October. Some details need to be added to the picture. As follows from the press release prepared by the Germans, the explosion of the bomb planted outside the synagogue in rue Notre-Dame-de-

---

showing the British connection with Georg Elser, the would-be assassin of Hitler in Munich on 8th November 1939.

219 L. Poliakov, op. cit., pp. 265–6.
220 IHTP, microfilm A 106, frame 5445, sheet 304.
221 Dr Knochen was not as ruthless in fighting the Résistance as Himmler would have expected him to be. He might, perhaps, have had some connections with the plotters who prepared the 20th July 1944 attempt on Hitler's life. In any case, he was degraded to the rank of SS private and conscripted into the Waffen-SS; cf. Bernd Kasten, *"Gute Franzosen". Die französische Polizei und die deutsche Besatzungsmacht im besetzten Frankreich 1940–1944*, Sigmaringen 1993, pp. 211–2.
222 Cf. Robert Wistrich, *Wer war wer im Dritten Reich. Ein biographisches Lexikon: Anhänger, Mitläufer, Gegner aus Politik, Wirtschaft, Militär, Kunst und Wissenschaft*, Munich 1983, pp. 31–32. O. von Stülpnagel was in office until 16th February 1942.

Nazareth wounded three Frenchmen living in a nearby tenement house (building no. 17).[223] Strikingly enough, the differences in the reported time the explosives were released appear quite significant. The explosion at rue Sainte-Isaure took place, according to Knochen, at 3:30 a.m., whereas a note prepared by the Jewish community said it was around 5:00 a.m.[224] The explosion outside the synagogue at rue Copernic occurred, as per Knochen's report, at 3:05 a.m., whereas the note has 5:15 a.m. The information quoted in the police report of 4th October 1941 is also worthy of note. As we learn, it was only on that day at 9:45 a.m. that the German authorities detonated two containers with explosives the attackers had placed in front of the synagogue in rue Pavée. In contrast to what Gen. Stülpnagel reported, not only the synagogue's interior was damaged (the police reported severe material loss): all the neighbouring buildings had their window panes blown out.[225]

What was the Parisians' response to the attacks against the synagogues? Let us look into the diary of the Jewish journalist Jacques Biélinky where we find an entry of interest to us: "At three in the morning, several bomb explosions woke up the whole of Paris. Later, it was made known that time bombs had been planted under the main synagogues, causing serious damage: in rue de la Victoire (the adjacent *L'Illustration* house was affected, window-panes were smashed all over the quarter), in rue Notre-Dame-de-Nazareth, rue des Tournelles, rue Pavée [actually, no explosion occurred there at that time – T.S.], rue Julien-Lacroix [a synagogue was located there, at no. 75, but was not an object of the attack – T.S.], and so on. No bomb exploded at [28] rue Buffault, probably owing to the adjacent hotel."[226]

The report by Egon Steinfeld-Clayton, which has already been referred to, brings a few very interesting pieces of information. As it turns out, many a Parisian was convinced that their city had been bombed by the British – hearsay that was transmitted by local taxi drivers, for instance. In the morning, however, rumours circulated that some synagogues had been blown up. "There were such," the report goes on, "who stated that it was the Germans who did this." When

---

223 AN, fund AJ40, box 884, file (dossier) 1, c. 595.
224 A document titled *Note sur les attentats comis contre diverses synagogues dans la nuit du 2 au 3 octobre 1941*, dated 15th October 1941, has been attached as an annex to: Jacques Biélinky, *Journal 1940–1942. Un journaliste juif à Paris sous l'Occupation*, ed. by Renée Poznanski, Paris 1992, pp. 302–5.
225 AN, fund AJ40, box 877, dossier 2 (no page numbering).
226 J. Biélinky, op. cit., p. 153 (the record date given, *2 Octobre*, is erroneous; the correct is 3rd October).

Steinfeld-Clayton protested, claiming that only the French could have done it, he was told, "And who blew up the synagogues in Germany?" Clearly, the French people did not forget the *Kristallnacht* pogrom od 1938. One should not believe, the agent replied, that the Germans could have brought their people from the Reich to carry out such an action; at this point his interlocutors could not think of an answer. They seemingly did not hit upon the idea that such a thing could have been done by the hands of others.[227]

As I mentioned earlier, Dr Helmut Knochen sent General Stülpnagel his second report on the attacks on 4th October 1941, focusing this time on "the first obtained picture of public opinion." Frankly speaking, the content of this report would not make us think highly of the intellectual ability that has usually been associated with this Doctor of English Studies. Knochen is primarily interested in opinions regarding the perpetrators and in the assessment of the anti-Jewish occurrence. He does not hesitate to open his report with the following statement: "The opinion most frequently heard is that the attacks were made by the Jews themselves in order to elicit compassion from the wide masses." Let me remind the reader that the Rev. Stanisław Trzeciak interpreted the pogroms in Poland before the war in similar terms.[228] Yet, the report in question quotes other opinions as well. According to the French Police, "given the manner in which the action was prepared, Deloncle is the only possible bet"; as we know, the professionals were not wrong. Another view had it that the attackers relied on using the religious element to cause an anti-German affair and instigations against the "Jewish regulations inspired" by them. There were such, too, who pointed out that due to the curfew, only Germans could have appeared in the streets in the night, and "although it cannot be absolutely ascertained that the Germans were the perpetrators, it is definitely certain that French people ought to be excluded from deeds of such sort."

The final passage is significant: "The fact that something noticeable was finally undertaken against the Jews has been animatedly welcomed, especially by the youth, who basically don't care who stood by the perpetrators. In the Anti-Jewish Institute circles, the stance has been assumed that the Jews were taught a lesson

---

227   L. Poliakov, op. cit., p. 260–1.
228   Cf. Alina Landau-Czajka, *W jednym stali domu... Koncepcje rozwiązania kwestii żydowskiej w publicystyce polskiej lat 1933–1939*, Warsaw 1998, p. 176.

in public, which is a good thing."[229] I will add here that a reports that reached one of the London units of General de Gaulle's Free France (on 3rd February 1942) informed that the people of Paris had condemned the attacks, and that the perpetrators were sought among those surrounding Jacques Doriot.[230]

There is yet another document worth quoting, a copy of which I have found at the Centre de Documentation Juive Contemporaine, namely a declaration agreed upon at a meeting of Le Conseil de l'Association des Rabbins Français (the Council of the Association of French Rabbis) on 15th October 1941 which concerned the attacks on the Paris synagogues. The Rabbis recall that synagogues in Marseilles and Vichy had been the objects of similar attacks earlier on – with less serious consequences, though. As they found, "This time, the press and the radio announced that walls alone remain of the profaned synagogues, and that two people were killed." The source of this false information is unknown. The Rabbis would not have deliberated or written their declaration in Paris; they probably convened somewhere in unoccupied French territory. The Rabbis render thanks to God that the attack had not occurred the day before, during the Jewish feast of Yom Kippur, when a plethora of the faithful visited the temples. Shocked with the desecration of the sacred places, they ask: "where will this sacrilegious madness lead to, and when will all the synagogues of France, like those in Germany, fall into ruins, resembling the Galilean ones where Jesus prayed?" The document ends with a sort of ecumenical call: "What a consolation it would be for us and for our frightened brethren if we could discern an echo of our feelings in the hearts of all those who praise God, the One and only, to whom we appeal in synagogues, churches, and mosques, and if the faithful of the other religions and their spiritual leaders would manifest their condemnation for these godless crimes which intend to deal a blow against the glory of this same God!"[231]

What was the actual purpose of the action of blowing up the Paris synagogues at the hands of French collaborationists? As was the case with the German *Kristallnacht* of November 1938, the intent was to achieve propagandist purposes – to show the "people's wrath" that "spontaneously" arises against the Jews,

---

229 L. Poliakov, op. cit., p. 259–260.
230 AN, fund F/60 (*Délégation générale du gouvernement français dans les territoires occupies*) box 1678 (*Politique anti-Semite*) [no page numbering].
231 Archives du Centre de Documentation Juive Contemporaine, Paris, ref. no. CCXIX-86.

striving for their removal from the country. This particular attempt failed as the contribution of the Germans had failed to be kept secret. However, the additional purpose of spurring the military administration to take more energetic action toward implementing the design described as the "final solution to the Jewish question" did, indeed, prove successful.[232]

---

232 I would like to point out that a similar purpose stood behind the anti-Jewish riots in Antwerp which took place on 14th April 1941 (I cover this topic at some length in the next chapter). Among other ends, they were provoked in order to force General Alexander von Falkenhausen to initiate steps against Jewish people; cf. Maxime Steinberg, *L'Etoile et le fusil*, vol. 1: *La question juive 1940–1942*, Bruxelles, 1983, chapter 7: *Le pogrome d'Anvers: un défi SS à l/autorité militaire?*, pp. 155–66.

Chapter 3 The Hague and Amsterdam. Antwerp

The two capital cities of the Netherlands

Attacked by Nazi Germany on 10th May 1940, the Netherlands, with a population of less than nine million, offered resistance for a mere few days. After Queen Wilhelmina left the country, the Government emigrating with her, and the day after the barbaric bombing of Rotterdam on 14th May 1941, with 800–980 killed,[233] General Henri Winkelman signed the capitulation. Three days later, Hitler appointed Arthur Seyss-Inquart Civil Commissioner for the Occupied Netherlands – officially: *Reichskommissar in den besetzten niederländischen Gebiete*. An Austrian by birth, Seyss-Inquart had previously acted as deputy to Hans Frank in the Generalgouvernment.

An astute and cynical politician, Seyss-Inquart enjoyed Hitler's trust and fondness.[234] Assuming his office on 30th May 1940, he delivered a proclamation to the Dutch nation during a ceremony at the Royal Palace in The Hague. He said on that occasion: "We are not willing to apply imperialistic oppression with respect to this country and its population, or superimpose our own political convictions." He made reference to "observance of the law, respect for the morals and institutions of public life of the Dutch people," and remarked on their Germanic "blood community."[235] Since the behaviour of the German soldiers and officers in the conquered country was unobjectionable, the earlier news from occupied Poland, emphasising the prevalence of terror, came to be seen as much exaggerated, if not as propagandist lies. This is by no means to say that the Dutch came to terms with their lost independence.

---

[233] Resulting from the bombing, 25,000 buildings were destroyed and 78,000 inhabitants were left homeless. For more on this air raid, see: H.A. Jacobsen, *Der deutsche Luftangriff auf Rotterdam (14. Mai 1940). Versuch einer Klärung*, 'Wehrwissenschaftliche Rundschau', 1958, Heft 5, pp. 257–284.

[234] So is he portrayed by Czesław Madajczyk in his book *Faszyzm i okupacje 1938–1945: Wykonywanie okupacji przez państwa Osi w Europie: Ukształtowanie się zarządów okupacyjnych*, Poznań 1983, pp. 290–291; for a biographical note of A. Seyss-Inquart, see R. Wistrich, *Wer war wer im Dritten Reich*, Munich 1983, pp. 250–251.

[235] *Deutsche Zeitung in den Niederlanden*, no. 1, 5th June 1940.

To quote the co-authors of a book on "underground Europe":

> The 15th of May 1940, the first day the Germans took power in the Netherlands, saw the publication by Bernard Ijzerdraat of the first illegal bulletin titled *Geuzenbericht – The Geuze Message*. The group editing the periodical [...] assumed the character of an organised conspiratorial formation which soon afterwards undertook sabotaging and diversionary activities.[236]

The extant reports of commanders of the Netherlands' Police and Security Service (specifically, SS-Standartenführer Dr Nockermann, replaced from July 1940 by Dr Wilhelm Harster[237]) allow us to very minutely follow the accumulating anti-German sentiments and various forms of objection and resistance, beginning with the first mass patriotic manifestation on 29th June 1940, the birth date of Prince Bernhard, the successor to the throne.[238] These reports tell us about anti-German leaflets being circulated, whistling and stamping in cinema-theatres to the newsreels displayed, letters containing threats sent to members of the fascist collaborationist formation Nationaal Socialistische Beweging in Nederland (NSB), and even about attacks on German soldiers committed after dark in The Hague. It has to be remarked that the dissatisfaction with the invaders' rule was heightened by the worsening material situation of the population and scarcity of provisions. One more element – discrimination of the local Jewish population – came to the stage in the autumn of 1940.

It could initially seem that the Germans abandoned addressing the "solution to the Jewish question" in the Netherlands. A 21st July 1940 report of SS-Standartenführer Nockermann tells us that people whose attitude is pro-German marvel that rather than attacking the Jews, the Germans are shopping

---

236 E. Duraczyński and J.J. Terej, *Europa podziemna 1939–1945*, Warsaw 1974, p. 220. The underground organisation of "Gueuze" was smashed a few months afterwards, and its 43 members brought before the court in The Hague, on 24th February 1941. Eighteen of them, including Ijzerdraat, were sentenced to death, on 4th March.
237 For more on W. Harster, see: G. Meershoek, "Machtentfaltung und Scheitern. Sicherheitspolizei und SD in den Niederlanden", [in:] *Die Gestapo im Zweiten Weltkrieg*, Darmstadt 2000, p. 385–388.
238 Cf. T. Szarota, *V – jak zwycięstwo. Symbole, znaki i demonstracje patriotyczne walczącej Europy 1939–1945*, Warsaw, 1994, pp. 78–79. Harster's report of 5th November 1940 states: "The attitude of the Dutch populace is assuming increasingly negative forms, and an expanding hostility towards the Germans is observable in all parts of the country."; the Institut für Zeitgeschichte (hereinafter, IfZ) in Munich, microfilm MA-9(1).

at stores belonging to them.²³⁹ The testimony of De Monchy, Lord Mayor of The Hague, is enormously interesting: "I immediately asked the first German officer I came across what the German position was like with respect to the Jews in the Netherlands. His reply was that there is no Jewish problem existing for the Germans in the Netherlands. The Dutch Jewry are going to be treated on equal terms with the Dutch, and the alien Jews present there put on equal footing with the other foreigners. Freedom of action should be restricted with respect to fugitive German Jews, most of whom are 'tax evaders' anyway. And yet, in spite of my insistence, no such declaration has been published. I was sharing this good message further on with anyone willing to hear it."²⁴⁰

The actual position of the German occupation authorities was thus presented by SS-Standartenführer Wilhelm Harster: "With regard to the Jewish question, it can generally be said that preparations have been undertaken so that at the appropriate time, the Jews in the Netherlands can be targeted. Soon, Jewish shops will be marked with signboards saying 'No entry for Germans' as the first step."²⁴¹ On this occasion, mention was also made of a camp for Jews being prepared in Westerbork and the planned deportation of Dutch Jews "overseas" via Belgium, France, Spain, and Portugal. In other words, Harster had in mind carrying out the plan to dispatch the Jews to Madagascar. It is worth noting as well that rather than notices forbidding the Jews to enter "Aryan" shops or restaurants, reference is made here to a ban on the frequenting of Jewish shops by members of the *Herrenvolk*.

The day Harster wrote his report coincided with the date the German authorities issued their first decree concerning Jews.²⁴² The decree imposed the obligation for Jewish enterprises to be registered, defining on this occasion the notion of "Jew" in accordance with the Nuremberg Laws. Thus, anyone with three members of the family of their grandparents' generation being members of a Jewish community, or only two such members if he (or she) was a member of such community or married to a Jew or Jewess would be identified as a Jew. The obligatory marking of Jewish shops was not yet decided.

---

239 Ibidem, report no. 5, dated 21ˢᵗ July 1940.
240 *So begann die Zeit des großen Schweigens. 10.-14. Mai 1940. Der deutsche Überfall auf die Niederlande, dargestellt aus niederländischer Sicht*, ed. by M. Burgarth-Holberg [no publication date given], pp. 40–41. Mayor Monchy was dismissed by the Germans after the demonstration of 29ᵗʰ June 1940.
241 IfZ, microfilm MA-9(1), no. 18, 22ⁿᵈ October 1940.
242 *Deutsche Zeitung in den Niederlanden*, no. 146, 28ᵗʰ October 1940.

Two days after this decree was passed, representatives of the six Protestant churches active in the Netherlands submitted an official protest to Seyss-Inquart, recognising the occupiers' actions as contrary to the legal and ethical standards binding in their country.[243] A month later, on 23rd November 1940, another decree discriminating the Jewish populace was issued, this time requiring civil servants to submit a sort of "declaration of Aryanness" (*Arischerklärung*). Since one of the aims was to eliminate Jews and people of Jewish origin teaching in schools and universities, their colleagues and students pleaded for them this time. Demonstrations were held in parallel at the Universities of Leiden and Delft which lasted two days (25th–26th November 1940) and eventually led to the closing down of both institutions by the Germans.[244]

The occupational authorities resolved to continue the actions aimed against the local Jewish population. A decree was issued on 8th January 1941 banning Jews from visiting cinemas, the reason allegedly being that Jews tended to arrange anti-German demonstrations in cinema theatres. Dutch public opinion reacted instantly: calls were made to boycott the cinemas as a manifestation of solidarity with the Jews. A leaflet distributed on this occasion summoned: "Leave the movies to the Germans and NSB members. Show your self respect and don't go to cinema!"; another, titled *Keine Kino-Besucher im Februar*, read: "A part of our fellow-countrymen has again been classed as tenth-category citizens. The Dutch Jews have been forbidden to attend cinemas, effective 9th January. This disgraceful ordinance arouses anger and abhorrence in us." Calling for the boycott of cinemas, an appeal was made to make "a small sacrifice for a greater cause."[245]

Members of the local Police and Security Service finally realised that the advancing discriminatory measures against the Jews would not find understanding in Dutch society, which was emphatically attested to by a study compiled by Eisatzkommando 3 of Amsterdam in autumn 1941. Entitled *Die Judenfrage in den besetzten niederländischen Gebiete*, it stated that:

---

243 For an English translation of the protest, see in: H.C. Touw, "The Resistance of the Netherlands Churches", [in:] *The Netherlands during German Occupation*, publ. by N.W. Posthumus, *The Annals of the American Academy of Political and Social Science*, special issue, vol. 245, May 1946, 156–157.

244 A.J. Herzberg, "Kroniek der Joden-Vervolging", [in:] *Onderdrukking en verzet. Nederland in oorlogstijd*, ed. by. J.J. van Bolhuis, C.D.J. Brand, H.M. van Randvijk and B.C. Slotemaker, vol. 3, Arnhem–Amsterdam 1954, p. 49.

245 Cf. Harster's reports: no. 29, 21st January 1941 and no. 31, 4th February 1941 (as in footnote 9).

> The solution of the Jewish question in the territory of the Netherlands under occupation has, since the beginning, been executed in view of separating the Jews spatially from the rest of the society. Since, on the one hand, the people of the Netherlands have no worldview background and therefore do not consider Jews to be a foreign body, but rather sympathise with them, whilst, on the other hand, the Jewry have been intertwined with the Dutch economy to an excessively strong degree, the German authorities could only push forward the solution to this issue step by step.[246]

It cannot be excluded that the local fascists and anti-Semites might have encouraged, or might have intended to encourage, the Germans to accelerate the relevant actions. It likely, however, that the Germans made use of members and sympathisers of NSB to persuade the rest of the society that the people "spontaneously" demand a settling of accounts with the Jews.

On Sunday, 26th January 1941, a pastoral letter protesting against racial discrimination was delivered in all churches of the Netherlands.[247] The initiative stemmed directly from a decree of 10th January 1941 making the registration of Jewish people mandatory (as from 24th January). The Dutch fascists counteracted on the following day (Monday, 27th January), launching an anti-Semitic campaign in Amsterdam. Three days afterwards, the largest cinemas in The Hague and Amsterdam (the "Asta" and "Rembrandt", respectively) released a film by Veit Harlan, *Jud Süss*, with the same purpose in view. Let us remark that the German authorities had earlier dissolved the Dutch board evaluating motion pictures for distribution, as the body had opposed the showing of this film.[248]

The 2nd of February 1941 saw anti-Jewish riots on the streets of The Hague. The action was instigated by members of an armed band affiliated with NSB, a party set up in 1931 and headed by its cofounder Anton A. Mussert. Modelled after the Nazi SA, the formation was named Weer Afdeling ("Defensive Squad"; hereinafter, "WA"). The young men wore black shirts, and their task much resembled their spiritual kinsmen's doings in the streets of Warsaw in March 1940 or in the streets of Paris in August 1940. Thus, the 2nd of February 1941 saw the WA boys set fire to a synagogue in The Hague and place stickers telling the Jews they were not welcome – "*Joden niet gewenst*" – on almost all local restaurants and cafes. Jewish customers who happened to be inside those places at the time began leaving them, while some of the restaurant owners started removing the

---

246 Rijksinstitut voor Oorlogsdocumentatie, Amsterdam, Reports and statements of the Sipo and the SD, file 52a, report of 17th November 1941.
247 Ibid., file no. 37 d, report as for January 1941, 5th February 1941.
248 Report of Commander of Sipo and the SD for February 1941, 5th March 1941 (as in footnote 14), file 37 d.

139

stickers; those placed on the window-panes were covered up by roller blinds. In the evening of the same day, representatives of the restaurant and hotel keepers' trade unions met in the city to deliberate on these developments and resolved that the labels should be removed.[249]

The labels consequently disappeared, so the squad's members decided to move the scene of their actions to Amsterdam. Amsterdam was the largest Jewish hub in the Netherlands, with some 80,000 Jewish inhabitants (57% of the Dutch Jewish population of 140,000) accounting for about 10% of the city's population. A German report called Amsterdam the "Jewish metropolis of Western Europe."[250]

The 8th of February 1941 marks the beginning of anti-Jewish incidents in Amsterdam.[251] The following day, the Jewish cabaret "Alcazar" had its building at Thorbeckeplein destroyed.[252] In the neighbouring streets and squares, the storefronts were broken in Jewish shops, and passers-by with Semitic features or recognised by their attire were beaten. The Jews counteracted from the start; they organised a self-defence structure which put up a fight against the attackers. The native fascist militants encountered armed resistance also from members of "Unie", a mass organisation that had been functioning legally since the summer of 1940, as well as from local communists, described in the Sipo and SD report as "Marxists". Small combat squads (*Knokploegen*) began to be formed, and clashes with the WA formation occurred.[253] On 11th February 1941, a WA member named Hendrik Kott was wounded and died three days later, becoming

---

249 Cf. Harster's report no. 31, 4th February 1941 (as in footnote 9).
250 Special report of Sipo and the SD for 1942, IfZ, microfilm MA-9(2). The statistics as for April 1941 had it that the Jewish population in Amsterdam equalled 79,352, including 10,241 foreigners – with a total of 140,245 Jews in the whole of the country; or more precisely, 56.6% of the Jewish population in Amsterdam alone. Cf. *Amsterdam pendant la deuxième guerre mondiale. Annuaire statistique*, Amsterdam 1949, p. 72.
251 For the most detailed description of these events, describing the role of individual exponents of the authorities, see: F. Roest and J. Scheren, *Oorlog in de stad. Amsterdam 1939–1941*, Amsterdam, 1998 (Chapter 8: "De Jodenbuurt en Joodse Raad" [The Jewish district and the Jewish Council], pp. 225–245). The book by B. Beuys, *Leben mit der Feind. Amsterdam unter deutscher Besatzung 1940–1945*, München, 2012, adds no new elements to the picture.
252 J. Presser, *Ondergang. De vervolging en verdelging van het Nederlandse jodendom 1940–1945* [The doom. The persecution and extermination of Dutch Jewry], vol. 1, Den Haag 1965, pp. 64–65.
253 W.B. Maas covers these developments in his memoirs, *The Netherlands at War: 1940–1945*, London–New York–Toronto 1970, p. 64.

the first "martyr" of the Dutch fascists. Tension and determination were growing on both sides. The 11th of February 1941 saw one more occurrence that possibly added fuel to the fire: an ordinance came out introducing a *numerus clausus* for Jewish tertiary students. On that same day, Dutch patriots sympathising with the Jews attacked Germans for the first time; vitriol and ammonia were poured onto the heads of WA fighters and German soldiers out of house windows. The German Order Police, the Orpo, intervened in the evening, detaining nineteen young Jews who were later presented as bandits overcome with lust for murder and destruction; their portraits, with axes in their hands, were published in the press.[254]

The riots moved to The Hague on 12th February 1941. The German plenipotentiary for the city of Amsterdam, Hans Böhmcker (his function was largely analogous to that exercised by Ludwig Leist in Warsaw), called in representatives of the local Jewish religious community on that day and presented to them a plan to build a ghetto in the town. The proposal was rejected, and at the last minute, the German authorities quit the idea to develop an enclosed Jewish quarter. The preparations had been in an advanced stage, though; on 13th February, a Jewish Council was established.[255] As testified by the surviving photographs (see Fig. 8), bilingual yellow notice boards reading *"Juden-Viertel/ Joodsche Wijk"*, *"Juden-Strasse/Joodsche Straat"*, or *"Juden-Platz/Joodsche Plein"* had been placed in many points of the city.[256] Trestles with barbed wire had been deployed in several places (Fig. 9) to separate the ghetto area from the "Aryan" district. As we learn from Abel J. Herzberg, anti-Jewish incidents intensified in the streets of Amsterdam; he even refers to them as a "pogrom" on 13th February.[257] A possible interpretation is that WA's actions were meant to show the Jews the consequences of their rejection of the Germans' offer to arrange a ghetto for them.

A 17th February 1941 report sent from Amsterdam to the German Foreign Ministry thus anticipated the consequences of the anti-Jewish riots: "The *Reichiskommissariat* has taken advantage of the opportunity created by the riots to energetically set about solving the Jewish question in the Netherlands, which has many a time been described by *Herr Reichiskommissar* as crucial. The first step in

---

254 One such photograph is published in Presser, op. cit., following p. 64.
255 For more on the establishment of Amsterdam's Jewish Council and its cast of members, see: J. Michmann, *Planning for the Final Solution against the Background of Developments in Holland in 1941*, Yad Vashem Studies', vol. XVIII, 1986, pp. 145–152.
256 Cf. Herzberg, op. cit., pp. 85, 87.
257 Ibidem, p. 88.

this field will be the future closing of the Jewish quarter. The Aryans living within it will be relocated and exchanged for undesirable Jews from the remainder of Amsterdam. Aryans will be forbidden to enter the Jewish quarter area. The Jews inhabiting it will each receive an ID in the Hebrew and Dutch languages and will be allowed to cross the district's limits based on production of the ID. A Jewish Council has been set up with the purpose to maintain order."[258] Nevertheless, the ghetto was not created.

Let me now return to a previous remark that linked the increase in anti-German sentiments in the Netherlands with the deterioration of living standards and conditions. As early as on 11th November 1940, two hundred women protested in a demonstration convened in front of the Amsterdam Stock Exchange building. On 3rd December, the city witnessed a "hunger march" of local workers. Again, on 29th January, Amsterdam set the scene for a great demonstration of the jobless.[259] As we read in the book *Europa podziemna* ("Underground Europe") by Polish authors E. Duraczyński and J.J. Terej:

> Another demonstration followed on 17th February 1941. The workers came up with the demand to have welfare payments for the unemployed raised, to stop the deportations to Germany, and to discontinue anti-Jewish actions. When the directors of the city's largest shipyard announced – as if in reply to those demands – a recruitment of workers for labour in Germany, all the shipyards in Amsterdam and, following them, the other local shipyards stopped their operations on 18th of May and went on a strike that expanded to almost the entire city. [...] Seyss-Inquart responded almost immediately by declaring, along with summoning the workers to resume work, that dispatches of labourers to Germany would be discontinued immediately. This calmed down the moods for a while. Yet, a mere few days later, on 25th February, a general strike began in Amsterdam.[260]

---

258 Report of Enrst-Günther Mohr, in: *Die faschistische Okkupationspolitik in Belgien, Luxemburg und den Niederlanden (1940–1945)*, a collection of documents edited and with an Introduction by L. Nestler, Berlin 1990, pp. 141–2.

259 Cf. Harster's report no. 31, 4th February 1941 (as in footnote 9); Report of Commander of the Sipo and the SD ad for January 1941, 5th February 1941 (as in footnote 15). (Some 2,000 workers went into the streets of Amsterdam on 29th January 1941.).

260 The Sipo/SD Commander's report as for February 1941 (cf. footnote 16) thus explained the reason for the strike: "The strike has directly been caused by the arrest of approximately 400 Jews, which had become imperative after Jewish elements attacked one of the German Security Police patrols. No social moments came to the fore in the course of the strike." The history of this particular strike is recounted in: B.A. Sijes, *De Februari-staking 25–26 Februari*, Den Haag 1954.

While the previous workers' strikes included the cessation of anti-Jewish actions among other demands, this one was the first strike action in history taken in defence of persecuted Jews; within two days it overwhelmed almost the entire country. The developments unfolded as follows. On 19th February, during an inspection at an Amsterdam restaurant, a German police patrol came across an émigré from Germany, a Jew named Ernst Cahn. He incidentally had with him a bottle containing a caustic liquid, which he spilled on the Germans, clumsily or deliberately. Arrested on the spot, Cahn was put before a German military court a few days later, sentenced to death, and executed by firing squad on 3rd March 1941.[261] In retaliation for this offensive act against the German uniform, the occupying authorities carried out a repressive action against the Jews in Amsterdam on 22nd and 23rd February. A manhunt was organised and, as one report has it, 427 young Jews were arrested (Fig. 10), most of whom were dispatched a few days later to the Buchenwald concentration camp and then redirected to Mauthausen. The roundup has been called the first great "*razzia*" of the Dutch Jews.[262]

The Dutch people responded to the roundup with the above-described general strike of 25th–26th February (the *Februari-staking*). This was the first anti-German action of this size in occupied Europe as a whole.[263] On 26th February, General Friedrich Christiansen, German military commander in the Netherlands, introduced a state of emergency countrywide. Assemblies and street manifestations, the activity of political parties, and wearing of uniforms, badges, and decorations were all barred. A penalty of up to fifteen years' imprisonment was imposed for exhorting to strike, and in ordnance factories or establishments working for the military, capital punishment could be imposed.[264] That this was no empty threat is testified by the condemnation and execution, on 6th March 1941, of a worker named L. Schijvenschuurder for his "exhortation to strike";[265] the man had been

---

261 For more on E. Cahn, see in: M. Gilbert, *The Holocaust. A History of the Jews of Europe During the Second World War*, New York 1985, p. 143.
262 Cf. Harster's report no. 35, 5th March 1941 (as in footnote 241).
263 Historian E.G. Groeneveld finds that "This was the first-ever general strike against a pogrom"; cf. E.G. Groeneveld, "The Resistance in the Netherlands 1940–1945", [in:] *Europäischer Widerstand im Vergleich*, ed. by G. van Roon, Berlin 1985, p. 313.
264 Cf. *Procès des grands criminels de guerre*, vol. XXXVI, Nuremberg 1950, pp. 705–706.
265 *Deutsche Zeitung in den Niederlanden*, the German-edited newspaper issued in Amsterdam, published a notice (no. 273, 7th March 1941) headed "Penalty of death for a Jewish strike incendiary. The sentence was delivered immediately."; the description read: "A certain Jew who was posting an exhortation to strike in Amsterdam

posting leaflets to this end in Amsterdam. As per the police report dated 5th March 1941, nine people were killed as the strike was being suppressed, twenty-three were heavily wounded, and another twenty-one lightly injured. Altogether, 200 strike participants were detained over the course of the two days.[266]

There is no question that the attitude of the Dutch people toward the discrimination and persecutions of their Jewish fellow-citizens during the first months of the occupation deserves the utmost respect, if not admiration. However, it is not to be denied that when considering the period 1940–1945 in overall terms, it turned out that the percentage of Jews saved in the Netherlands was not very significant, much smaller than, for instance, in France or Belgium. There were many reasons behind this outcome – one of the crucial reasons possibly being the bloody suppression by the Germans of the Dutch people's protest action and rebellion in February 1941.[267]

---

was caught red-handed and arrested. The Amsterdam military court sentenced to death. The verdict was carried out Thursday by firing squad."

266 See footnote 30. A tribute of 15 million guilders was imposed on the city of Amsterdam; the state of emergency was maintained till 8th March 1941.

267 An estimated 100,000 to 115,000 Dutch Jews out of 140,000 were killed, which represents 71%–82% of the Netherlands Jewish population. The question why so few of the Jews managed to survive has been tackled by J.C.H. Blum in "The Persecution of the Jews in the Netherlands. A Comparative Western European Perspective", *European History Quarterly*, vol. 19, 1989, pp. 333–351. In his opinion, the lack of organised resistance at the time the Jews were deported, along with the "segmentation" or "pillarisation" (*verzuiling*) of the society, characteristic to the Dutch, were the key factors.

Figure 8: Notice board indicating the Jewish district in Amsterdam

Figure 9: A barbed-wire barrier at the border of the ghetto (under preparation) in Amsterdam, February 1941

Figure 10: The "razzia" (roundup) – a hunt for Jews in Amsterdam, 22nd February 1941

Figure 11: Facsimile of the report by Egert Reeder, chief of the German military administration for Belgium, for April 1941. The pictured passage refers to the incidents in Antwerp of 14th and 16th April 1941

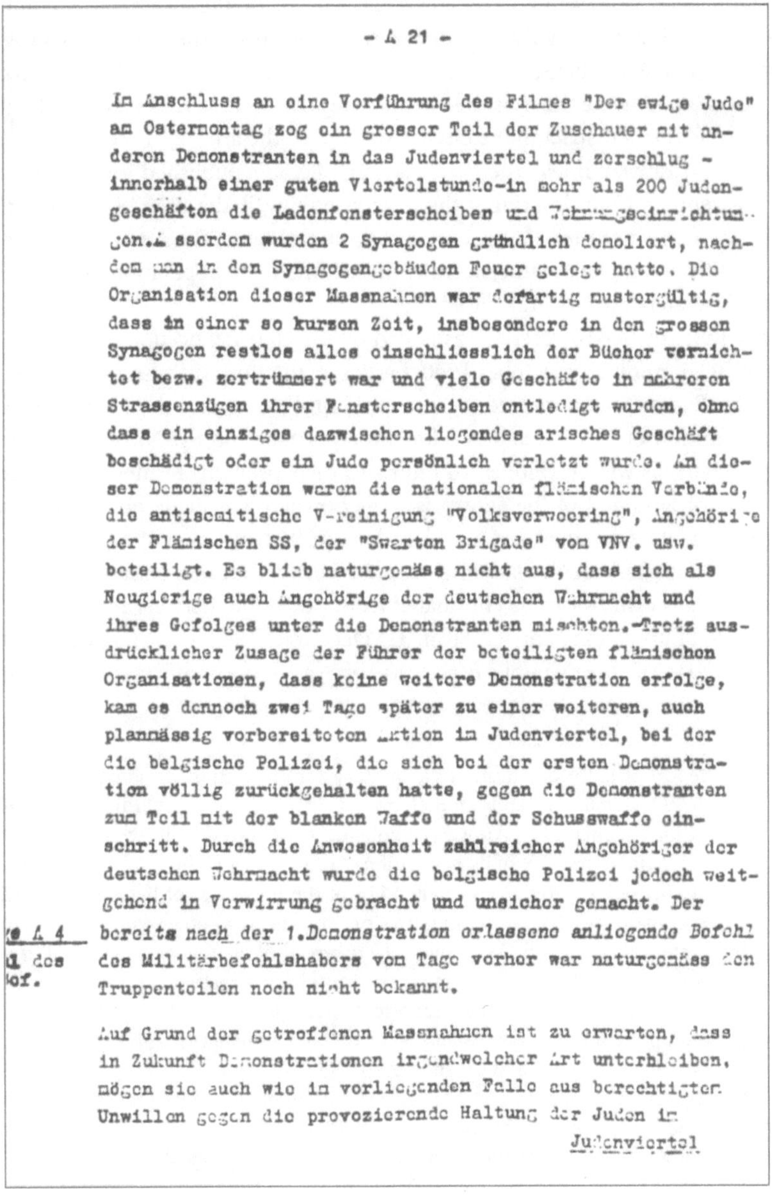

- A 21 -

Im Anschluss an eine Vorführung des Filmes "Der ewige Jude" am Ostermontag zog ein grosser Teil der Zuschauer mit anderen Demonstranten in das Judenviertel und zerschlug - innerhalb einer guten Viertelstunde-in mehr als 200 Judengeschäften die Ladenfensterscheiben und Wohnungseinrichtungen. Ausserdem wurden 2 Synagogen gründlich demoliert, nachdem man in den Synagogengebäuden Feuer gelegt hatte. Die Organisation dieser Massnahmen war derartig mustergültig, dass in einer so kurzen Zeit, insbesondere in den grossen Synagogen restlos alles einschliesslich der Bücher vernichtet bezw. zertrümmert war und viele Geschäfte in mehreren Strassenzügen ihrer Fensterscheiben entledigt wurden, ohne dass ein einziges dazwischen liegendes arisches Geschäft beschädigt oder ein Jude persönlich verletzt wurde. An dieser Demonstration waren die nationalen flämischen Verbände, die antisemitische V-reinigung "Volksverwering", Angehörige der Flämischen SS, der "Swarten Brigade" von VNV. usw. beteiligt. Es blieb naturgemäss nicht aus, dass sich als Neugierige auch Angehörige der deutschen Wehrmacht und ihres Gefolges unter die Demonstranten mischten. Trotz ausdrücklicher Zusage der Führer der beteiligten flämischen Organisationen, dass keine weitere Demonstration erfolge, kam es dennoch zwei Tage später zu einer weiteren, auch planmässig vorbereiteten Aktion im Judenviertel, bei der die belgische Polizei, die sich bei der ersten Demonstration völlig zurückgehalten hatte, gegen die Demonstranten zum Teil mit der blanken Waffe und der Schusswaffe einschritt. Durch die Anwesenheit zahlreicher Angehöriger der deutschen Wehrmacht wurde die belgische Polizei jedoch weitgehend in Verwirrung gebracht und unsicher gemacht. Der bereits nach der 1.Demonstration erlassene anliegende Befehl des Militärbefehlshabers vom Tage vorher war naturgemäss den Truppenteilen noch nicht bekannt.

Auf Grund der getroffenen Massnahmen ist zu erwarten, dass in Zukunft Demonstrationen irgendwelcher Art unterbleiben, mögen sie auch wie im vorliegenden Falle aus berechtigtem Unwillen gegen die provozierende Haltung der Juden im
Judenviertel

Antwerp

Antwerp, the second largest city in Belgium, has been referred to as Jerusalem on the Scheldt. According to a census carried out by the Germans in autumn 1940, some 22,500 Jews lived in Antwerp at the time. The Jewish population largely consisted of aliens, émigrés from other countries, among whom the comers from Poland were the most numerously represented.[268] The Jews were largely concentrated in a district in the city's eastern part, the area of the central railway station and railway lines. The Brussels "rag" *Le Soir* published a reportage on 13th November 1940 describing the district, giving it the title "*Aux cent mille juifs. Le Ghetto d'Anvers*" ("One hundred thousand Jews. The Antwerp Ghetto"). Apparently, to emphasise the enormity of the threat, the population of local Jews was deliberately multiplied fivefold.

The first anti-Jewish decree was issued by the German occupational authorities in Belgium on 28th October 1940. Earlier, regulations discriminating Jews in Western Europe had appeared in Luxembourg, France, and the Netherlands.[269] The definition of "Jew" was based for these purposes on the Nuremberg Laws. Jewish refugees were forbidden to return to their previous residences. The registration of Jews and of the enterprises they owned was made obligatory; such establishments were supposed to be labelled by 30th November 1940 in three languages: "*Jüdische Unternehmen // Entreprise juive // Joodsche onderneming*". The local Jewry was meant to be eliminated from public life here earlier than in the other West European countries. From 31st December 1940, Jews were deprived of the right to perform any public functions, serve as clerks or officials with the state

---

268 Cf. Report of E. Reeder, head of the military administration, for January 1941, IfZ, MA 677/2, c. 966 (Alexandrian materials, T-501, reel 103). According to a similar report for October 1940, Antwerp numbered 191,678 residents, which means that Jews accounted for 7.7% of its population. According to H. Bernard (*La Rèsistance*, 2nd ed., Bruxelles, 1969, p. 63), only 4,115 of the Jews were of Belgian nationality, while as many as 62,536 were migrants or refugees from other countries. According to the data quoted by W. Weber (*Die innere Sicherheit im besetzten Belgien und Nordfrankreich 1940-44: ein Beitrag zur Geschichte der Besatzungsverwaltungen*, Düsseldorf 1978, pp. 120–121), there reportedly were approximately 115,000 Jews living in Belgium before the war (excluding those below the age of 15), including some 35,000 refugees from the Reich and approx. 45,000 former Polish citizens. Antwerp was itself home to approx. 55,000 Jews. Thus, it can be concluded that 45,000–50,000 Jews had left the country by the autumn of 1940.

269 Cf. Szarota, T., *Życie codzienne w stolicach okupowanej Europy*, Warsaw 1995: chapter *Segregacja rasowa i dyskryminacja Żydów*, pp. 107–117.

administration, be active with any associations or societies, work as attorneys or lawyers, teachers, or as journalists with the press or radio.[270]

What was the Belgian people's response to such an *ordonnance*? An attempted answer can be found in the article "*Le problème juif*", published in December 1940 by *Le Clandestin*, a conspiratorial magazine (no. 6), which found that: "It would be pointless to conceal this: even though our people are not violently anti-Semitic, they nonetheless approved – with at least partial satisfaction – the measures that have been applied by the occupiers against the Jews. [...] At the present moment, it is the Germans who are our enemy, and those Belgians who are offering their services to them are traitors of their homeland [...] and the most bloodthirsty anti-Semites. [...] If, from the social point of view, anti-Semitism is a socialism of imbeciles, then from the national standpoint it is a symptom of a degenerated national sentiment. Let us think of France, and let us remind ourselves of the Dreyfus affair." The reactions among the Belgians must have been quite diverse; still, it is a matter of fact that this very drastic stroke of the occupational authorities did not trigger any sort of outraged protest. Those who condemned it for the most part remained silent.

The attitude of the German occupational authorities with respect to the "solution to the Jewish question" in Belgium was openly disclosed in a report for January 1941 of SS-Brigadeführer Eggert Reeder, head of the military administration (*Militärverwaltungschef*).[271] From this document we learn, "The wide-ranging actions aimed against the Jews would be pointless, since the Belgians, partly because they do not know their Jews, have no understanding for the decrees concerning them; and, moreover, due to the incitements against the German Reich that have been going on for years, they are particularly sensitive about this particular point. The military board will proceed in a way so as to eliminate the Jewish influences from public and economic life without spectacular actions."[272]

---

270   *Le Soir*, no. 274, 7th November 1940; *Brüsseler Zeitung*, no. 120, 6th November 1940.
271   Although Reeder held an honorary rank of General with the SS, he was not a fanatical Nazi; he actually represented a moderate approach and was considered to be an excellent administrator. Cf. Madajczyk, op. cit., pp. 311–312, and numerous references to this figure in a study by A. De Jonghe, a leading expert on the subject-matter: A. De Jonghe, "La lutte Himmler-Reeder pour la nomination d'un HSSPF a Bruxelles, Part 1: La Sicherheitspolizei en Belgique", [in:] *Cahiers d'Histoire de la Seconde Guerre Mondiale*, vol. 3, 1974, pp. 103–172; "Part 2, Prélude", ibidem, vol. 4, 1976, pp. 5–158 (hereinafter, quoted as: "De Jonghe, 2").
272   Cf. Reeder's report (as in footnote 268).

This does not clearly tell us what was actually intended for the Jews remaining in Belgium after depriving the sources of income for at least some of them. Reeder does not mention options such as the deportation of Jews, their removal from Belgium, or arranging camps or ghettos for them inside the country. The concept of the military decision makers to solve the "Jewish question" in a gradual manner and on the quiet did not at all meet the expectations of the local nationalist or overtly fascist formations. It was moreover contrary to the objective set by the Belgium-based agency of Goebbels's department, the *Propaganda-Abteilung*, which theoretically reported to its military superiors – that is, General Alexander von Falkenhausen (*Militärbefehlshaber*) and E. Reeder; the latter dealt with civil affairs on behalf of the former. In reality, as will become apparent soon, the *Propaganda-Abteilung* frequently operated behind the backs of the occupational military authorities and contrary to their position.[273]

Of the Walloon and Flemish nationalist formations that had functioned in Belgium before the war, only the latter ones will be of our present interest in regards to the anti-Jewish incidents that took place in Antwerp in August 1941: Among the largest organisations was, no doubt, the Vlaams Nationaal Verbond (Flemish National Union; VNV). Founded by Staf De Clercq, it numbered some 60,000 members by mid-1941. Its leader offered his cooperation with the German occupying authorities as early as June 1940. In a speech to VNV members in Brussels on 10th November 1940, De Clercq stated: "Belgium has been our enemy. The Germans are not our enemy. We trust the Führer."[274] The Flemish hoped that they could take advantage of the Germans in implementing their idea of a Flemish community linking the inhabitants of two subdued countries – Belgium and the Netherlands. VNV, which organisationally was a political party, had its own militia that functioned as a fighting squad; its name was *Zwarte Brigade* – the Black Brigade – because of the colour of the shirts they wore.[275] Let me point out the formation's close similarity to the French *Gardes Françaises* and the Dutch *Weerafdeling*. All three have been modelled after the German *Sturm-Abteilung*. We know today that the French and Dutch fighting groups participated in the anti-Jewish riots; as we will see in a moment, their Flemish counterparts did as well.

The Duits-Vlaamse Arbeidsgemeenschap – German-Flemish Labour Community, abbreviated as "DeVlag", was a social-cultural association whose goal was to strengthen the contacts between Flemish politicians and intellectuals, on

---

273 De Jonghe, 2, pp. 66–69.
274 Ibidem, p. 29.
275 This formation was headed by Raimond Tollenaere, who was killed on 22nd February 1942 in the Eastern Front.

the one hand, and with their partners representing the Third Reich, on the other. On the Flemish side, the central figure was Jef Van de Wiele, his main German contact being Rolf Wilkening, an activist with the Nazi youth movement.[276] There are apparent analogies here again, as DeVlag had a part to play which was very similar to that of the *Comité France-Allemagne* formed by Otto Abetz. Both organisations had made contacts before the war with people whom they won over for the idea of a "New Europe" under German hegemony. Those people were the first to become collaborators once their respective countries were seized.

Owing to its Flemish aspirations and overt Catholicism, De Clercq's VNV aroused the objections of Gottlob Berger, commander of the SS Head Office (*SS-Hauptamt*) and Himmler's confidant.[277] DeVlag, on the other hand, enjoyed Berger's support from the very beginning; he even extended his care to this organisation. Of particular note is the fact that Rolf Wilkening, DeVlag's German contact, arrived in Belgium together with the German army and was employed with the Propaganda Office.

The military authorities were reluctant about establishing SS formations within Belgium from start of the occupation. On his part, Himmler strove for it as he treated recruitment with the SS as a means to gradually broaden the competencies of RSHA and as a method to take over power from the military administration. Recruitment for *Algemeene SS-Vlaanderen*, the Flemish SS, began in September 1940. The formation's first commander was SS-Hauptsturmführer René Lagrou, an attorney; Antwerp was to be their assigned headquarters. On the German side, their "supervisor" was SS-Brigadeführer Konstantin Kammerhofer.[278]

Lastly, let us mention a relatively little-known organisation called *Volksverwering* (People's Defence). Founded in 1937 in Antwerp by René Lambrichts, a local lawyer,[279] it had its own press organ there since 1st February 1942, *L'Ami du Peuple*, sub-headed *Hebdomadaire d'action racique contre les forces occulte*. Although I have only seen citations from this publication and no actual issues, it seems somehow similar to the Parisian *Au Pilori*. If one looks for further French-Belgian analogies,

---

276   De Jonghe, 2, p. 64.
277   SS-Brigadeführer Gottlob Berger enjoyed Himmler's trust and was in charge of the affairs of occupied Belgium on his behalf. Before then, he had organised the *Einsatzgruppen* that operated in Poland in September 1939. Berger was a primitive man of low-IQ; cf. De Jonghe, 2, p. 23.
278   Ibidem, p. 49.
279   Steinberg, M., *L'Etoile et le fusil*, vol. 1: *La question juive 1940–1942*, Bruxelles, 1983, chapter "Le front antijuif des nazis flamands et wallons", pp. 133–154 (A. De Jonghe does not mention the organisation or its leader).

a counterpart of Lambrichts's *Volksverwering* would be P. Clementi's *Parti Français National-Collectiviste*.

Let us, however, move on to the occurrences being focal to our present considerations – that is, the anti-Jewish riots witnessed by Antwerp in April 1941.[280] Before large-scale street brawls took place in the city, several other noteworthy incidents occurred. The first of them was, perhaps, the premiere release of Fritz Hippler's quasi-documentary *Der ewige Jude* (*The Eternal Jew*), which took place on 6th April 1941. The film showed, among other things, scenes from the Łódź ghetto and the ritual slaughter of animals, which was supposed to demonstrate Jewish cruelty. After the show, the head of the *Volksverwering*, which had prepared the release, delivered a speech in which he said, "The last Jew should leave Flanders and Wallonia, we ought to be free from his presence and destroy his wretched influence on our country."[281] Although the audience received Lambrichts's oration enthusiastically, they quietly exited the cinema, and there were no excesses following the show. The copy of the film must have been provided by the German Propaganda Office.

Four days afterwards, young fascist volunteers for the *Algemeene SS-Vlaanderen* – the Flemish SS – entered the arena. They went to Lange Kievitstraat and did exactly what their French counterparts had done on Champs Elysées in August 1940: they smashed the windows of shops owned by Jews. The action was renewed on 12th April – this time, on a larger scale, as it extended beyond a single street. The perpetrators were more numerous now, as members of other nationalist formations joined in. The attackers rushed into the Rotary Club office at 18,

---

280 For the most detailed description of these events, see the book by Lieven Saerens on the history of Jewish populace of Antwerp in the period 1880–1944. Very importantly, this author observed an interdependence between what occurred at the time in Antwerp and the earlier developments in The Hague and Amsterdam: L. Saerens, *Vreemdelingen in een wereldstad: Een geschiedenis van Antwerpen en zijn joodse bevolking (1880–1944)* [Foreigners in a metropolis. A history of Antwerp and its Jewish population, 1880–1944], Antwerp, 2000. The chapter of importance for the purpose of my present book is titled "*Een Antwerpse 'Kristallnacht' (April 1941)*", pp. 568–576. I owe a German translation of this particular chapter to Mr. Dominik Scholz of the Joods Museum van Deportatie en Verzet, Mechelen (for which I should like to express my thanks).

281 In his book *L'Etoile et le fusil* (which has been quoted above), M. Steinberg included a separate chapter describing these events titled "Le Pogrome d'Anvers: un défi SS à l'autorité militaire?", pp. 155–166 (the quotation is from p. 156). There is strong evidence to support his statement that the pogrom was a challenge cast by the Police to the military authorities.

rue Quellin and forced its directors to put up a notice banning entry to Jews.[282] Later on that same day a performance was interrupted at the Antwerp music hall "L'Ancienne Belgique". As the Brussels "rag" *Le Pays Libre* explained, this had happened because "the Flemish artists were repeatedly booed by certain Jews and francophone snobs." Another legally published magazine, *Volksche Aanval*, added: "If there is some Jew unwilling to listen, there is only one thing left for him: a German blow of the fist to his mug. This is, after all, the only language a Yid can understand."[283]

The developments recounted so far occurred in the days before the Easter of 1941. Let us recall that the anti-Jewish riots in Warsaw of the previous year had taken place in a corresponding period. On the Monday after the Easter Sunday, the film *Der ewige Jude* was shown for a second time at the "Rex" cinema on Keyserlei Street; its enormous auditorium of 1,500 seats was full to capacity. As is known, this screening would also not have been possible without the Propaganda Office lending a copy. There is a controversy, though, regarding who organised that particular presentation: Lambrichts's organisation again, or DeVlag? The latter option is possible because of the organisation's very close contacts with the *Propaganda-Abteilung* through Rolf Wilkening. For the French researcher Joseph Billig, it was DeVlag who had organised the film as well as the following pogrom on the orders of Holm, head of the Antwerp *Sicherheitspolizei*.[284] It is also not out of the question that the *Volksverwering* and DeVlag cooperated. René Lambrichts again delivered an oration, reportedly quite resembling his 6th April speech. The audience applauded several times during the show. Special applause was given to the fragment of Hitler's famous speech at the Reichstag of 30th January 1939 announcing "the destruction of the Jewish race in Europe" in the case of war.[285]

The spectators would perhaps have peacefully gone home afterwards – if not for some three men who called the crowd to follow them. Some two hundred followed, that is, every seventh or eighth member of the audience. Among them were

---

282   E. Schmidt, *L'histoire des juifs à Anvers*, Anvers, 1969, p. 156 (I thank José Gotovitsch of Brussels for sending me a photocopy of a fragment of this book).
283   *Le Pays Réel* of 12th May 1941, and *Volksche Aanval* of 19th April 1941; quoted after: Steinberg, op. cit., pp. 155–156.
284   See: J. Billig, *Les premières persécutions policières et les pogroms à Anvers (avril 1941-juillet 1942)*, Centre de Documentation Juive Contemporaine, Paris, ref. no. CCC-58, pp. 19–20.
285   For the text of the Hitler speech, see: Domarus, M., *Hitler. Reden und Proklamationen, 1932–1945*, vol. III, München, 1965, p. 1058.

members of the Black Brigade (the VNV fighting squad), members of DeVlag, young people from the Flemish SS, and approximately 100 members of the *Volksverwering*. It could be supposed that Lambrichts, the organisation's leader, would have been the man at the head the crowd who led it to the Jewish quarter. Indeed, a figure of leader/ringleader did appear, but it was not Lambrichts. Maxime Steinberg, the Belgian historian, has presumed that the man who acted in this capacity was someone connected with Gustave Vanniesbecq, who rivalled with Lambrichts. This author unambiguously hints that the mob's leader performed the task entrusted to him by his principals, who preferred to remain behind the scenes. As we finally learn from L. Saeren's book, the man's name was Pieter Verhoeven, a construction foreman whose countenance is known.[286]

After the public exited the cinema, a procession soon formed and marched toward Pelikaanstraat and Simonsstraat, streets leading to a quarter of the city that had a considerable concentration of Jewish people, located behind the railway tracks in the area of Oostenstraat and Van den Nestlei Streets. As we learn from a report of the German military authorities (more on this report to come in a moment), a few uniformed Germans joined the mob out of curiosity. There is something important to note, however, which suggests that the whole action had been planned and prepared. All of a sudden, wooden clubs and metal crowbars appear in the hands of some of the participants, and a standard with the inscription "*Juda verrecke*" ("Perish, Jew!") started to be waved above the crowd's heads. As they marched on, some of them began sticking slips of paper on Jewish shops and service outlets, probably calling for their boycott. A certain hairdresser started protesting, and immediately had his storefront broken. When two Belgian policemen intended to intervene, the crowd leader approached them, shouting that SS members were untouchable (some of those in the crowd wore uniforms). Then, two German gendarmes appeared. It is not known what the ringleader told them, but they left with smiles on their faces. The news spread that the occupational authorities had consented to the demonstration; this sufficed for the mob to believe they could go on unpunished.

The further course of the events of 14th April 1941 in Antwerp quite closely resembles that of *Kristallnacht* of 9th/10th November 1938 in Germany. The resemblance is not limited to the breaking of shop windows, as synagogues were also set on fire and destroyed. The city on the Scheldt River had two synagogues located

---

286 L. Saerens, op. cit., p. 571 (information on P. Verhoeven); p. 572 (photograph of P. Verhoeven).

not far from each other: one at the corner of Van Den Nestlei St./Oostenstraat and the other 300 meters away, at 42 Oostenstraat. The house of Rabbi Markus Rottenberg was located next to the latter. The assailants formed three groups, each of which started destroying its "assigned" object. The synagogues were set on fire after their interiors had been demolished, the sacred books and objects of cult defiled. One Belgian policeman tried to stop them, but was thrown down to the ground by the vandals. When another asked for the ID of one of the aggressors, he was surrounded by a menacing crowd who threatened to lynch him. Within a quarter of an hour, three buildings were on fire. The fire brigade turned up and started extinguishing the fires only after 45 minutes. The attackers dispersed to "square accounts" with the Jews in the neighbouring streets. As an underground communist bulletin *Les Temps Nouveaux* reported in its May issue, an old woman was seen crying on Somersstraat, standing on the sidewalk beside a bed that had been thrown out of her flat's window. A furrier was spotted in Koornstraat whose shop had been plundered and now was escaping, holding a very small child in his arms.

How were these events portrayed in the report sent to the *Oberkommando der Wehrmacht* by Eggert Reeder, head of the occupational military administration? An extensive fragment of this report (facsimile – see Fig. 11) is worth quoting for a number of reasons. Reeder writes:

> In connection with the screening of the film *Der ewige Jude* [in Antwerp – T.S.] on Easter Monday, a large group of the spectators, together with the other marchers, headed for the Jewish district and within a matter of a quarter of an hour, broke the windows in more than two hundred shops and apartments owned by Jews. Moreover, having first been set on fire, the two synagogues were demolished thoroughly. The undertaking was organised so exemplarily (*mustergütlig*) that within a short time, particularly in the great synagogues, everything, including books, was destroyed or shattered, numerous shops along the whole street lines were deprived of their windows and displays, whereas none of the nearby Aryan shops suffered any loss, and no Jew was personally injured.

I would like to interrupt Reeder's report at this point since the last part of it deserves some commentary. In my conviction, the particular mention that no harm was done to any "Aryan" business during the anti-Jewish action gives a clear indication of who inspired and, quite likely, commissioned the entire propaganda venture. That the instructions were given by the Germans is attested by the coincidence of what happened in the streets of Antwerp and what was stated in the guidelines set forth by Reinhard Heydrich, head of the Sipo and SD, distributed to all the outposts of the Police and Security Service in the famous message (*Geheimes Blitzfernschreiben*) sent from Munich on 10th November 1938, at 1:20

a.m.[287] One of those guidelines clearly instructed: "In the streets where shops are located, one has to observe particular caution so that non-Jewish shops are necessarily safeguarded against any losses." Although elsewhere in these guidelines the devastation and plundering of Jewish shops and apartments was forbidden, as was the maltreatment of detained Jews, such instructions were not observed at that time in Germany itself. Goods were robbed from Jewish shops in Antwerp, but no Jews were arrested, while one of the aims of *Kristallnacht* was to arrest Jews: within a few days, some 20,000 people were put in concentration camps.

We continue with the Reeder report: "The demonstration," we are told, "was attended by Flemish national associations, the anti-Semitic union *Volksverwering*, members of the Flemish SS, the *Zwarte Brigade* affiliated to the VNV, and others. By nature of things, they were joined by persons being members of the German Wehrmacht, out of curiosity, blending in with the crowd of marchers."[288] As we can learn further on, although the "leader of the participating Flemish organisations" promised to desist from such actions in the future, there were more anti-Jewish incidents two days later, on 16th April. However, insofar as the Belgian police were completely passive during the Monday riots, perhaps fearing to intervene in the presence of German soldiers, this time they dispelled the aggressors, not even hesitating to use cold steel to do the job. What is no less important is that Gen. Alexander von Falkehnausen, the *Militärbefehlshaber* and Reeder's superior, ordered on 17th April 1941 that Wehrmacht soldiers who incidentally find themselves in the vicinity of a demonstration should immediately withdraw from the area. It was remarked that their presence at such occasions hindered the dispelling of the crowds by the Belgian police.[289]

Reeder presumed in his report that owing to an "aversion that is justified by the defiant attitude of Jews," someone may want to organise similar riots in the Jewish district in a future. To his mind, such designs ought not to be indulged or permitted. He enumerates a few specified reasons for his stance, proposing arguments very close to those used by the authorities of the military occupational forces in France as they condemned the anti-Jewish incidents in Paris of the summer of 1940. In Reeder's words, "With no worse an organisation as was the case with Antwerp, it would be possible, in the guise of anti-Semitic incentives,

---

287 Recently, the text of this message was published by Karol Jonca in an annex to his book *"Noc kryształowa" i casus Herschela Grynszpana*, 2nd ed., Wrocław 1998, pp. 362–364.
288 Cf. Reeder's report for April 1941, dated 9th April 1941, IfZ, MA 677/3 (Alexandrian materials, T-501, reel 104), cc. 352–5 (A21–A24).
289 Falkehnausen's order: ditto, c. A23, overleaf, attached as an annex.

to also take by assault German outposts within an astonishingly short time." And, he adds: "It is entirely possible that [...] communist or other anti-Semitic elements will in the future participate in such manifestations in order to diminish the authority of the occupational authorities, summoning others to disturb the peace and order." Reeder concludes this part of the report dealing with the Antwerp events with a telling statement: "The problem of the removal (*Abschiebung*) of the Jews can only be regulated in a planned and centralised fashion."[290]

Maxime Steinberg, whose study has been referred to several times in this chapter, titled a section of his book on the riots in Antwerp "*Le Pogrome d'Anvers: un défi SS à l'autorité militaire?*" ("The Antwerp pogrom: Did the SS challenge the military authorities?"). To his mind, it was an attempt to force the military authorities to take resolute steps aimed at bringing about a "solution to the Jewish question" in Belgium. Steinberg has pointed to certain analogies between the actions taken by the Sipo and SD in Paris as part of the preparations for the arson of the synagogues in the night of 2nd/3rd October 1941 and what happened on the 14th and 16th of April in Brussels. Steinberg has no doubt that those managing the anti-Jewish action felt supported by "an authority no less mighty than the military one." The participation of *Algemeene SS-Vlaanderen* in the incidents would indicate that it was the German SS that patronised the action. The fact that DeVlag members joined it attests to a central role of the *Propaganda-Abteilung*. Another argument in support of this thesis is that the riots were filmed by the Germans – as was the case in Warsaw in March 1940. The already-quoted communist conspiratorial bulletin *Les Temps Nouveaux* stated in a May 1941 issue: "The moment the disturbances started, the German officers were already there with their movie camera ready to go and then filmed the whole pogrom. Their camera was installed on Oostenstraat, near the synagogue." Maurice Bénédictus, a Jewish notable and witness to the events, submitted an account after his flight to Portugal in which he wrote: "Everything was being filmed by the Germans from the *Propaganda-Staffel III B* (the propaganda column)."[291]

---

290 Ibidem, c. A23. The annual report of the military occupational government in Belgium as for 10th May 1940–10th May 1941 thus presented the stance regarding the solution of the "Jewish question": "In spite of its rather low significance, the planned action against Jews was, in any case, necessary, so that the issue be resolved in a manner similar to that applied in the other areas under German occupation or influence."; IfZ, MA 677/3, c. 752.
291 Quoted after: Steinberg, op. cit., pp. 162–163.

How did the inhabitants of Antwerp react to what happened on the streets of their city? E. Schmidt writes of "universal outrage" in his *L'histoire des juifs à Anvers*. The Jewish quarter became a site of pilgrimage for many days, as the locals wanted to see for themselves the effects of the acts of vandalism that their compatriots had committed following instructions received from the occupiers. As punishment for the street riots, the German authorities imposed a curfew, fixing it at 10 p.m. Two days later, "Aryans" were released from its observance, whereas for Jews it was changed to the earlier hour of 8:00 p.m.[292] Then, something extraordinary occurred in Antwerp. The city council's lay-judge panel, chaired by officiating mayor Delwaide, resolved to compensate the Jews for their incurred losses from municipal funds. The city recognised itself as responsible for the pillage that had occurred during the riots and the damages caused. They cited on this occasion a regulation from the French Revolutionary period (from the year 1796!). A year later, the German authorities banned any payments to be made on this basis.[293] In 1943, the collaborationist magazine *Volksche Aanval* recalled the riots; in the opinion of the editors, "they were provoked by the scandalous attitude of the Jews themselves. [...] There could not have been any plan conceived in advance. The response was a manifestation of the spontaneous anger of the inhabitants of Antwerp."[294]

Of course, the same sort of spontaneity could be observed in the streets of German cities during *Kristallnacht*; in Warsaw, in March 1940; in Paris, in the summer of 1940; and in The Hague and Amsterdam in February 1941. As for Kaunas – after the Red Army withdrew and before the Germans entered in June of 1941 – one can indeed speak of improvised, if not spontaneous, actions of the local nationalists.

---

292 As in Steinberg, op. cit., p. 160; a letter of Rüstungs-Inspektion Belgien, sent from Brussels on 2nd May 1941 says that "with the view of keeping order," the curfew was fixed for Antwerp at 9:00 pm; CDJC, Paris, ref. no. CDXCII-16.
293 Schmidt, op. cit., p. 157.
294 Cf. *Volksche Aanval* of 23rd January 1943; quoted after Steinberg, op. cit., p. 159.

Chapter 4 Kaunas/Kovno

From an independent state to a (forcedly established) Soviet republic

The Lithuanian Activist Front in Berlin and the Underground at home

At the onset of the Second World War, Kaunas (referred to by its Jewish population as Kovno) was the capital city of Lithuania. A temporary capital, as it were, for the Lithuanians considered Vilnius – which had been seized by Poland (and was referred to as Wilno in Polish) – to be their traditional and proper capital as noted in their Constitution. The anniversary of seizure of Vilnius by General Lucjan Żeligowski, 9th October 1920, was commemorated by the Lithuanians as a national day of mourning. Diplomatic relations between the two countries were only established in the spring of 1938, following an ultimatum from Poland. Before this occurred, demonstrations under the banner "Vilnius is ours!" were held in Lithuania, whereas crowds exclaimed, "Leader, lead us to Kowno [i.e. Kaunas]!" in Poland. In 1939, Poland and Lithuania clearly endeavoured to come to agreement and reconciliation, but ultimately failed to arrive at a political and military alliance.[295]

The Third Reich did not observe the emerging Polish-Lithuanian rapprochement passively. Endeavours were taken to incite the Lithuanians to stand up against Poland and regain Vilnius. A few days before the war broke out, Colonel Kazys Škirpa, the Lithuanian envoy to Berlin, arrived in Kaunas and tried to persuade the Lithuanian Government to take steps to this effect. A Germanophile, Škirpa was envoy to Warsaw in 1938 but earlier had served for ten years as Lithuania's military attaché in the German capital. Soon thereafter, Professor Augustinas Voldemaras came to Lithuania. Living in France at that time, Voldemaras, an extreme nationalist, had once been Prime Minister. His return home probably had something to do with the Germans' intention to use him in a political game that was to lead to Lithuania's involvement on their side. Voldemaras was arrested when he crossed the border, and the Lithuanian Government was

---

295 An admirably unbiased discussion of the difficult issues stemming from these two neighbouring of nations can be found in two basic monographs on this subject-matter authored by Piotr Łossowski: *Po tej i tamtej stronie Niemna. Stosunki polsko-litewskie 1883–1939*, Warsaw 1985; and, *Stosunki polsko-litewskie 1921–1939*, Warsaw 1997.

warned by France and Great Britain of the consequences that might be inflicted in case their Polish ally was confronted. As a result, Lithuanian President Atanas Smetona declared his country neutral on 1st September 1939. This status was maintained throughout the Polish campaign, although Germany continued to pressure Lithuania to stand up against Poland.[296]

Resulting from the German-Soviet agreements, following its forty-day occupation of Wilno (19th September to 27th October 1939), the Red Army withdrew from the city and Lithuanian troops entered it on 28th October 1939. This by no means meant that Stalin had quit the idea to seize Lithuania; for the time being, he watched the European developments attentively. The day the German army entered Paris, the Lithuanian Government received an ultimatum demanding that Lithuania be subjected to the Soviet Union's interests. The following day, 15th June 1940, saw Soviet troops seize the country again. On 21st July 1940, the newly "elected" People's *Seimas* (parliament) announced in Kaunas the establishment of the socialist republic of Lithuania and resolved to join the Soviet Union,[297] which was eventually declared on 3rd August 1940. Lithuania was to regain its independence fifty years later: the free Republic of Lithuania was proclaimed on 11th March 1990.

It is not my task to describe life in Lithuania under the so-called "second Bolsheviks", that is, between 15th June 1940 and 22nd June 1941. Even though the poorer sections of the populace, including destitute Jews as well as some members of the progressive (that is, Left-inclined) intelligentsia, could have initially entertained some hope for the slogans of social justice to be put into practice, with ethnic feuds coming to an end, these illusions were soon to be dispelled. The Soviet occupation entailed political repressions, shortages of goods, widespread pauperisation, and hindered, if not obstructed, religious practice. The Polish and Lithuanian people grew disillusioned, and so did the Jews, as they were being deprived of their shops and craft workshops, religious schools, and houses of prayer. However, Soviet authority was supported by a significant portion of Jewish youth who willingly joined the local Komsomol.

---

296   This topic is touched upon by P. Łossowski in his earlier book *Litwa a sprawy polskie 1939–1940*, Warsaw 1982.

297   It is regrettable that no monograph similar to Jan Tomasz Gross's *Studium zniewolenia. Wybory październikowe 22 X 1939*, Krakow, 1999, dealing with the elections for the National Assemblies of West Ukraine and West Belarus, has been written so far about the election in Lithuania. According to Henryk Wisner, the decision to move the Lithuanian capital to Vilnius (Wilno) was taken on 26th August 1940; cf. H. Wisner, *Litwa. Dzieje państwa i narodu*, Warsaw 1999, p. 223.

The subject of our central interest here is the situation in Kaunas region – a part of Lithuania that housed no sizeable clusters or hubs of Poles, and where Jews constituted a considerable proportion of the inhabitants, particularly in cities and small towns. Describing the sentiments in the area, General Stefan Rowecki, Commander of the Home Army, wrote in a report dated 19th February 1941: "The Lithuanians' hatred toward the Bolsheviks is widespread."[298] These feelings further intensified as on 14th June 1941 the Soviet authorities commenced the deportations of some 30,000–40,000 inhabitants of Lithuania – including approximately 7,000 Poles and 6,000–7,000 Jews – into the depths of the USSR, an action that lasted a number of days.[299] As the Lithuanian-American historian V. Stanley Vardys wrote: "Since these mass cruelties, with no provoking incentive behind them, occurred a mere week before the outbreak of the German-Russian war, they were a decisive factor in the Lithuanians' attitude to the German attack. The offensive was joyously welcomed by a majority of almost all strata of the population, as it seemed to be the only possibility to be liberated from the unmerciful Bolshevik regime. This attitude toward Hitler's war against the Soviet Union is clearly different from the stance prevailing in the Western Europe. For instance, Germany's invasion of Denmark was rightly deemed to have been an aggressive act. But the Lithuanians, similarly to the Latvians and Estonians, perceived the German troops in the first days of the war roughly in the manner the Dutch saw the British seizing Amsterdam in 1945."[300]

It is true that the expectations of the Lithuanians of the coming of the Germans as liberators was to a great extent caused by the system of Soviet rule. However, it should not be forgotten that both at home and abroad there were those who never accepted that their own state had ceased to exist. Most of them expected the Third Reich to prove helpful in regaining it for themselves – but they were wrong, as it occurred soon after. The 17th of November 1940 saw the setting up in Berlin, on the initiative of Col. Škirpa, of a *Lietuvių aktyvistų frontas* – Lithuanian

---

[298] *Armia Krajowa w dokumentach*, vol. I, London 1970, p. 462.
[299] The number of the deportees varies by source. Michael MacQueen mentions 35,000 (incl. 6,000 Jews and 7,500 Poles); cf. M. MacQueen, "Polen, Litauer, Juden und Deutsche in Wilna 1939–1944", [in:] W. Benz and M. Neiss (eds.), *Judenmord in Litauen. Studien und Dokumente*, Berlin, 1999, p. 61. Referring to the documents published in 1990 by Henrikas Sadzius, H. Wisner makes the number much lower – 12,682; cf. Wisner, op. cit., p. 224.
[300] V. Stanley Vardys, "Litauen: Sowjetrepublik mit Widerwillen. Die Entwicklung seit 1940", [in:] *Die baltische Nationen Estland, Lettland, Litauen*, ed. by B. Meissner, Köln 1990, p. 173.

Activist Front (LAF), whose role was that of a national committee in exile. It was formed of representatives of a number of political parties or factions, but the truly powerful ones were the followers of former President Smetona, on the one hand, and the adherents of his rival, Augustinas Voldemaras, author of the failed fascist putsch of 7th June 1934, on the other. Once Lithuania was made part of the Soviet Union, a wave of refugees flowed into Germany, among whom were numerous politicians and military officers. Berlin became a hub of Lithuanian irredentism. For fairly obvious reasons, the German authorities took steps to make a use of the strivings of the Lithuanians for their own purposes; the Lithuanians, on their part, cared very much about establishing contacts with the Germans and gaining their support.

Due to a shortage of documents, not much can be said today about the details concerning the Berlin talks between the Lithuanians, on the one hand, and the exponents of the Reich Security Main Office (*Reichssicherheitshauptamt*, RSHA), the German Ministry of Foreign Affairs, military intelligence – i.e. the Abwehr, as well as NSDAP and the Wehrmacht, on the other. The Germans reportedly tied their expectations, to some extent, to General Stasys Raštikis, the former Lithuanian Commander-in-Chief. It seems that the Foreign Ministry soon withdrew its support for Col. Škirpa. Instead, as time went on, the position of Voldemaras's followers was growing in the Germans' perception, particularly in military and police circles. Among the underlying factors was the group's radically anti-Semitic ideology, close to the National-Socialist one, along with the existence in Lithuania of conspiratorial units of the clandestine organisation Geležinis Vilkas (Iron Wolf), which had been established in 1929.[301] When the "Barbarossa" plan was developed in Germany, diversionary actions to be possibly taken by the local people against the withdrawing Red Army were also taken into account. It is quite probable that already at that point the Germans were looking at the possibility of taking advantage of the Lithuanian anticommunists, who were filled with hatred towards Jews, in carrying out the *Endlösung* programme.

As there were extant proclamations, instructions, and leaflets prepared and printed in Berlin by Lithuanian emigrants and then distributed by couriers to

---

301 The organisation was set up after President Smetona dismissed Voldemaras as Prime Minister. Members of the underground "Iron Wolf" organisation perpetrated anti-Jewish pogroms in Lithuania in the years 1935–1936 and in 1939; cf. Stang, K., "Das Fußvolk und seine Eliten. Der Beginn der Kollaboration in Litauen 1941", [in:] *Judenmord in Litauen* … (see footnote 5), p. 74. SS-Sturmbannführer Heinz Gräfe, head of Tilsit's *Stapostelle* in 1937–1940, played the first fiddle in maintaining contracts with the Lithuanian nationalists.

clandestine organisations at home, the LAF's plans and intentions are no secret. Here is a fragment of their instruction of 19th March 1941 (as quoted by Maria Wardyńska):

> The hour of liberty for Lithuania [is] near. You shall be notified of the march commencing from the west by radio or otherwise. At that moment, local uprisings ought to kick off in the enslaved towns, settlements, and villages of Lithuania; putting it otherwise, taking control into our own hands. [...] Get organised into secret and quantitatively not-quite numerous [sic] groups. [...] After the actions are started, seize the bridges, important railroad junctions, airports, factories, and other [such objects]. [...] Once the actions are commenced in the rear, a parachuting sortie will be carried out. Communicate with them [the sortie crew] immediately and offer them assistance, if need be.[302]

As it irrefutably follows from this text, the central objective for LAF was to make use of the German-Soviet war for the purposes of rebuilding a Lithuanian state which would be allied to the Third Reich while maintaining a status similar to that of Slovakia. It would be hard to deny that there were arguments in favour of perceiving the LAF's doings in terms of patriotic activity.[303] Yet there is no doubt, at the same time, that the planned "local uprisings" and diversionary acts were meant to contribute to the Reich's war machine.

As it turns out, LAF endeavoured to prepare their compatriots at home for cracking down on the "Judeo-commies" as a sort of additional action. The following passage appeared in the above-quoted instruction: "[...] traitors will be forgiven only when they truly prove that they have liquidated at least one Jew."[304] The struggle against the "Judeo-commies" is clearly mentioned in the LAF proclamation of 24th March 1941, titled *Lietuvai Išlaisvinti Nurodymai* (Directives on the liberation of Lithuania). The reinforcement of anticommunist

---

302 The content of this instruction, issued by the LAF's Lithuanian Information Office in Berlin, was first published in its original language version in 1965 in Vilnius: *Masinės žudynės Lietuvoje, 1941–1944. Dokumentų rinkinys* [The mass crimes in Lithuania, 1941–1944. A collection of documents], ed. by B. Baranauskas and E. Rozauskas, based on the documents collected by G. Erslavaite and K. Rukšenas, Vilnius 1965 pp. 49–50. My quote follows the Polish translation by Maria Wardyńska, published in: M. Wardyńska, *Sytuacja ludności polskiej w Generalnym Komisariacie Litwy (czerwiec 1941 – lipiec 1944)*, Warsaw 1993, p. 29.

303 It is worth noting that a State ceremonial burial was held for Col. Kazys Škirpa, the initiator of LAF, who died in 1995.

304 This passage is quoted by Saulius Sužiedėlis, an American historian of Lithuanian descent, in his "Lithuanian Collaboration during the Second World War: Past Realities, Present Perceptions", [in:] *"Kollaboration" in Nordosteuropa. Erscheinungsformen und Deutungen im 20. Jahrhundert*, ed. by Joachim Tauber, Wiesbaden 2006.

and anti-Jewish actions was meant to be indispensable for the unity of a nation that saw itself founded upon the principles of Christian morality. As we further read therein:

> It is very important on this occasion to shake off the Jews. For this reason it is necessary to create within the country such a stifling atmosphere against the Jews that not a single Jew would dare to even allow himself the thought that he would have even minimal rights or, in general, any possibility to earn a living in the new Lithuania. The goal is to force all the Jews to flee Lithuania together with the Red Russians. The more of them who leave Lithuania at this time, the easier it will be to finally get rid of the Jews later. The hospitality granted the Jews during the time of Vytautas the Great [the Lithuanian duke who ruled from 1392 to 1430 – T.S.] is hereby revoked for all time on account of their repeated betrayal of the Lithuanian nation to its oppressors.[305]

Particularly characteristic is a manifesto issued by LAF just before the outbreak of the German-Soviet war. Allow me to quote an extensive passage from it:

> Dear Compatriots, brothers and sisters! [...] The crucial day of reckoning has come for the Jews at last. Lithuania must be liberated not only from Asiatic-Bolshevik slavery, but also from the Jewish yoke of long standing. The Lithuanian Activist Front on behalf of the Lithuanian people solemnly declares: [...] 1. The old rights of sanctuary granted to Jews in Lithuania by Vytautas the Great are abolished forever and without reservation; 2. Hereby all Jews, without any exception, are strictly ordered to immediately leave Lithuania; 3. All Jews who have singled themselves out by betraying Lithuania, and persecuting and torturing Lithuanians shall be separately brought to trail [trial] and receive condign punishment. Should it become known that at the decisive hour of retribution and Lithuania's resurrection, Jews guilty of grave crimes, manage to escape in secret, the duty of all honest Lithuanians is to take measures on their own initiative to stop such Jews and, if necessary, punish them. [...] The new Lithuanian state will be rebuilt by Lithuanians themselves, by their energy, heart and wisdom. All Jews are excluded from Lithuania forever. Should anyone of them dare to expect any refuge in new Lithuania, let him know the irrevocable sentence passed on them: not a single Jew shall have any citizenship rights nor any means of sustenance in Lithuania reborn. Hereby the errors of the past and evils committed by the Jews will be set right and a firm foundation for the happy tomorrow and creative work of our own Aryan nation will be laid. Thus we all must prepare for the struggle and a victory for the freedom of Lithuania, the purification of the nation, the independent Lithuanian state, and for a happy future.[306]

---

305 Ibidem, loc. cit.
306 The English version is quoted by Alex Faitelson in his *The Truth, and Nothing but the Truth. Jewish Resistance in Lithuania*, Jerusalem–New York, 2006, p. 13. Other fragments are quoted by Algis Kasperavičius, "Stosunki litewsko-żydowskie na Litwie w latach 1935–1944", [in:] *Świat NIEpożegnany. Żydzi na dawnych ziemiach wschodniej Rzeczpospolitej w XVIII–XX wieku // A World We Bade no Farewell: Jews in the eastern*

The racist phraseology seems to attest that the backers of Voldemaras had a decisive say within LAF at the time.[307]

"Self-cleansing actions": a task of the *Einsatzgruppen* and a stage in the Holocaust

The *Einsatzgruppen*, and the *Einsatzkommando*s and *Sonderkommando*s forming part of them, were formations of the Nazi Security Police (Sipo) and Security Service (SD) tasked with special responsibilities and equipped with extensive competences who collaborated with the military leadership. Their central, though nowise exclusive, task was to "cleanse" the frontline's logistics support of factual and potential opponents or enemies. Part of their task was, as it were, to prepare the territory seized by the Wehrmacht for the future occupational authorities. The formations were used for the first time during the September 1939 campaign in Poland. As the cruel repressive methods applied by them triggered protest among the German generals, these formations were not used in the course of the 1940 campaign in Western Europe.

When preparing the "Barbarossa" plan, no one opposed their inclusion in this military undertaking, whose profile was political as well as ideological. The attack on the Soviet Union was intended not only to seize the vast territories in the East and subject the local population ("of little racial value") to the will of their German master, but also to abolish the communist system. The image of Slavs, communists, and Jews, in the perception of most Germans on the eve of the Second World War, full of stereotypes inherited from their ancestors, facilitated the approval for applying to an enemy of this sort methods whose use would have been impossible against any other enemy, at least at the start of the war.[308] This

---

territories of the Polish Republic from 18*th* to 20*th* century, ed. by Krzysztof Jasiewicz, Warsawa–Londyn/Warsaw–London 2004, pp. 322–324.

307 The history of LAF is dealt with in a book by Valentinas Brandisauskas discussing the attempts at restoring the Lithuanian state in WW2 years: V. Brandisauskas, *Siekiai atkurti Lietuvos valstybinguma (1940.06–1941.09)* [Efforts to restore the Lithuanian state, June 1940–September 1941], Vilnius, 1996. M. McQueen, the U.S. historian, sees Brandisauskas' monograph as "groundbreaking" for the research on the LAF, and marvels at the author's courage in dealing with the subject-matter; cf. M. McQueen, "Massenvernichtung im Kontext: Täter und Voraussetzungen des Holocaust in Litauen", [in:] *Judenmord in Litauen* …, p. 24.

308 Cf. H. Dmitrów, *Obraz Rosji i Rosjan w propagandzie narodowych socjalistów 1933–1945*, Warsaw, 1997; also, J.W. Borejsza, *Antyslawizm Adolfa Hitlera*, Warsaw, 1988; E.C. Król, *Propaganda i indoktrynacja narodowego socjalizmu w Niemczech*

being the case, the *Einsatzgruppen's* participation in the delivery of the "Barbarossa" plan became not only desirable but indispensable.

The formation of *Einsatzgruppen*, including the recruitment and training of its members, was the task of the Reich Security Main Office (RSHA), managed by Reinhard Heydrich, a man we have already met and know quite well,[309] who reported to SS-Reichsführer Heinrich Himmler. An important part in completing the crews was played by SS-Brigadeführer Bruno-Heinrich Streckenbach, head of RSHA's Department I (Personnel); he had been promoted to the post – which was of equal rank with that of the Gestapo head, Müller – because of his "merits" in Poland.[310] The centre for the training of personnel was at the frontier police school in Pretzsch on the Elbe, not far from Torgau, where the U.S. Army was to meet the Red Army troops in 1945. Four *Einsatzgruppen* were formed, each identified with subsequent letters of the alphabet. We shall soon take a closer look at the activities of *Einsatzgruppe A*, commanded by Dr Franz Walter Stahlecker,[311] which was to be sent to the Baltic countries and then moved further on toward Leningrad. *Einsatzgruppe B*, operating in Byelorussia and expected to reach Moscow, was commanded by Arthur Nebe. Dr Otto Rasch was commander of *Einsatzgruppe C*, tasked to go to the north of Ukraine. Lastly, the command of

---

1919–1945, Studium organizacji, treści, metod i technik masowego oddziaływania, Warsaw 1999.

309 An excellent biography of Heydrich has been penned by Robert Gerwarth, *Hitler's Hangman: The Life of Heydrich*, London 2011 (a German version was published, in parallel, in Munich; a Polish translation came out in 2013).

310 In September and October 1939, Streckenbach commanded one of the *Einsatzgruppen* operating in Poland; in January 1941, he was promoted to head of the Sicherheitspolizei and Sicherheitsdienst (Sipo/SD) in the Generalgouvernement (GG). He directed the action of arresting 183 Polish scientists and scholars in Krakow on 6th November 1939 (the so-called "*Sonderaktion Krakau*"); he also contributed to the formation of ghettos within the GG.

311 Regrettably, no biography of Stahlecker has appeared as yet. Born in 1900, Stahlecker joined the NSDAP in 1932 and two years later managed the political police in Wurttemberg. Made head of the Security Service in Vienna in 1938, he later was Territorial Commander of the Sipo/SD for the Protectorate of Bohemia and Moravia and, subsequently (May 1940), in Norway. Promoted to SS-Brigadeführer and Major-General of the Police, he took command of *Einsatzgruppen A* in June 1941. Wounded in a skirmish with partisans, he died on 23rd March 1942. Heydrich delivered a funeral speech at the Prague castle in commemoration of "a hero of the uncompromising fight against the enemies of the Reich"; cf. "SS-Mann im Leben und im Sterben", *Deutsche Polizei* No. 8, 15th April 1942, pp. 113–114. (I extend my cordial thanks to Dr Elke Fröhlich of Munich for having sent me a photocopy of the speech.).

Einsatzgruppe D, whose area of operation was southern Ukraine and Moldavia, was entrusted to Dr Otto Ohlendorf.[312]

For many years, historians from all over the world specialising in the history of the Second World War have disputed whether there existed an explicit order from Hitler to liquidate all the Jews – and, if so, when it was issued.[313] A sort of offshoot of this dispute is the discussion regarding the orders received by the commanders of the *Einsatzgruppen, Einsatzkommandos,* and *Sonderkommandos* before their deployment to the Eastern Front. Those who assume that the formations were ordered to carry out the annihilation of the Jewish people, regardless of their sex and age, have tried to find answers to the inevitable questions of who issued the order, and when and where it happened. Having become acquainted with a considerable portion of the relevant publications, my conclusion is that, in the course of the ongoing discussion, the difference between oral utterance, command, or even a directive set in a conversation, on the one hand, and a written order, on the other, is all too rarely perceived. As time goes on, I am increasingly inclined to accept the opinion of the late Franciszek Ryszka,[314] an eminent expert on the subject, whereby a written order to carry out the *Endlösung* with Hitler's signature never existed; had it existed, the one-million dollar prize established by someone in the United States would have gone to the finder long ago. No one, however, challenges the fact that many a time and at various occasions, Hitler did speak about the necessity to eradicate the Jewish race, a concept advocated by many other Third Reich leaders. The war in the East finally provided an opportunity for the "final solution of the Jewish question", and so it is not surprising that those who were entrusted with the task were addressed in such a spirit.

To establish what the phrasing of those oral commands, instructions, or general directives was, those participating in the conferences held in Pretzsch would

---

312 A map showing the directions of the actions pursued by each of these EGs is featured in the U.S. edition of *The Einsatzgruppen Reports. Selections from the Dispatches of the Nazi Death Squads' Campaign Against the Jews in Occupied Territories of the Soviet Union, July 1941–January 1943*, ed. by I. Arad, S. Krakowski, and S. Spector, New York: Holocaust Library, 1989.

313 With respect to this topic, cf. P. Longerich, *Der ungeschriebene Befehl: Hitler und der Weg zur "Endlösung"*, Munich and Zürich 2001.

314 Professor Franciszek Ryszka (1924–98) has authored the excellent book *Państwo stanu wyjątkowego. Rzecz o systemie państwa i prawa Trrzeciej Rzeszy* [The State of emergency. The state organisation and legal system in the Third Reich], first published 1964 and then republished twice in Poland; unfortunately, no foreign-language edition of this monograph has ever been produced.

have to be questioned – as well as those who took part in the most important briefing that was held on 17th June 1941 in the RSHA conference room at 8 Prinz-Albrecht-Strasse.[315] After the war, only one of the four *Einsatzgruppen* commanders, namely Otto Ohlendorf, could give testimony. Believing that Bruno Streckenbach was dead, he said that it had been Streckenbach who transmitted the order to liquidate the Jews. The other lower-level commanders interrogated either confirmed this or pointed to other persons – most frequently, Heydrich, but Müller was mentioned too. The matter of the orders given to the *Einsatzgruppen* was brought up already at the great trial of Nuremberg, and was resumed in the course of another lawsuit that was brought against members of this particular formation in 1948. The supplementary material available to historians today consists of the transcripts of testimonies, kept in the court archives or at the documentation centre in Ludwigsburg, given by the Nazis during their interrogations regarding the charges brought against them by courts of the post-war Federal Republic of Germany. These testimonies have partly been published.[316]

It is obvious that testimonies made by individuals accused of having committed the severest of crimes ought to be approached with extreme care. It is a natural human tendency to try to save one's own skin, diminish one's responsibility, and put the blame on others – preferably, one's superiors. Many a German war criminal adopted a line of defence, probably suggested to them by their counsels, which was based on pointing to the necessity of subjecting to and executing orders given from the above. This was all the easier since the major figures – Hitler, Himmler, and Heydrich – were by then dead. Based on the records of the testimonies they gave after the war, it is extremely difficult to reconstruct the course of deliberations and conferences the *Einsatzgruppen* members attended before moving to the front. In order to single out the true pieces of information from utterances blending apparent lies and the truth, only one efficient method is applicable to my mind: that is, mutually confronting several independent sources. Whether we like it or not, any testimony is such a source.

---

315 The exact date of the conference is known to us because Heydrich referred to it in a teletype of 29th June 1941 sent to the heads of the EGs; for the teletype's content, see: *Die Ermordung der europäischen Juden: Eine umfassende Dokumentation des Holocaust 1941–1945*, ed. by P. Longerich and D. Pohl, 2nd ed., Munich and Zürich 1990, pp. 118–119.

316 For the purposes of this book, the documents published by Hans-Heinrich Wilhelm have proved of particular value, cf.: H.-H. Wilhelm, *Rassenpolitik und Kriegsführung Sicherheitspolizei und Wehrmacht in Polen und in der Sowjetunion 1939–1942*, Passau 1991.

To me, personally, of the highest importance are the two nearly completely overlapping testimonies submitted by two individuals who attended a briefing at the RSHA headquarters in Berlin on 17th June 1941, reconstructing its course years later. The first was *Oberregierungsrat* (senior government official) and SS-Obersturmbannführer Walter Blume, former commander of one of the *Sonderkommando*s. Interrogated on 2nd August 1958 as a witness in a criminal action against Streckenbach (who in 1955 returned to Germany after being released by the Soviets), he testified that at the said briefing a few participants delivered their reports, among them Heydrich, Streckenbach, Müller, and someone representing the Foreign Ministry. As we read in the record: "Heydrich was personally explaining that a campaign against Russia was near, partisan warfare was to be expected, and that there were many Jews living in that area who had to be eradicated, through liquidation. When one of the attendees exclaimed to him, 'How is it that we should perform this?', he replied, 'You'll see for yourselves.' He then said that the Eastern Jewry should be destroyed, as the germinal cell of worldwide Jewry. There was no way to understand this," Blume comments, "other than that all the Jews, whatever their age or sex, ought to be wiped out."[317] Quoting this same piece of evidence by Blume, Ralf Ogorreck refers to a passage where Blume mentions the receipt of the order to liquidate "communist functionaries and Eastern Jewry."[318]

The other testimony I wish to refer to comes from SS-Standartenführer Karl Jäger, whom we will encounter later as the story evolves. Jäger commanded *Einsatzkommando 3*, forming part of the operational group led by Stahlecker, one of those primarily responsible for the crimes committed in Kaunas and in the whole of Lithuania.[319] During an interrogation of 15th June 1959, six days before he committed suicide in his cell, Jäger testified as follows:

---

317 Quoted from a fragment of Blume's testimony included in the indictment of 30th June 1973 of the Public Prosecutor's Office, Land Court of Hamburg versus Bruno Streckenbach, in: Wilhelm, op. cit., p. 218.
318 R. Ogorreck, *Die Einsatzgruppen und die "Genesis der Endlösung"*, Berlin, 1996, p. 69. This author would not preclude that Blume erroneously interpreted Heydrich's statement; he also quoted another testimony by Blume, given in 1969 during another case, where he deemed it possible "that individual commanders of the *Einsatzkommandos* when the war with Russia broke out did not yet know that the Jews had to be exterminated." According to Ogorreck, this would attest that Heydrich's utterances were "not quite unambiguous." I personally do not share this opinion.
319 A biography of this criminal has recently been published: W. Wette, *Karl Jäger: Mörder der litauischen Juden*, Frankfurt a. Main 2011.

If I am not mistaken, this must have been a few weeks before the Russian campaign started, when I was called for a commanders' conference at the RSHA in Berlin, on Prinz-Albrecht-Strasse. […] I can recall that the conference was held in one of the grand RSHA rooms. A large number of SS commanders were gathered, and of chiefs of the State police. While I cannot make it certain, I suppose there were some fifty of us, SS commanders, there. I cannot possibly give the reason for why we had been convoked there, nor can I define how long the meeting lasted. I can only recall that Heydrich declared in his speech that in case there was a war with Russia, the Jews in the East must all be executed. I would like to note that I cannot recall whether he said that *all* the Jews had to be executed, or that Jews had to be executed. What I have managed to recall, moreover, is that one of the State police chiefs asked, literally, "Should we be shooting the Jews?", to which Heydrich replied, roughly, that this was pretty obvious.[320]

Undeniably, the sense of this statement is close to the testimony that Blume had given a year earlier, completely independently. I emphasise that both testimonies have pointed out a meaningful exchange between Heydrich and one of the delegates. One thing is certain to me: no order or command was read out in the course of that conference, and none of the attendees received any such order in writing whatsoever.[321] There can be no doubt, though, that the delegates were given sufficiently clear guidelines as to who was the Third Reich's enemy and how this enemy ought to be dealt with.

There is no document available today that would be dated before 22nd June 1941 that contains instructions telling the *Einsatzgruppen* what to do and how to act in the territory of the Soviet Union. Detailed written guidelines appeared, perhaps, only in Heydrich's order of 2nd July 1941, some ten days after the campaign in the East kicked off. Any earlier similar instructions have not survived, or simply never existed. The most important fragments of the 2nd July order read: "All the following are to be executed: officials of the Comintern (together with professional Communist politicians in general); top- and medium-level officials and radical lower-level officials of the Party, Central committee, and district and sub-district committees; people's commissars; Jews in Party and State

---

320 Karl Jäger's testimonies are kept at the *Zentrale Stelle der Landesjustizverwaltungen zur Aufklärung nationalsozialistischer Verbrechen* in Ludwigsburg; quoted after: Wilhelm, op. cit., p. 187.

321 At his interrogation on 18th June 1962, Jäger testified: "Heydrich's speech from Berlin, where he avowed that the Jews are to be executed during the operations in the East, has never been repeated. It was not said, either, that there had been any strict order given to execute the Jews in the East. I consider it absolutely out of the question that a written order [to this end] might have come from anyone. As for myself, I certainly never saw any such order, including later on, in Kaunas"; Wilhelm, op. cit., p. 188.

employment; and other radical elements (saboteurs, propagandists, snipers, assassins, inciters, etc.), so long as they are not, in individual cases, of use for giving political or economic directions of special importance for security actions or the further economic reconstruction of the Occupied Territories. It should be particularly considered that the economic, trade-union, or commerce corporations not be definitively liquidated in case that individuals capable of giving the competent information are not available."[322]

Comparing this fragment of Heydrich's written order with the reports of what he said on 17th June in Berlin, one readily notices that there is no mention of the eradication of Jews in the later-dated order. To draw the conclusion that Blume and Jäger gave false testimonies would, however, be unjustified. I should think that Heydrich avoided formulating in writing a message (and thus, leaving evidence of it) that he could pass orally, within a circle of his trusted men. Besides, at the Berlin meeting, the goal was set for what was intended to be achieved resulting from the conquests in the East, whereas the written command concerned immediate tasks – the first stage of dealing with the "Judeo-commies" – at the time. The command was not overly precise, after all; the criterion whereby somebody would be classed as a "radical functionary" is unclear, and one cannot tell where exactly the boundaries were set between high-, medium- and low-level officers. Let me emphasise that he remarks on the necessary caution to be observed not to liquidate those who might still prove of use. What this bit demonstrates is that some enemies were to be wiped out at a later date, rather than immediately and simultaneously with the others.

The second part of Heydrich's order dated 2nd July 1941 strictly refers to the topic of this chapter as well as of the whole book, as it concerns so-called "self-cleansing actions". As we can read there: "No obstacle is to be placed in the way of the self-cleansing efforts [*Selbstreinigungsbestrebungen*] of the anti-Communist and anti-Jewish circles in the newly occupied areas. Rather, they are to be fostered, without leaving evidence that would allow the local 'self-defence circles' any opportunity to later claim that they acted on orders or were given political assurances. Because such conduct, for reasons easy to guess, such actions are only possible during the initial period of military occupation, the *Einsatzgruppen* should, in their dealing with the military posts, endeavour to enter the respective newly-occupied territories as soon as possible with at least one advance troop [*Vorkommando*] each."

---

322 The text has been published by P. Longerich and D. Pohl in: *Die Ermordung der europäischen Juden* ..., op. cit., pp. 116–118; also, in: *Der Krieg gegen die Sowjetunion 1941–1945. Eine Dokumentation*, ed. by R. Rürup, Berlin, 1991, pp. 103–104.

A document referring to the "self-cleansing actions" that I would deem the most important one is Heydrich's teletype regarding these very actions, sent on 29th June 1941 to the *Einsatzgruppen* heads. Although the sender makes reference "to the instructions already given, on 17th June, in Berlin," which clearly implies that the matter of the "self-cleansing actions" was already touched upon at the Berlin conference, none of the individuals interrogated after the war ever mentioned this fact. True, the teletype's content is similar to what we find in the 2nd July 1941 order, but these texts are not identical at all. The teletype instructs that "self-cleansing actions" should not only be triggered but also "intensified, when required, and channelled onto the proper path," and that this should be, of course, accomplished "*spurenlos*" – without leaving evidence. An additional instruction appears: "It is recommended that the formation of permanent self-defence troops, with a central executive, be initially avoided; it is purposeful, instead, to bring about pogroms [*Volkspogromme*] locally."[323]

It can be said, in conclusion, that the Nazi *Einsatzgruppen* which were following the front very closely had two basic tasks to do. The first was to purge the logistics support of the frontline, following the army, of real and potential enemies, while the second was to provide support to the local people in settling accounts with the communists and Jews – the "self-cleansing actions" – or initiating such actions and channelling them in "the right direction."[324] As it will be made apparent in a moment, what the channelling of their activities meant in practice was focusing the "public wrath" on the Jews.

Kaunas in Lithuanian hands, 23rd–24th June 1941: A national uprising, or a settling of accounts with the "Judeo-commies"?

The outbreak of the German-Soviet war on Sunday, 22nd June 1941, came as a surprise to all in Lithuania – the communist authorities and the Red Army troops stationed there, as well as those Lithuanians in the Underground who (as instructed by the LAF) were waiting for the opportunity to organise local uprisings, seize power, and subsequently salute the entering German troops in the capacity of host. Let me draw attention to the fact that this concept, developed by the Lithuanian activists in Berlin, was essentially quite similar to the plan prepared in 1943 by the

---

323 *Die Ermordung*…, op. cit., pp. 118–119.
324 Helmut Krausnick, co-author of a book of critical importance to our subject-matter here, has warned against mistaking *Reinigungsaktionen* for *Selbstreinigungsaktionen*; see: H. Krausnick and H.-H. Wilhelm, *Die Truppe des Weltanschauungskrieges. Die Einsatzgruppen der Sicherheitspolizei und des SD 1938–1942*, Stuttgart 1981, p. 162.

main command of the Polish Home Army, envisioning armed action within the "Tempest" operation. In both cases, the point was to demonstrate aspirations for independence and the existence of an apparatus of an own nation-state. Yet, the Lithuanians were not notified by the Germans about the planned date of attack on the USSR, and no parachuting sortie appeared in their territory. The Wehrmacht command saw no need for military support from the Lithuanians, while Hitler considered contracting any political obligations with respect to them to be out of question.

Our focus is the developments in Kaunas. The city's 1940 population was approximately 154,000, of which Jews probably accounted for more than 40,000.[325] It is possible that by the outbreak of the German-Soviet war, this population had grown to approximately 160,000, of which 45,000 were Jews, as of June 1941. This figure must have started to diminish once the war began, as the communist authorities fled in panic, along with the Red Army garrison and local Jews, in terror of the approaching Germans. We can infer what was occurring at that time in Kaunas mainly from entries in the diary of the physician, Dr Elena Kutorgienė-Buivydaitė,[326] and the recollections of William W. Mishell[327] and Helene Holzman,[328] written down based on the notes both of them were taking at the time.

---

325 This is the number quoted by K.-M. Mallmann, A. Angrick, J. Matthäus, and M. Cüppers, editors of *Die "Ereignismeldungen UdSSR" 1941. Dokumente der Einsatzgruppen in der Sowjetunion I*, Darmstadt 2011, p. 57.

326 The diary of this local physician is doubtless one of the most important sources regarding Kaunas of the wartime and occupation years. Vasily Grossman and Ilya Ehrenburg edited it and prepared it for publication just after the war, as part of *The Black Book* documenting Nazi crimes in the territory of the USSR. The publication was prevented due to numerous interventions from the censors; it was first published in book form several dozen years later, in various language versions, with the interventions of the Soviet censorship authorities marked in the text. I am indebted to Antony Polonsky for having provided me with a photocopy of the U.S. edition: "From the Diary of Doctor Elena Buividaite-Kutorgene (June–December 1941)", [in:] I. Ehrenburg and V. Grossman, *The Complete Black Book of Russian Jewry*, translated and edited by David Patterson, New Brunswick, NJ 2002.

327 W.W. Mishell, *Kaddish for Kovno. Life and Death in a Lithuanian Ghetto 1941–1945*, Chicago, 1988. As this author is very precise in giving the dates and days of the week, I suppose that he made use of notes taken on the spot.

328 *"Dies Kind soll leben". Die Aufzeichnungen der Helene Holzman 1941–1944*, ed. by M. Kaiser and M. Holzman, Frankfurt a. Main, 2000. (A Polish edition, subtitled *Niezwykłe pamiętniki* [Extraordinary memoirs], was issued in 2002.) Cf. U. Herbert, "Genauer Blick auf das Grauen. Zeugnis einer Überlebenden: Helene Holzman in Kaunas", *Frankfurter Allgemeine Zeitung*, 2nd December 2000.

On the very first day of the war, German planes bombed the airport in Kaunas. The Soviet command resolved to withdraw their army from the town, which meant surrendering Kaunas without a struggle. By all indications, as there were no evacuation plans put in place, an atmosphere of complete chaos prevailed, with the result that 1,968 prisoners remained unevacuated.[329] Dr Kutorgienė noted that thoughout the night of 22nd/23rd June, withdrawing Red Army soldiers were pulling through the streets of Kaunas. On Monday, 23rd June, she wrote in her diary (a fragment that was removed in the post-war edition published in the USSR): "I saw whole crowds of Russian soldiers with and without their weapons wandering along the riverbank… Countless vehicles… They are retreating in disarray, without any order. Gunfire here and there continues." As it turns out, some "Lithuanian patriots" (quotation marks were used by the diarist) were shooting at the Red Army soldiers out of the windows and from the roofs of buildings; in her opinion, they were fulfilling orders they had received to kill every single Soviet soldier they encountered. Sounds of gunfire reverberated in the streets of Kaunas for the whole of the following night. "Who are they shooting at? Why? Perhaps out of fear, for their own reassurance, to shore up their 'patriotic courage'?"

At the same time, 22nd June marked the start of the flight of Jewish people from the town. The following day, the doctor noted down in her diary: "The Jews are leaving with baskets, baby carriages… . frightened faces… . Pale… ." She watches the family next-door get ready to go. She can see everything overturned in the room, the appliances scattered around, and the family so jittery that they cannot complete their packing and finally leave the room carrying only some handbags. The father, who decides to set off together with his adult son, leaves his wife and smaller children under the care of the doctor, convinced that the Germans would not be killing the women or children *as well.*

---

329 As of 10th June 1941, the Kaunas prison, with a capacity for 1,850, was home to 1,910 prisoners, although there is a list specifying a total of 1,952 prisoners, incl. 321 convicts. Yet another document (undated), titled *A breakdown of departures and traffic of transports from NKVD prisons of the Lithuanian S[oviet] S[ocialist] R[epublic]*, states: "Kaunas – no evacuation was carried out; 1,968 prisoners remained at the prison"; cf. Kokurin, A., "Ewakuacja więzień – w dokumentach Zarządu Więziennictwa NKWD", [in:] *Drogi śmierci*, Warsaw 1995, pp. 121, 125. An essay by Krzysztof Popiński, "Ewakuacja więzień – w relacjach", contained in the same book informs us that "The prisoners in Kaunas were murdered" (p. 26), which suggests that a situation occurred there similar to that in Lvov. However, none of the sources I know of mentions that corpses were found at the Kaunas prison.

It is hard to determine today whether the first killing of Jews on the streets of Kaunas by Lithuanians took place on Monday 23rd June or a day later. Ada Hirsz's account, written down in 1948 at the Szczecin branch office of the Jewish Historical Institute, reads: "The day before Kaunas was seized by the Germans, the Lithuanians organised a pogrom and killed some 200 Jews, who were buried in a common grave near the Wilja [River; Lith., Neris]."[330] Since the Germans entered the city on 24th June in the evening, this should mean that the killings she describes took place the day before. Helene Holzman recollects: "Tuesday came. A revolution is occurring in the streets. An army came out of the woodwork, dressed in civilian clothing, armbands on their arms: the partisans."

A note made by Dr Kutorgienė on 24th June suggests that railway connections were still functioning, and trains were departing the Kaunas station normally. Her building was empty; "All the Jews," she wrote, "have fled." How many Jews managed to do so, one cannot tell exactly. Taking into account the numbers related to those killed at a later date, as well as the figures referring to the Jews enclosed in the ghetto (30,000–35,000), it may be concluded that a maximum of a few thousand Jews escaped from Kaunas, saving their lives for the time being. Let us note that some of them might have been caught by the Germans and sent back to town.

On Monday, 23rd June, once the representatives of the governing communist regime had disappeared from Kaunas, and whilst the Red Army troops were withdrawing in panic from the town, the Lithuanians set about taking action: their aim was to restore the statehood their country had lost a year earlier. As the first step, they seized control over the radio broadcasting station; the second thing they did was form a Provisional Government. A radio communiqué announced that Colonel Kazys Škirpa was appointed Prime Minister; however, since the Germans prevented him from leaving Berlin, Juozas Ambrazevičius became the factual head of this Government. Let us add that initially, the Germans detained General Stasys Raštikis in Berlin as well. The Lithuanians wanted to make him Minister of National Defence; he arrived in Lithuania on 27th June but eventually resigned, fearing for his family who were in the Soviet Union.

Let us look again into Dr Kutorgienė's diary. In the afternoon of 23rd June, she noted: "A Provisional Government of Lithuania has been formed, which ordained that national flags be flown. They are playing the Lithuanian national anthem and promising an independent Lithuania, which will be annexed to a 'New

---

330 The Archive of the Jewish Historical Institute, Warsaw, Fund "Accounts of Rescued Jews", ref. no. 301/3325. The phrase "the day before" does not have to be understood literally; many inhabitants of Kaunas first encountered the Germans in the morning of 25th June.

Europe', under the leadership of 'the great' Hitler; the first ministers have just been appointed. They are continually playing Lithuanian songs on the radio." The broadcasting station turned out to be an extremely important centre of transmission of news and, on the other hand, of propaganda. The latter influenced the mood of the listeners. By disseminating the circulating rumours, they exacerbated an ambience of unrest and intensified the desire to deal with the recent oppressors and the lust for reprisal. As is apparent from Dr Kutorgienė's notes, the news claiming that the drinking water in Kaunas had been poisoned by "the Red bandits and barbarians" was repeated over and over again on the radio. The broadcasters also warned that the Jews were shooting with machine guns out of windows, and that for every German soldier killed one hundred Jews will be shot. Speeches were delivered on international Jewry, saying it had been formed by "a combination of the English plutocracy and the Red bandits of the Kremlin."

The family of William W. Mishell listened to the same radio broadcasts which Elena Kutorgienė mentions. This author recalls an announcement stating that the Soviet decrees abolishing private ownership of real property had been cancelled, which for him meant that a tenement house once seized from his father would now be returned. He also recalled "a vicious anti-Semitic statement by the commander of the Lithuanian forces in the city, a well-known colonel" (while he quotes no name, we know that he meant Col. Jurgis Bobelis) who stated that instances of Jews shooting at German soldiers within Lithuania had been established as fact. As the German army was expected to arrive at Kaunas very soon, it was announced that 100 Jews would be killed for each and every German soldier killed. For Mishell, "This was a clear invitation to a pogrom." He also emphasises on this occasion that the juxtaposition of the figures was meant to declare how cheap Jewish life was. As he states further on: "This announcement, issued on the sole initiative of the Lithuanian forces (the Germans had not yet even entered town), clearly demonstrates that the local anti-Semites did not intend to wait for German directives regarding the Jews and were ready to move on their own."[331]

It is a fact that both the Provisional Government and Colonel Bobelis did indeed fear that someone might suddenly start shooting at the entering Germans. Dr Kutorgienė noted that while the radio at first urged the public to give the Germans an enthusiastic welcome, on 24th June an announcement was broadcast instructing the locals to have their windows shut and the curtains drawn, or else the military patrols might open fire.

---

331 Mishell, op. cit., pp. 16–17.

The anti-Semitic elements clearly heard in the radio broadcasts, were prominent also in the periodical *I Laisve* (*To Freedom*) published in Kaunas by LAF from 24th June. Its first issue asserted as indisputable that "Jews and bolshevism are the same thing – two parts of an inseparable unity."[332] It is hard to deny that the superiors of the Nazi *Einsatzgruppen*, who assigned the relevant tasks for the area of the East, shared this opinion. The same issue of *I Laisve* published a proclamation to "the riflemen and the partisans" banning mob rule and announcing that those guilty of the crimes committed by the communist regime will be subject to their deserved and just punishment.[333]

We should take a closer look at who were the addressees of this proclamation. The "riflemen" were members of Šaulių Sąjunga, an organisation that had enjoyed extreme popularity in Lithuania since the twenties (its members were described with the Polonised word "*szaulisi*", which triggers in Poland the worst associations possible). The organisation combined the paramilitary Riflemen's Union, the Reservists' Union, and the Veterans' Union. The "partisans" addressed in the proclamation primarily referred to the raiding parties originating from "Iron Wolf" – that is, Voldemaras's followers. Even though the "partisans" might not initially have outnumbered the others, it must have happened very rapidly, as Lithuanian deserters from the Red Army started joining their ranks along with individuals previously persecuted by the Communist regime. Moreover, they were joined by regular criminals set free from prisons, as well as the dregs of society. Regrettably without quoting his source, Michael MacQueen informs us that more than 3,360 partisan fighters were registered in Kaunas as of June 1941.[334]

These "partisans" had no shared command: several troops concurrently operated, with their commanders rivalling one against the other, not recognising the authority of either LAF or the Provisional Government. The Government intended to gain control over them and subsequently transform into a germ of the national army. The groups, however, preferred to act on their own, getting

---

332 Quoted after: MacQueen, M., *Massenvernichtung im Kontext* ..., p. 25.
333 Alvydas Dargis quotes this proclamation in a polemic published in *Lietuvos rytas*, one of the most popular newspapers in Lithuania (no. 141, 19th June 1999; I warmly thank Ms. Jagoda Hernik Spalińska for providing me with a copy of the article, and I am grateful to Henryk Wisner for his translation of the text for my use), in reply to Aleksas (Alteris) Faitelsonas' text sent from Israel (this author has also published under the name Alex Faitelson). Clearly enough, Dargis does not even mention any other publication of *I Laisve*.
334 MacQueen, op. cit., p. 27.

even, summarily and bloodily, with the "Judeo-commies" and growing richer on this occasion though the pillaging of Jewish property.

The doctor's diary rather unexpectedly notes: "Kaunas Radio announced on 25th June at 6 a.m. in the name of the "partisans", that all the thieves, plunderers, and perpetrators of assaults will be executed on the spot." It does not seem quite plausible to me that this appeal was made by any of the "partisan" groups; instead, it was most probably issued by the Lithuanian commander of the city and the leader of the "Riflemen", that is, the Šaulių Sąjunga, Colonel Jurgis Bobelis (whom we have already met), who acted in close consultation with both LAF and the Provisional Government. The appeal was aimed at suppressing the banditries perpetrated by no other than the "partisans" themselves. It was obviously issued to no avail, as were Bobelis's other commands instructing that the arms possessed by Kaunas residents be registered or banning the "partisans" from moving around the city with firearms.[335]

Before the first troops of the German 16th Army entered the city, the streets of Kaunas became, from the morning of Tuesday, 24th June, the scene of the settling of accounts with those who in the eyes of the Lithuanian "patriots" embodied the hated Communist regime: that is, the Jews. It was probably on that day that the first killings occurred. As Dr Kutorgienė noted in her diary, "This is so dreadful, behind the windows, over and over again, the Jews, elderly and young alike, are led to a prison." And so goes the report by Aleksas (Alteris) Faitelsonas: "[Our] mother went off on 24th June, Tuesday, to the town (we lived in Vilijampolė [a district of Kaunas] at the time) to take care of some financial matters. [...] When she returned, she told us about the situation in the town: she'd heard about Jews being caught, thieves and murderers released from the gaol at 9 Mickievičius Street, attacks in the streets, the prison being filled with hundreds of Jews caught in the streets or taken away directly from their houses."[336] It should be added that the prison soon ran out of space, and subsequent batches of Jews were redirected to Fort VII, located at the northern edge of the city, which was soon to become the site of their torment.

There were no clashes in Kaunas between the Lithuanian partisans and the withdrawing Red Army troops; only solitary soldiers caught wandering around were killed. No encounter with the Bolshevik "nomenclature" took place, either, as the communist notables had managed to flee from the town. There is also no

---

335 A. Dargis refers to these commands; cf. footnote 333.
336 From an article by A. Faitelsonas, intertwined with personal reminiscences, entitled *Tiesa apie nusikaltimą visada būna skauci, bet ją žinoti reikia*; the title of the fragment I have quoted reads Mieste *prasidėjo pogromai* [A pogrom began in the town].

information of any Soviet offices or industrial facilities being taken over by force. Instead of the local uprising which LAF had hoped to inspire in its instructions, the "burst for freedom" among the Lithuanian anti-Semites and anticommunists was not limited to retaliation against the "Judeo-commies" but, in fact, to focusing all their accumulated hatred on the defenceless Jews. There were even such among them who, seeing with fright that Kaunas had fallen within the control of "hooligans", were waiting for the Germans to come in hope that they would protect them.[337]

A five-day a pogrom under German oversight (25th to 29th June, 1941)

The first German troops, part of the 16th Army commanded by General Ernst Busch, entered Kaunas late in the afternoon of 24th June.[338] As testified by the surviving photographs, they were enthusiastically welcomed on the following day by the locals, who showered them with flowers.[339] On the morning of 25th June, SS-Brigadeführer Walter Stahlecker, whom we have already encountered in this book, arrived in the town together with the soldiers of *Einsatzgruppe A* that he commanded as point men (*Vorkommando*).[340] As per the testimony given after the war by SS-Obersturmführer Horst Eichler, his former aide, and his interpreter Richard Waldemar Schweizer, a Lithuanian-born German, Stahlecker was accompanied by a Lithuanian journalist, former editor of the *10 centų* newspaper, named Algirdas Jonas Klimaitis (Klimaičius).[341] It was he who successfully solicited the meeting of the Sipo and SD crew with the two commanders of what were probably the largest "partisan" troops, Col. Kazys Šimkus and Lieut. Bronius

---

337 Mishell uses the phrase "... the town belonged to hooligans" and goes on to state that "... we were suddenly more afraid of yesterday's neighbours, people with whom we had lived for generations, than of the Germans. Now we waited for the Germans to protect us from the mob"; op. cit., pp. 14, 16.
338 I build here upon the findings of Christoph Dieckmann, author of the excellent two-volume work *Deutsche Besatzungspolitik in Litauen 1941–1944*, Göttingen 2011, p. 313 [joint page numbering].
339 One such photograph has been published by Franz W. Seidler in his book *Die Kollaboration 1939–1945*, Munich–Berlin 1995, p. 9.
340 Dieckmann, op. cit., p. 315.
341 This information is given by P. Stankeras in the book *Lietuvių policija 1941–1944 metais*, Vilnius, 1009, p. 237 (I thank Professor Piotr Łossowski for providing me with an extract from this book and its translation); also, cf. Dieckmann, op. cit., p. 317, giving the place and date of Klimaitis's death, i.e. Hamburg, 29th August 1988.

Norkus.³⁴² German historian Knut Stang describes the course of that fateful conference, based on the post-war evidence: "Stahlecker pushed the partisans not only to target their troops against the communist and activists but also against the Kaunas Jews, which the partisans did not see as their priority task. He advised them, at least, in order to improve their contacts with the Germans, to form a squad that should begin decimating the Jews in Kaunas and in Lithuania. He simultaneously threw out a question as to where would be the most suitable place for concentrating the Kaunas Jews; in reply, the Lithuanian party suggested Vilijampolė. That is where the ghetto was developed later on."³⁴³

Let us now turn our attention to a document whose significance for the Kaunas pogrom is of fundamental importance. I am referring to Stahlecker's report dated 15ᵗʰ October 1941 which was used at the Nuremberg Trials.³⁴⁴ Although annotated *"Geheime Reichssache!"* ("State Secret!"), the document was made in forty copies. I do not believe, however, that having prepared and written it with such complete candour, Stahlecker could ever have imagined that it would fall into the wrong hands. The commander of *Einsatzgruppe A* concealed nothing:

> Similarly, native anti-Semitic forces were induced to start pogroms against Jews during the first hours after capture [of the town], though this inducement proved to be very difficult. Following out orders, the Security Police was determined to solve the Jewish question with all possible means and most decisively. But it was desirable that the Security Police should not put in an immediate appearance, at least in the beginning, since the extraordinarily harsh measures were apt to stir even German circles. It had to be shown to the world that the native population itself took the first action by way of natural reaction against the suppression by Jews during several decades and against the terror exercised by the Communists during the preceding period.

In a later part of the report, entitled *Säuberung und Sicherung des Einsatzraumes* ("Cleansing and Securing the Area of Operations"), Stahlecker first discusses what he calls *Auslösung von Selbstreinigungsaktionen* – i.e. "instigating self-cleansing actions" – which, quite significantly, came before *Bekämpfung des*

---

342 C. Dieckmann has determined that B. Norkus, born 1914, committed suicide in 1942; op. cit., p. 136.
343 Stang, K., *Kollaboration und Massenmord. Die litauische Hilfspolizei, das Rollkommando Hamann und die Ermordung der litauischen Juden*, Frankfurt a. Main 1996, p. 115.
344 I quote the report's content as published in: *Trial of the Major War Criminals before the International Military Tribunal*, vol. XXXVII, Nuremberg, 1949, pp. 670–717. As "Document 180 L", a copy of the report was presented by an American prosecutor. Recently historians have been quoting a different copy of the document that was found in Soviet archives.

Kommunismus – "Combating communism." The following are sections of major importance to us:

> Considering that the population of the Baltic countries had suffered very heavily under the government of Bolshevism and Jewry while they were incorporated in the USSR, it was to be expected that after the liberation from that foreign government, they (i.e. the population themselves) would render harmless most of the enemies left behind after the retreat of the Red Army. It was the duty of the Security Police to set in motion these self-cleansing movements (*die Selbstreinigungsbestrebungen in Gang zu setzen*) and to direct them into the correct channels in order to accomplish the purpose of the cleansing operations as quickly as possible. It was no less important in view of the future to establish the unshakable and provable fact that the liberated population themselves took the most severe measures against the Bolshevist and Jewish enemy quite on their own, so that the direction by German authorities could not be found out (*ohne dass eine Anweisung deutscher Stellen erkennbar ist*).
>
> In Lithuania this was achieved for the first time by partisan activities in Kowno. To our surprise it was not easy at first to set in motion an extensive pogrom against Jews. Klima[i]tis, the leader of the partisan unit, mentioned above, who was used for this purpose primarily, succeeded in starting a pogrom on the basis of advice given to him by a small advanced detachment acting in Kowno, and in such a way that no German order or German instigation was noticed from the outside.

In other words, Stahlecker admits that the Germans initiated the action and entrusted its delivery to the Lithuanians.

From Wednesday, 25th June, onwards, the Lithuanian "partisans" found themselves under the care of Stahlecker's team. They were provided with food from field kitchens and with means of transport, and care was taken so that nobody would obstruct the action entrusted to them. For this purpose Stahlecker issued a large number of proxies and identity cards to the commanders of partisan troops, featuring his manual signature. The proxies were general and served as a blank cheque for the "partisans'" activities. Knut Stang quotes the texts of such documents, reconstructed in the course of the post-war interrogations of SS-Obersturmbannführer Erich Ehrlinger.[345] They read as follows, respectively (as translated into English):

> Proxy
> [It is hereby attested that] Mr. ..... is a member of the Lithuanian partisan unit .... and remains under my personal care. He acts on the instruction of the Security Police and the Security Service. Any and all official agencies and [military] departments are requested to extend care and assistance to the holder hereof, when appropriate.

---

345   Stang, *Kollaboration und Massenmord*, ..., p. 116.

Identity Card
….., the holder of this Identity Card, is member of ….., the Lithuanian national partisan unit. He is authorised to appear in the streets in the day and night and to carry firearms with him. …… [name of troop/squad] is in the service of the Security Police. Any and all official agencies and [military] departments are requested to extend care and assistance to Mr. ….., if need be.

Dr. Stahlecker, *SS-Brigadeführer und Chef der Einsatzgruppe A der Sicherheitspolizei und des SD*

Although the Wehrmacht command protested the granting of such proxies and IDs, their withdrawal lasted long weeks. For the time being, in the late days of June, the certificates proved enormously useful for the "partisans", allowing them free and armed movement and the ability to take action during the night. Let us refer again to the diary of doctor Elena Kutorgienė for an idea of what such actions were like. Her entry for 25th June – for her, the first day of the German occupation, but for a number (possibly, a majority) of her compatriots, the first day of what seemed to them regained freedom – reads as follows:

> A bright, sunny and warm day. The Germans are in the town. It has all begun… The town is richly decorated with Lithuanian national flags today… There are masses of armed people with armbands in the national colours milling about in the streets. All of them are unlikeable, some boors running around with rifles with bayonets fixed on their tops. The Jews are led away [to a prison], individually and in groups, I am watching them, full of sorrow. […] The mob surrounding Laisves Avenue is mocking those passing by, enjoying their distress, reviling them and laughing derisively at them. Some elderly woman came up to me and said, with tears in her eyes, "It's awful to see people capable of rejoicing a thing like this." I was shocked and devastated by everything I have seen.

Around 2 a.m. on Thursday, 26th June, the doctor was awoken by the noise of a lorry which was stopping by the neighbouring house; a few people got off the vehicle. They banged at the gate and were let inside by the caretaker, "who was one of the first to have put out the Nazi flag." Suddenly, a heartrending scream of a woman was heard, joined a moment later by a shout made by a man, begging something from the comers in Yiddish, and finally shooting could be heard, and everything grew silent afterwards. A man said, in Lithuanian, "You're not supposed to shoot without my authorisation." At a certain moment, two children were heard, crying. Someone fired the gun again and everything became silent – "which means," Dr Kutorgienė noted down, "four innocent people were killed." Moments later, she could hear shouts coming from somewhere else, followed by three gunshots, which led her to the conclusion that seven or eight people had been killed within an hour. "The Germans," she continues, "allow for this night-time shooting in the city they have conquered, where no-one is supposed to be on the streets at this time of the day. It is clear enough that the murderers act on the permission and consent of their new lords. [...] Therefore, innocent women and children, deprived of any help, can simply be murdered just because they are Jewish. And these are supposed to be people!!!" During the following night, when cars passing by and the sounds of gunshots could be heard again, Ms. Kutorgienė refers to the curfew imposed with this remark: "You are not supposed to appear in the street before 6 a.m. so that the killings can be done without a witness."

Who did the killing – who were the murderers? In the report I have already quoted, Stahlecker wrote:

> In Lithuania, activist and nationalists formed themselves into so-called partisan-units at the beginning of the Eastern Campaign, in order to take active part in the fight against Bolshevism. [...] Four great partisan formations emerged in Kaunas, with whom [our] leaders soon established contact. There was no uniform command over these groups. Rather, everyone tried to outrun the others and ensure a close as possible connection with the Wehrmacht.[346]

As we already know, two of the four "partisan" troops mentioned above were commanded, respectively, by Col. Šimkus and Lt. Norkus. I use the quotation marks intentionally, as partisans are generally associated with an armed groups operating in a forest or mountain area. In the summer of 1941, the "partisans" appearing in Lithuania were anticommunist and nationalist fighters, who after emerging from the underground, transformed themselves into hit squads commanded by warlords with astonishing speed. Based on what Stahlecker wrote, it could be inferred that the third group of "partisans" was commanded by Klimaitis, the Lithuanian journalist. This is not so certain, however, since Klimaitis arrived in Kaunas along with Stahlecker after previously living in exile in Germany, where he had no opportunity to form a troop of his own in conspiratorial conditions.

The part Klimaitis played in the Kaunas pogrom inspired by the Germans has never been fully clarified. Klimaitis is, overall, an extremely mysterious figure; in all probability, he had been connected from the mid-thirties with Voldemaras's followers who operated in the underground in Lithuania. For RSHA, he was an official representative of "Iron Wolf".[347] The Lithuanian historian Arūnas Bubnys tells us the following about Klimaitis and the role he played:

---

346 Stahlecker's report, as in footnote 44, p. 677.
347 Based on information from various testimonies kept in Ludwigsburg (provided to me in a letter dated 13th February 2000 from Knut Stang), it seems quite plausible that Klimaitis had already collaborated with German intelligence before the outbreak of the Second World War.

The troop of A. Klimaitis that was organised by Stahlecker should by no means be considered a partisan troop. It was assembled by the Nazi Security Police with former political prisoners and other individuals who had suffered from Soviet authority, and with the criminal elements that had joined them. Klimaitis's troop was not part of the Lithuanian Activist Front (LAF) and had no political goals to meet. It is just that the Germans used the troop for their criminal purposes. Stahlecker's staff equipped Klimaitis's troop with armament and transport facilities. The Lithuanian Provisional Government instructed General Stasys Pundzevičius and General Mykolas Rėklaitis to talk to Klimaitis and resolutely warn him against fomenting pogroms or organising massacres any longer. When talking to these governmental representatives, Klimaitis admitted that he had delivered Stahlecker's orders and was threatened with getting killed if he failed. The generals condemned the offences perpetrated by Klimaitis's troop and commanded him to leave Kaunas and hide from Stahlecker.[348]

It is a real pity that we are not told when the conversation between the generals and Klimaitis took place. He did, in fact, disappear from Kaunas at some point, leaving no trace, reappearing years later as a peaceful car dealer in Hamburg, where he was eventually tried in court in 1983.[349] Stahlecker also admitted that Klimaitis's troop had been formed by the Germans, saying: "Since military use of the partisans was out of the question for political reasons, an auxiliary squad was formed within a short time of trustworthy elements from the undisciplined partisan groups numbering at first 300 members, the command of which was entrusted to the Lithuanian journalist Klima[i]tis."[350] We are regrettably not told what was meant by "within a short time" and when exactly the squad commenced its activities.

Who were the people that walked armed down the streets of Kaunas? Who brought the Jews to the prison and later to Fort VII? Who attacked their apartments in the night, pillaging them and killing their dwellers? The documents and memoirists tell us about partisans or persons wearing white armbands on their left arms; hence their name, the *Baltaraiščiai* ("white-armband wearers"). This tells us unambiguously that they were members of "partisan troops" commanded

---

348 Bubnys, A., *Vokiečių okupuota Lietuva (1941–1944)*, Vilnius, 1998, p. 199. (Again, I was able to make use of this book on Lithuania under the German occupation thanks to the help of Prof. P. Łossowski. I had no access to its English edition, published in Vilnius in 2003.).
349 As is apparent, based on what can be read in Dieckmann, op. cit., p. 317.
350 Stahlecker's report, as in footnote 44, pp. 677–678. An analysis of *Einsatzgruppen* reports has been published by Roland Headland: Headland, R., *Messages of Murder. A Study of the Reports of the Einsatzgruppen of the Security Police and the Security Service, 1941–1943*, Rutherford, N.Y. 1992.

by Šimkus and Norkus – neither of whom, unlike Klimaitis, were disavowed by either the Provisional Government or the LAF. They should have been, indeed!

As we already know, the first anti-Jewish riots which produced fatalities occurred in Kaunas before the Germans' arrival. I do not really think, however, that the occurrences taking place in Kaunas on 23rd and 24th June should be described as a "pogrom" – although the atmosphere prevailing in the town doubtlessly paved the way for a bloody encounter with the Jews. At some point, beating up or killing a specific Jew became insufficient: someone calls out to take revenge, and to discharge all the accumulated antipathy, now transformed into hatred, on every single Jew one comes across. I presume that such a slogan could have been shouted out by one of the "partisan" commanders without even being prompted to this end by the Germans. In my opinion, however, a slogan would have not sufficed for initiating a pogrom – that is, for taking an action. It was indispensable to be *reassured of impunity* and to receive consent to take action from the Germans.

The meeting of Stahlecker with Klimaitis, Šimkus, and Norkus must have taken place no earlier than in the morning of Wednesday, 25th June. It is not quite plausible that an event described years afterwards by Aleksas Faitelsonas (whom I have quoted earlier) resulted from that particular meeting: "Some thirty young Jews were caught by the Vilijampolė bridge. Cruelly beaten, they were forced to dance and sing religious songs, as well as Soviet ones. When the murderers got bored with this amusement, they forced the victims to dig out graves and kneel down by them, after which, showing gaiety, they shot them dead."[351] Thus, a pogrom was heralded, but had yet to occur: it was to begin on 25th June in the evening.

Before I report on the course of the events, let me share some pieces of topographical information. Like Praga, the right-bank district of Warsaw located on the other side of the Vistula River, opposite the historical downtown area, Vilijampolė (Slobodka) lies within Kaunas, on the other side of the Neris (the river by which Vilnius is situated further upstream). Neris, let us add, is the Lithuanian name for the river – the Polish being Wilia. Before the war, Vilijampolė was an area with a considerable concentration of Jews. Jurbarko Street leading from the only local bridge into the depth of the district, was similar in its role to Nalewki St. in Warsaw, or rue des Rosiers in Paris. It should be mentioned that for orthodox Jews, Vilijampolė was a very important centre of religious cult – not merely because of the several synagogues there, but primarily owing to the fact that a major rabbinate school (*yeshibot*) was situated there. It seems the very fact

---

351   Cf. footnote 333.

that the district was home to a considerable number of Jews was a sufficient reason for starting the action to "decimate" them, in Stahlecker's words, right there. Let me remind the reader that Vilijampolė was mentioned in his talk with the "partisans": the Lithuanians were said to have pointed to that particular district as the most convenient site for a ghetto-to-be. On the other hand, it is equally possible that Stahlecker asked where the largest number of Jews lived at the time, and having been told "Vilijampolė", he might have recommended or suggested that this particular part of Kaunas would be suitable for kicking off a "self-cleansing action".

There are several eye-witness accounts available, corresponding with one another as to their details, regarding what occurred in Vilijampolė (Slobodka) on 25th June 1941. The most important report, to my mind, is that of Rabbi Ephraim Oshry, written down over fifty years later and published, in English, in the United States in 1995. Here is a passage from his memoirs:

> That Wednesday evening at dusk, Lithuanian Nazis, accompanied by mobs of ordinary Lithuanians, marched into the Jewish section of Slobodka with axes and saws. They began the Slobodka pogrom on Yurborger [Jurbarko] Street, moving from house to house, from apartment to apartment, from room to room, killing every Jew they encountered, old and young alike. They chopped off heads with axes, sawed people in half and – I learned afterwards – they took their time doing it in order to prolong their victims' agony.[352]

William W. Mishell, the author I have already quoted, did not in fact witness the pogrom as he lived in another part of Kaunas; he learned of the developments on the following day from an acquaintance of his, who did not fail to inform him that the pogrom killed all his more distant family. The survivor namely recounted: "Last night, a large band of partisans and some college students descended in Slobotke [sic] with rifles, guns, knives, and axes and carried out a vicious pogrom. As soon as it got dark, they rushed the area and systematically killed every Jew from Jurbarko Street all the way to our house. The screams could be heard for miles."[353]

Let us resume Rabbi Oshry's reminiscences. As he tells us, the murderers (whom he calls the "butchers") made their first stop at Jurbarko St., by the house of Mordechai Jatkunski and his wife Dr Stein-Jatkunska, a dentist. They were both killed, their arms and legs chopped off, the woman had her breasts and the man his genitals cut off; their son was slaughtered afterwards as well. Moving deeper into the district, "Indiscriminately they killed every Jew encountered – rabbis,

---

352 Oshry, E., *The Annihilation of Lithuanian Jewry*, translated from Yiddish by Y. Leiman, New York, 1995, p. 2.
353 Mishell, op. cit., p. 20.

professionals, Zionist activists, intellectuals, Communists. The butchery was overwhelming." What this report also tells us is that on one street, twenty-six people were lined up against a wall and shot. On the bank of the Neris, right beside the bridge, thirty-four Jews were buried alive. The *yeshibot* students (all of them, according to Mishell) were killed during that night.

It would seem that the nightmarish occurrences of that night were all equally harrowing. Nevertheless, nearly all the sources available to us today describe and are in agreement on the martyr's death of Zalman Osowski, the rabbi of Slobodka. The bandits found him at his home dressed in a ritual garment. He was seated at his desk, reading a Talmud volume. They bound his arms and legs to the chair and chopped his head off, then placing it on the opened book. Afterwards, the rabbi's corpse was displayed to the public with a sheet of paper attached to it, claiming, "This is what we shall do with all the Jews." Rabbi Oshry adds that Zalman's son Judel, who was also a rabbi, was also killed, while Judel's wife was shot dead. Zalman's five-year-old granddaughter Esterka, who hid under a bed, and her mother Rachel, who was not home at the time, were the only ones to survive; a month later, both were killed in the ghetto. Thanks to the publication in 1999 of Alex Faitelson's memoirs, we now know the name of the man who slaughtered Rabbi Osowski: the killer was Lieut. Viktoras Vitkauskas, a resident of Vilijampolė. As he set off to confront the Jews, he took a sabre with him and used it to cut off Zalman's head.[354]

The descriptions of this pogrom mention one more occurrence, highlighted by nearly all the witnesses and authors of the accounts. Someone wrote on the wall of one of the houses, in Yiddish, "Jews! Take revenge!" (See fig. 17) Years later, it was found that the inscription had been made with a finger dipped in his own blood by a Jewish locksmith named Akiba Puchert as he was dying.[355] It should be added that Rabbi Ohsry is the only one to mention the Germans. He namely writes that some German soldiers were standing on the bridge, shooting at those Jews who tried to swim across the Neris, treating them like targets in a sports contest.[356]

---

354 Faitelson, A., *Nepokorivshiesja* [Defiant], Tel Aviv, 2001, pp. 26–27. Lieutenant Vitkauskas later served under the command of Maj. Kazys Šimkus; after the war, he struggled against the Soviet regime and was eventually killed in December 1950.

355 A photograph of this inscription is reproduced in Rabbi Oshry's memoirs, op. cit., p. 3. The full name of the inscription's author is given in a footnote in: *Černaja kniga*, Vilnius, 1993, p. 523. The same source (p. 279) tells us that the rabbi's dead body remained unburied for a week; and that Jews had their tongues cut off and eyes put out. I thank Ms. Roza Bielauskiene of Vilnius for having sent me a copy of this edition.

356 Oshry, op. cit., p. 3.

As we can read in his *Kaddish for Kovno*: "The pogrom in Slobotke [*sic*] was monstrous. It was infinitely worse than the pogrom in Kishineff [Kishinev] [of 12th April 1903 – T.S.], which had stirred the conscience of the entire civilized world and brought about the condemnation of the czarist regime by all decent people. This pogrom cost the Jewish people forty-five dead, eighty-six seriously and five hundred lightly wounded. It was like a Sunday school picnic compared to the pogrom in Slobotke."[357]

As Mishell estimates, a thousand Jews, if not more, were killed in Vilijampolė. Israeli historian Yitzhak Arad cites 800 victims.[358] The relevant paragraph of the Stahlecker report reads as follows: "During the first pogrom in the night from 25. to 26.6 the Lithuanian partisans did away with more than 1,500 Jews [*beseitigt*, in the German original: A typical example of *Lingua Tertii Imperii* in Victor Klemperer's concept! – T.S.], set fire to several Synagogues or destroyed them by other means and burned down a Jewish dwelling district consisting of about 60 houses. During the following nights about 2,300 Jews were made harmless in a similar way."[359]

Stating that 1,500 Jews were killed by the Lithuanians within a single night, the *Einsatzgruppe A* commander has in mind the outcome of the pogrom not for the Vilijampolė district as such, but for the whole of Kaunas, I should think. On that very night of Wednesday/Thursday, Jews were also killed in the downtown area, which Dr Elena Kutorgienė noted down in her diary. The Jewish Historical Institute in Warsaw keeps a copy of the account of Leon Kuperberg, who lived in Kaunas at the time. As we do not know what his address was there, we do not know whether what he writes refers to Vilijampolė or to the centre of the city, on the right bank of the Neris: "The bodies of a few hundred Jews, many women with children among them, were strewn on the streets of Kaunas. The corpses appeared the most numerously in the area of the bridge."[360]

On the morning of 26th June, the town must have looked utterly appalling. It was necessary to bury the dead bodies as soon as possible, if only for sanitary reasons. Col. Bobelis, the city's commander, ordered all the municipal services

---

357 Mishell, op. cit., p. 21. Other sources have it that the 1903 Kishinev pogrom killed forty-nine Jews; cf. Doron, D., *Kišhinevskoye getto – posledniy pogrom*, Kishinev 1993, p. 15.
358 Arad, Y., *The "final solution" in Lithuania in the Light of German Documentation*, Yad Vashem Studies, vol. 11, 1976, p. 240.
359 Stahlecker's report, pp. 682–683.
360 The Archive of the Jewish Historical Institute, Warsaw, Fund "Accounts of Saved Jews", ref. no. 301/2085.

to take part in removing them.³⁶¹ In the Vilijampolė district, the Jews who had survived the pogrom were forcefully engaged for the action. And thus they buried those killed, many of them members of their own families, in mass graves excavated along the bank of the Neris.³⁶²

When writing about the Kaunas pogrom, historians have quite a lot to say about the instigators and victims, much less about the witnesses and bystanders, and the least about the perpetrators.³⁶³ It is very rare that someone taking part in a pogrom would speak of it. William Mishell quotes an utterance of one such participant. On Friday, 27ᵗʰ June, a group of "partisans" appeared at his home to arrest him. As he reports,

> One of them, apparently some chief, began an interrogation of me. After a lengthy antisemitic outburst, he said, "You Jews are all communists. You probably were one too, weren't you?" "No, sir," I replied, "I was never a communist. We had an apartment building which was nationalized by the communists, not exactly a friendly act." "Oh, so that is it, you were a Jewish capitalist pig." This was a no-win situation, I thought to myself. If I was a communist, that was bad, but if I was a capitalist, that was wrong again. For all it was worth, I could be the pope, but as long as I was a Jew, it was the wrong thing to be. "No," I replied, "we were not capitalists, but hard-working people who saved enough money to buy a piece of property."³⁶⁴

Mishell was eventually saved thanks to his good command of Lithuanian – and the declaration that he had volunteered for labour the day before; he had helped to bury the victims of the pogrom, to be sure.

On that same day, the 27ᵗʰ of June, Dr Kutorgienė noted the following in her diary (a passage that was almost entirely deleted by the censors for the Russian edition prepared just after the war):

---

361 *Einsatz im "Reichskommissariat Ostland": Dokumente zum Völkermord im Baltikum und in Weißrubland 1941–1944*, ed. by W. Benz, K. Kwiet and J. Matthäus, Berlin 1998, p. 176.

362 Mishell, op. cit., p. 19–21.

363 The work by Raul Hilberg, considered a classic, is entitled *Perpetrators Victims Bystanders: The Jewish catastrophe, 1933–1945*; "bystanders" has been rendered in the German version (1992) as *"Zuschauer"* (similarly to the Polish edition: *"świadkowie"*). I find the English word, not completely equivalent to the words in German or Polish, to be the most accurate and pertinent one.

364 Mishell, op. cit., p. 23. Let us consider that the arguments given by the Lithuanian nationalist perfectly show the symbiotic relationship between anti-Semitism of rightist provenance, which makes use of the stereotype of the "Judeo-commies" (or "Judeo-Bolshevism") and the leftist variety of anti-Semitism, with its social accents and the image of Jewry as a plutocracy.

> All the yard keepers are murderers and thieves; they betray the Jews, call in the partisans, and plunder the Jews' apartments themselves. My soul is torn apart. [...] The sadistic, patriotic frenzy has continued all day long: with the permission and approval of the government they are torturing and murdering the Jews... All the Lithuanians, with very few exceptions, are of one mind in their hatred for the Jews, especially the intelligentsia, who under the Soviet authorities suddenly lost everything. Since they were inclined toward nationalism and felt they had been usurped by the Jews, the intelligentsia did not actively set out to work; moreover, they suffered materially from the nationalization of their homes and their capital. Now they are taking revenge for their suffering and humiliation. Although she condemns the way the "partisans" murder the Jews at night without a trial, a physician I know is looking for an explanation and justification in Jewish "dominance". [...] All day long people wearing national Lithuanian armbands saunter about the streets with an air of victory; in broad daylight they break into Jewish homes and load their goods onto carts, without the slightest compunction about grabbing every last pitiful thing. It is a kind of epidemic, a debauchery of greed... Everyone is carrying a gun. Unfortunately, they dare to "fight" only with the permission of the government (red or black, it's all the same; I remember that when the Soviets came, all the hoodlums were also wearing red sashes during the first days). Everywhere you see either the national colours or white bands with a red cross. The ambulances are assigned the task of gathering the bodies of murdered Russians and Jews. [...] Black terror is made all the more terrible by the fact that the Jews are doomed to death because of race, because of blood, that is, because of something over which no human being has any control... their fate... It is horrible... inhuman... Under the pretence that they are "communists", the "partisans" murder people who were perhaps enemies of the Soviet regime... hypocrites...
>
> An announcement has been posted on the doors of Outpatient Clinic Number 1 where I work: "Not a single Jew will be served in this establishment."
>
> Everything nationalistic is disgusting to me; it makes me nauseous. I have seen blood and suffering all because of nationalistic hatred. The partisans attract either stupid boys who have been deceived by slogans about an "independent" Lithuania or the dregs of society drawn to plunder and murder without being answerable to anyone.

The conclusive phrases of Elena's note from the tragic Friday of 27th June read as follows:

> The city is dead. There is no shooting in our area today; they are not murdering anyone... I did not know that gunfire could be so loud... People are talking about all kinds of humiliations that have been inflicted upon the Jews; they are forced to haul excrement with their bare hands. I saw a group of Jews who had been arrested being driven along carrying shovels. Yesterday a patient (Morkunaite) told me that she saw them using boards to beat Jews who were digging graves at the cemetery.

An awkward error was made in the translation of the last sentence: the Russian original has *vecherom* (in the evening), which had been read as *vchera* and thus translated as "yesterday".³⁶⁵ The German version of the *Black Book* has the accurate phrase, *Am Abend*, and when it comes to digging the grave, it is said (without remarking) that the Jews were digging "a grave for themselves."³⁶⁶

When writing these words in her diary, Dr Kutorgienė did not realise that they actually referred to an extremely horrifying event, of which everyone in Kaunas spoke at the time and what is nowadays, several dozen years later, described over and over again. The occurrence that took place on 27th June 1941 at the yard of the "Lietukis" ("Lithuanian homestead") cooperative garage, situated at 43 Vytautas Boulevard, cannot possibly be passed over unnoticed by anyone dealing with the history of Lithuania during the Second World War and the course of the Holocaust in the region.³⁶⁷ The story of the massacre of several dozen Jews committed at that site continues to be retold for a series of reasons. To my mind, essential to the matter is that there exists a series of photographs taken by German soldiers who witnessed the event which have been reproduced multiple times.³⁶⁸ Another important reason is the continually growing set of

---

365 *Černaja kniga* (see footnote 61), p. 303.
366 Grossman, W., Ehrenburg, I., *Das Schwarzbuch. Der Genozid an den sowjetischen Juden*, ed. by A. Lustiger, Reinbek bei Hamburg 1994, p. 633.
367 Lithuanian author Saliamonas Vaintraubas has collected the statements of witnesses as well as historians: Vaintraubas, S., *Garažas: aukos, budeliai, stebėtojai; ši knyga skirta Holokausto Lietuvoje pradžios 60-mečiui* [The garage: Victims, perpetrators, observers ...], Vilnius, 2002. I thank Professor Aivas Ragauskas and Professor Henryk Wisner very much for sending me a copy of this book and for translating fragments of it for my use, respectively.
368 The first two photographs published in the German weekly *Vorwärts* of 15th August 1958 were taken by Karl Reder, who was assigned to military bakery no. 562; for reproductions of these photographs and an English translation of Reder's 1959 testimony, cf. the book by A. Faitelson (see footnote 306, pp. 20–25). Reder took only two photos as the film in his camera was at its end. After he removed it and put it in his pocket, an SS officer took his camera with new film loaded inside it. Wilhelm Gunsilius, who used an official camera and was authorised to take pictures, managed to take a whole series of photographs. He successfully resisted the attempt to have his camera taken away. For reproductions of most of these pictures, see: *"Schöne Zeiten". Judenmord aus der Sicht der Täter und Gaffer*, ed. by E. Klee, W. Dreßen, V. Rieß, Frankfurt am Main, 1988, ff. p. 37; Gunsilius's testimony (without his name being given) is included in this publication as well, pp. 38–39. The photographs made by Reder and Gunsilius have been used as illustrations in, among others, books by Daniel Johan Goldhagen and Laurence Rees; recently, also in Witold Mędykowski's book *W cieniu gigantów. Pogromy Żydów w 1941 roku w byłej sowieckiej strefie okupacyjnej. Kontekst historyczny, społeczny i kulturowy*, Warsaw 2012, ills. 77–83.

written testimonies or accounts regarding the event, which have been gathered in Germany and Lithuania, some of them being published.[369] It has also to be borne in mind that what happened at the "Lietukis" garage yard forces a critical evaluation of not only the Lithuanian Provisional Government which functioned at the time, but also of the very "burst for freedom" of June 1941, which for a part of Lithuanian society represents a part of the glorious national tradition.[370] It should also be taken into consideration that some of those taking part in the massacre were killed after the war in the struggle against the communist regime imposed on their country, thus becoming national heroes.[371]

Before I discuss the course of those events, I would like to outline a picture of the scene of the events. The cobblestoned garage yard was a rather small square of an area of several dozen square yards. The entry and the gateway were situated on the boulevard side. There were some buildings on one side of the square, and there was a wooden fence on the other, behind which was the former Polish "A. Mickiewicz" junior high school (at Misku St.). Just on the opposite side of Vytautas Boulevard was a Catholic cemetery occupying a large area.[372] It was in that cemetery that the physician's patient saw the Jews digging graves. As we can learn from Christoph Dieckmann's book, it was already on 26th June and in the morning of 27th that funerals of Lithuanians killed fighting the Red Army were taking place at the cemetery;[373] hence, it is not impossible that some Jews were coerced to dig the graves. Some German military camp, quite presumably equipped with horses, occupied the garage space. Not far from the garage, military barracks were arranged, where the Wehrmacht staff were quartered in those days. There is one more important detail: in the middle of the garage yard was a sort of drain with a running water facility connected to it and a tap which was enabled to fit a rubber hose, and the facility was thus used for washing vehicles.

C. Dieckmann is right when he says that the behind-the-scenes, or the origins, of the killings committed in the "Lietukis" garage yard have not yet been

---

369   See footnotes 302, 306, 367, 368.
370   2012 saw the ceremonial burial of Juozas Ambrazevičius, Prime Minister of the Provisional Government, whose remains had been brought from abroad. The date the Government was established, 23rd June 1941, has begun to be celebrated as Lithuania's Independence Revival Day.
371   I will resume this thread while discussing specific examples.
372   Apart from the testimonies or accounts of the witnesses, I am using here a map of Kaunas published in Helene Holzman's memoirs (see footnote 328).
373   Dieckmann, op. cit., p. 322; the same source specifies that 161 Lithuanians were killed during the struggle in Kaunas, p. 422.

completely explained. It cannot be precluded that it was not the Lithuanians but the Germans – in specific, members of the said military camp – who began abusing the Jews in that very place. This is what we are told, at least by Julius Vainilavicius, who testified in 1959:

> I spotted some working people in the garage backyard. The Germans were dealing with them in a churlish way. I could see a small group of Jews gather horse manure with their bare hands and carry it onto a single heap. [...] Once those people gathered up the manure, they were told to freshen up. A German drove them to the tap and released the water. They were washing themselves one after the other. As they were washing themselves, each was forced to take the hose into his mouth and to wash his mouth under a strong jet of water. Some of the Jews refused to do so and fled aside. At that time, one German soldier wanted to give a Jew a kick and as he took a swing, the man suddenly dodged and the German lost his balance and fell on the ground. Then the massacre started. The Germans and the people staying beside the garage (10–15 people) with white armbands (*Baltaraiščiai*) began lashing the Jews.[374]

Some comments should be made at this point. Let us recall the entry in the diary of Dr Kutorgienė, who had heard that some Jews were "hauling excrement with their bare hands." No existing German account mentions such a fact whatsoever, which attests, to my mind, that those witnesses were not watching the events from the very beginning. The testimonies given by the Germans present a picture of a civilised people who observed the behaviour of the Lithuanian barbarians with astonishment and dismay, and emphasise that their compatriots were only watching what was happening. For me, a historian of Warsaw under the German occupation, Germans forcing Jews to gather horse dung with their bare hands is something that sounds quite plausible. Just to make the point: moments afterwards the rubber hose was used by the Lithuanians, as is clearly shown in one picture.[375] Vytautas Petkevičius's account tells us that the Jews had the tip of the hose inserted into their anuses, which caused a disruption of their body and an agonising death.[376]

---

374 A testimony of 1959, in: *Masinės žudynės Lietuvoje* ... (as in footnote 302), p. 231; Professor Piotr Łossowski has kindly offered me its translation. Pranas Baleniūnas, questioned by the Russians in Kaunas, identified a Lithuanian named Jozefas Vaitkiavičius who, reportedly, was putting the hose into the Jews' mouths; cf. Faitelson, op. cit., p. 34.
375 Faitelson, op. cit., p. 28.
376 Vaintraubas, *Garažas* ..., p. 56.

Although it was the Germans who, I believe, began abusing the Jews at the garage yard, the killing was carried out entirely by the Lithuanians. As Leonardas Survila testified in 1961:

> At the garage yard, I spotted five or six young men who, having pulled off their jackets, were beating the men of Jewish nationality with rubber hoses and iron crowbars, who had been brought in groups of two to three from the street – based on what I could grasp – from the cemetery on the opposite side, where they were digging ditches. The cobble surface of the yard was strewn with mutilated dead bodies and heavily covered with blood. The men were pulling the hair of those being brought in there, hustling them, beating their heads with crowbars, pouring water on them from the hoses used for washing cars. They were tormenting them until the victims died. I could see a group of German soldiers and officers at the edge of the garage backyard, but they were not beating the Jews.[377]

Whilst the author of the above-quoted account was at the site of the events at around 10 a.m., Wilhelm Gunsilius, assigned with the commanding staff of 16th Army as a photographer, arrived in the afternoon. This was the picture he saw, according to his own words:

> [...] on the left-hand side of a large yard was a group of men aged thirty to fifty. There were about forty-five to fifty of them. They had been forced there by some civilians. These civilians were armed with rifles and wore armbands as can be seen from the photographs which I took.
>
> A young man (a Lithuanian) aged about sixteen, with rolled up sleeves[,] was armed with an iron bar. From the group of men standing by, one man was led up to him at a time and with one or more blows on the nape of the neck he killed each one. In this way, in the course of an hour, he killed all the forty-five to fifty. I took a number of photographs of the corpses, which I discovered in my archive years after the war and am prepared to lend them as documentary material under the condition that either they or copies will be returned to me. After he had killed them all, the young man set the iron bar aside, fetched an accordion and clambered up above the corpses. Getting up on the "hill", he played the Lithuanian national anthem. I was familiar with the melody and people standing near me confirmed that this was their anthem.
>
> The conduct of the civilians, amongst whom there were women and children, was unbelievable. After every blow of the iron bar they applauded and when the murderer began to play the Lithuanian anthem, they began to sing it to the accompaniment of the accordion. In the front row of the crowd there were women with children in their arms, watching all that was happening.[378]

---

377 *Masinės žudynės* ..., p. 232, a testimony from 1961; I have relied on Prof. Łossowski's translation here once again.
378 I use the English translation, in: Faitelson, op. cit., pp. 25–26.

Figure 12: Welcoming the Germans to Kaunas – 26th June 1941

Figure 13: Lithuanian "partisans" driving Jewesses through the streets of Kaunas

Figure 14: The massacre of Jews at the "Lietukis" garage yard in Kaunas on 27th June 1941 with German soldiers looking on

Figure 15: Lithuanian "partisans" monitoring the course of the killings

Figure 16: A bloody harvest

Figure 17: A message written in blood on a wall in the Slobodka neighbourhood: "Jews! Take revenge!"

Figure 18: The report of 11ᵗʰ July 1941 of Reinhard Heydrich, head of Sipo and SD regarding, among other topics, Kaunas

1) In K o w n o wurden nunmehr insgesamt 7 800 Juden erledigt, teils durch Pogrom, teils durch Erschiessungen von litauischen Kommandos. Sämtliche Leichen sind beseitigt. Weitere Massenerschiessungen sind nicht mehr möglich, es wurde daher ein jüdisches Komitee von mir vorgeladen, und ihm erklärt, daß wir bisher keinen Anlaß gehabt haben, in die inneren Auseinandersetzungen zwischen Litauern und Juden einzugreifen. Voraussetzung für eine Neuordnung:

Die Errichtung von einem jüdischen Ghetto, die Kennzeichnung aller Juden durch einen gelben Davidstern in Größe von 8 x-10 cm Durchmesser auf der linken Brustseite und die Unterbringung von eventuell auf unseren Befehl durch die Litauer freizulassenden Frauen und Kinder durch ein jüdisches Hilfskomitee in dem neuen Ghetto.

Als Ghetto wurde die Stadt V i l i a m p o b bestimmt.

Die Umsiedlung muß in 4 Wochen durchgeführt sein. Die Gefängnisse werden nunmehr noch einmal durchgekämmt. Juden, soweit besondere Gründe vorliegen, verhaftet und erschossen. Es wird sich dabei um kleinere Exekutionen mit 50 bis 100 Leuten handeln. Um ein Zurückströmen von Juden nach K o w n o zu verhindern, wurde mit dem Höheren SS- und Polizeiführer vereinbart, daß Ordnungspolizei einen Gürtel um Kowno zieht und keinen Juden herein läßt. Nötigenfalls wird auf die Juden geschossen. Sämtliche Wehrmachtsstellen wurden von der getroffenen Regelung unterrichtet.

Etwa 205 Mann der litauischen Partisanen wurden von uns als Sonderkommando belassen, unterhalten und zu eventuellen Exekutionen, auch auswärts, herangezogen.

Figure 19: SS-Brigaderführer Walter Stahlecker and a fragment of his obituary in Die Deutsche Polizei

Figure 20: The murderer poses for a photograph (at the "Lietukis" garage yard)

Colonel Lothar von Bischoffshausen is the only witness who quoted, years afterwards, the exact date of the events: 27th June 1941. As an aide with the staff of the Heeresgruppe Nord, commanded by General Wilhelm Ritter von Leeb, he arrived in Kaunas on that very day, tasked with establishing contact with the commander of 16th Army. As we read in his 1959 account,

> Driving through the town, I arrived near a petrol station [i.e. the "Lietukis" garage – T.S.] which was beleaguered by a dense crowd of people. A number of women were there, who lifted their children or, to have a better view, stood on chairs or boxes. With applause, cheers, ovations and laughs bursting over and over, I initially drew the conclusion that it was some victory parade, or a sports event. Having asked what was happening there, I received the answer, though, that a "Kaunas Killer" [*Totschläger von Kowno*] was at work at that moment. The collaborators and traitors are finally getting their just punishment!

Let us pay attention that in this testimony as well as in the one of Gunsilius, the central figure is the same young Lithuanian man. Bischoffshausen's report goes on to state:

> On the concrete yard of that petrol station stood a man, aged roughly twenty-five, blond-haired and medium-tall, who happened to be taking a rest, leaning against an arm-thick pole, reaching up to his breast [this is how he was portrayed by Gunsilius – T.S.]. There were some fifteen to twenty dead or dying people lying at his feet. Water continued to flow off the rubber hose, washing up the blood spilled around into the sewage drain. Some twenty people stood a mere few steps behind that man; guarded by a few armed civilians, they were submissively waiting for their turn to meet the cruel execution on the verdict. At a short nod, the next victim to go stepped out of the line and was brought to death bestially, with a wooden club, each blow being accompanied by the ecstatic shouts of the spectators.[379]

When Gunsilius asked some Lithuanians who spoke German about who was that young man who was killing the Jews, the reply he heard was: "The parents of this boy who was murdering the other people were drawn from their bed two days ago, arrested, and executed immediately, for, as nationalists, they were suspect individuals, and now is the time the young man is taking his revenge. Quite nearby," the photographer adds, "a row of corpses lay of those who, according to what the civilians declared, had been killed two days earlier by the withdrawing commissars and communists."[380] A word of comment is needed here. Writing of what he saw at the yard of the "Lietukis" garage, the occurrence is dated as 25th June 1941; then, the killing perpetrated by the NKVD could indeed have occurred on 23rd June. I would also like to point out the mention of the corpses of

---

379 The 1959 testimony of Col. L. von Bischoffshausen has been published (without specifying his name) in *"Schöne Zeiten"* …, p. 35–38.
380 This fragment of W. Gunsilius's testimony is not included in the English version quoted by A. Faitelson; I am quoting it from *"Schöne Zeiten"* …, p. 39.

Lithuanians killed in the struggle with the withdrawing Red Army lying nearby. Evidently, the dead bodies were waiting to be buried at the cemetery adjacent to the garage. It can be supposed that the Jews were forced to dig graves for the Lithuanians and, subsequently, to prepare a grave for themselves not far from the site, into which the victims of the murder committed at the garage yard were thrown afterwards.[381]

Today, we know quite a lot about the perpetrators of that atrocious slaughter. No doubt, those most ardently engaged in settling accounts with the Jews were the Lithuanian political prisoners released by the Germans who were burning with the desire to take revenge for the sufferings they bore from the "Judeo-commies" they so hated. Karl Reder, a witness to the events and author of the first two published photographs, when asked who perpetrated that crime replied, "They were being beaten by Lithuanians freed from jails."[382] Hubert Schmaink, Reder's colleague from that same "Bakery 562", wrote in his testimony, "The beatings were carried out by six men dressed in civilian clothes of different make. Of course, I asked who were the men carrying out the beatings. I was told that they were Lithuanian and Latvian fighters for freedom. [...] They all had carabines [i.e. machine guns], each one wore a white armband."[383] Leonardas Survila, the Lithuanian whom I have already quoted, confirms: "Those who watched that scene were saying to one another that the settlement had been organised by political prisoners who, in the first days of the war, had got out from the prison in Kaunas, which means, they had been set free by the Germans." Their desire for revenge and retaliation could be understood; nevertheless, their oppressors and those who had caused their torments were no longer in Kaunas. These Lithuanians' accumulated hatred was retargeted at completely innocent people.

Among the accounts being gathered, there are some which come from those who participated in the murder. One of them was Henrikas Zemelis, who had earlier been tortured at the NKVD prison. He admitted that he "took part in the execution," as he was utterly craving for revenge – and it was only with time that he realised he had killed innocent people.[384] Alex Faitelson quotes an account of Jonas Barskeitis concerning the figure of Juozas Lukša, a man who had also

---

381 A. Faitelson quotes (in an English translation) the 1960 testimony of Hubert Schmaink, K. Reder's colleague from bakery no. 562, reading: "I saw a mass grave there. It was long, approximately seventy meters in length and about two-and-half meters deep. I watched as the Jews were thrown into the grave."; op. cit., p. 31.
382 Faitelson, op. cit., p. 22.
383 Faitelson, op. cit., p. 31.
384 Vaintraubas, *Garažas* ..., p. 59.

been held for some time at the NKVD's "Yellow Prison" as he had been an activist with LAF; he was eventually released thanks to the Germans. In the autumn of 1944, recognised as a murderer of Jews at a Kaunas meeting with the novelist Ilya Ehrenburg, he fled abroad. He later returned to his home country as a partisan warrior, nom-de-guerre "Daumantas", who fought against the communists. Then, he escaped again, went to the United States, and was parachuted back into the country to continue the struggle. He was eventually killed in September 1951, not far from Kaunas. When Lithuania regained independence, a street in the town was named after him.[385]

Some of those watching the crime protested. In her reminiscences, Helen Holzman writes: "An enormous crowd gathered to watch the horrible spectacle and instigate the blind fury of the murderers with encouraging cries. There were voices expressing outrage at such bestiality. 'This is a disgrace to Lithuania!', dared say those brave ones, but they were instantly forced to keep silent."[386]

The Jews being killed offered no resistance to their butchers; it would be rather hard to figure out how, exactly, defenceless and helpless, they could have stood up to them. Reder, the German soldier, remarked that "the Jews were saying prayers before they got killed. [...] Some of them, when already badly wounded and lying on the ground, still offered their prayers."[387] A most diverse variety of stories began circulating about what had happened at the "Lietukis" garage yard. Ada Hirsz's 1948 account tells us that "There were rather frequent incidents of seizing Jews and Poles [what she means by the latter is unclear – T.S.] to the garages, where the Germans, helped by Lithuanians, were slitting the people's stomachs and poured petrol and diesel into the open wounds."[388] We cannot say much today about the victims of the crime. The notes in the diary of Alphonsas Bira reveal to us the names of very few of them – members of local intelligentsia or petty bourgeoisie, who were completely incidentally captured by the Kaunas "insurgents".[389]

The news about what had occurred at the "Lietukis" garage yard was brought to a meeting of the Provisional Government by Vytautas Žemkalnis-Landsbergis, Minister of Municipal Economy, who arrived late at the meeting. Asked why the police had not prevented the massacre of those Jews, Jonas Šlepetys, the Minister

---

385 Faitelson, op. cit., p. 33–34. Faitelson's memoirs *Nepokorivshiesja* (see footnote 354) includes a photograph of Juozas Lukša as a partisan; p. 40.
386 Holzman, op. cit., p. 25.
387 Quoted based on the German translation of the testimony, *"Schöne Zeiten"* ..., p. 40.
388 See footnote 300.
389 Faitelson, p. 36.

of Interior, replied that the Bolsheviks are to blame, as it is they who had "destroyed the personnel." While the minutes of that meeting express objection against public executions, the attendees supported eradicating Jews and communists, however, with the use of different means.[390] The news about the terrible occurrences, moreover, reached Archbishop Juozapas Skvireckas, who made a related point in his diary under the date of 28th June 1941. He was asked to intervene; what is known is that he sent his assistant Kazimieras Šaulys to "the authorities of Kaunas," with a mission asking that they refrain from excesses.[391]

The day following the massacre, General Robert von Pohl, who represented the German military authority in Kaunas and headed the Field Command no. 821, ordered Bobelis, head of the Lithuanian police, to take away the arms from the locals of Kaunas, which meant that the "partisans" would be disarmed as well.[392] On that same day, 28th June, officers of the 16th Army Staff met Walther Stahlecker, commander of *Einsatzkommando A*, to discuss the situation as they were concerned about the doings of the Lithuanian "partisans".[393]

Col. von Bischoffshausen, who witnessed the massacre at the "Lietukis" garage, recalls that when he reached the 16th Army Staff headquarters, he noticed that the officers were already aware of the mass executions in the town and he shared their dismay and outrage at the news. It was explained to him, though, that these were the "spontaneous actions of the Lithuanian people, taking their retaliation against the collaborators from the time of the former Russian occupation and traitors of the homeland." Such barbarian excesses ought to be approached as "purely internal political conflicts," which the "Lithuanian state" was supposed to solve on its own, without the Wehrmacht interfering, according to higher-level orders. In the evening of this same day, Col. von Bischoffshausen was having dinner with his host Colonel-General Ernst Busch, Commander of

---

390 Dieckmann, op. cit., p. 323. Minutes of meetings of the Provisional Government have been published in Lithuanian by Arvydas Anusauskas, Vilnius, 2001; the record related to 27th June 1941 is quoted, in an English translation by S. Sužiedėlis (see footnote 304), op. cit., p. 155. It was remarked there that public executions of Jews were committed by people with no connection with LAF, the partisan staff, or the Provisional Government whatsoever. This was certainly true at least for the latter-mentioned organisation.
391 Sužiedėlis, op. cit., pp. 155–156. We do not know whether Archbishop Skvireckas would intervene with the Germans or with the Lithuanians.
392 *Die "Ereignismeldungen UdSSR" 1941* ... (as in footnote 325), p. 86 (dispatch no. 14 of 6th July 1941).
393 Dieckmann, op. cit., p. 324.

16th Army, when the latter suddenly received the news about the ongoing pogrom. In reply, Busch stated that "this is about internal political conflicts" – as Bischoffshausen had already heard. Yet, he added quite an important remark, saying that he personally "is temporarily powerless and can make no step in this matter as he has been forbidden to do so, but hopes to soon receive some different instructions from his superiors."[394]

General Franz von Roques, commander of German Army Group Rear Area, received news about the Kaunas massacre of the Jews when his staff was still in the territory of the Reich. A few days later, he arrived in Kaunas, and Stahlecker informed him that "this was perpetrated by the Lithuanians, on their own initiative." Having reported with Field Marshall Wilhelm Ritter von Leeb Commander of the Heeresgruppe Nord, on 8th July 1941, Roques noted that Leeb shared his own indignation, but also heard that this officer, a top-level one, "has, regrettably, his hands tied as well." As for Ritter von Leeb himself, he noted in his diary:

> General von Roques, commander of the Army Group Rear Area, complains about mass executions of Jews in Kaunas (thousands!) performed by Lithuanian protective units [orig., *Schutzverbände*, i.e. auxiliary police – T.S.] on instruction of [orig., *auf Veranlassung*, which may also mean "persuaded to this end by" – T.S.] the German police authorities. We have no influence on these actions. Nothing remains for us but to stay away. Roques's reasoning is quite apt as he observes that the Jewish issue cannot possibly be solved in this way. It would be the most certain solution to arrange the sterilisation of all the Jewish males.[395]

The day after the garage yard massacre, on 28th June, SS-Sturmbannführer Dr Erich Ehrlinger arrived in Kaunas at the forefront of *Einsatzkommando 1(b)* and took over the German police authority of the town for the following few days.[396] Moments after he arrived, he would report that "Over the past three days, groups of Lithuanian 'partisans' have killed already several thousand Jews."[397] On that same day, when Col. Bobelis, the Lithuanian city commander, ordered, as instructed by the German Field Command, that the 'partisans' be disarmed,

---

394 *"Schöne Zeiten"* …, p. 36.
395 The statement of Gen. von Roques of 22nd October 1947 and note from the diary of Marshall von Leeb are quoted after Krausnick and Wilhelm, *Die Truppe des Weltanschauungskrieges* … (as in footnote 324), pp. 207–208.
396 In 1939, Ehrlinger commanded one of the EKs in Poland; in 1940–1941, he was an advisor to Quisling in Oslo, Norway. Sentenced to twelve years of imprisonment in 1963, he was released 1969 due to poor health. He died in 2004. Cf. *Die "Ereignismeldungen UdSSR" 1941* …, p. 57.
397 Ibidem, p. 55 (dispatch no. 8 of 30th June 1941).

recruitment of volunteers began for an auxiliary police battalion which was being formed by agreement with the Germans. What is significant, however, is that while the German name of the formation was *Polizeihilfsbataillon Kaunas*, which exactly meant "the auxiliary police battalion of Kaunas", its Lithuanian name was initially something completely different: *Tautinės Darbo Apsaugos Batalionas*, i.e. "batallion for the protection of national achievements",[398] which testifies that in the Lithuanians' mind, it was meant to be the beginnings of their national army. The battalion was meant to be composed of five companies, three of which were to consist of members of the Šaulių Sąjunga (the "Riflemen") and the remaining two, of members of the "Iron Wolf", with their commanders Col. K. Šimkus and Lt. B. Norkus, both of whom we have met. These two latter companies were directly subordinated to the *Einsatzkommando*, with a special role assigned to Company 4 commanded by Lt. Norkus: it was tasked with the continued killings of Jews – no longer carried out in public but, instead, within the enclosed area of Fort VII.

An *Einsatzgruppe A* report of 5th July 1941 notified Heydrich that, besides the auxiliary police units, two "continually independent groups" were formed of locals in Kaunas "in order to carry out pogroms."[399] But it was essentially not about continuing with pogroms, but about performing mass executions, with no witnesses present to see the murders being committed. Let it be added that Norkus's people would soon after be included in the notorious *Rollkommando*, commanded by SS-Obersturmführer Joachim Hamann, which in the summer and autumn of that same year would be killing Jews on the entire territory of Lithuania.[400] The so-called *Ereignismeldung* dated 6th July 1941, compiled by Heydrich on the basis of reports flowing in from the Eastern Front, thus pictured the situation in the town:

> The partisans in Kaunas and the people associated with them have been disarmed on order of the German Field Command. A squad of auxiliary police, comprised of five companies, has been formed of trustworthy partisans. Two of these companies have been subjected to the *Einsatzkommando*. One of these companies keeps guard of the

---

398 Cf. Stang, *Das Fußwolk* ... (as in footnote 301), p. 78.
399 Quoted after Longerich, P., "Vom Massenmord zur "Endlösung". Die Erschießungen von jüdischen Zivilisten in den ersten Monaten des Ostfeldzuges im Kontext des nationalsozialistischen Judenmords", [in:] *Zwei Wege nach Moskau. Vom Hitler-Stalin-Pakt bis zum "Unternehmen Barbarossa"*, ed. by B. Wegner, Munich–Zürich 1991, p. 259.
400 Knut Stang has devoted one of his books to the *Rollkommando* – cf. footnote 343; for a biographical note on Joachim Hamann, see Krausnick and Wilhelm, op. cit., p. 640.

concentration camp for Jews. Meanwhile, a place has been formed in Fort VII in Kaunas where executions are carried out. [...] A concentration camp will be organised at Fort VII for Jews, with two sections: 1. for Jewish males, 2. For Jewish females and children. At present, there are some 1,500 Jews in the Fort. The central prison houses: 1,860 Jews, 214 Lithuanians, 134 Russians, 1 Latvian, and 16 Poles. Another concentration camp for Jews is envisioned at Kaunas's Fort IX.[401]

The appearance in Kaunas of Ehrlinger's *Einsatzkommando* and the commenced action of disarming the "partisans" by no means put an end to the pogroms. As William Mishell noted in his diary, on 28th June 1941:

> On Saturday the excesses against the Jewish population continued. Again the same ploy was used: the Jews were shooting from the windows at the German troops. This accusation was utterly ridiculous: first of all, the Jews never had arms in Lithuania; and secondly, no German soldiers were present where most of the Jews were being arrested, beaten up, and manhandled. Saturday, the Jewish Sabbath, only made the partisans' zeal higher. Groups of Jews were made to dance in front of jeering crowds and then were beaten in full view of the population, including Germans, but nobody intervened. Jews who were accustomed to going to synagogue stayed at home and went into hiding.
>
> It was futile to hope that the entry of the German army would provide a semblance of order. Under every international convention, an occupying army was responsible for maintaining law and order. But the Germans did not seem to bother. They observed the slaughter heartlessly and some of them even took pictures of the bloodbath.[402]

Last Hopes is the title given by the author of these reminiscences to the chapter describing the occurrences of Saturday, 28th June and Sunday, 29th June. As it turned out, the Jews held these last hopes for the condemnation of the perpetrators of the pogrom in the Sunday sermons of local Catholic clergy and for their restraining further repressive moves against them. Mishell writes:

---

401 Die "Ereignismeldungen UdSSR" 1941 ..., p. 86.
402 Mishell, op. cit., p. 27. In Dina Porat's words, "When the Germans entered Kovno, they filmed the massacre of the Jews by the Lithuanians so as to 'make clear that it was the local population that spontaneously took the first steps against the Jews'"; cf. Porat, D., "The Holocaust in Lithuania: Some Unique Aspects", [in:] *The Final Solution. Origins and Implementation*, ed. by D. Cesarani, London–New York 1994, p. 164. It was evidently for propaganda purposes that the Germans were taking photographs during the pogrom in Warsaw in March 1940. As we know, Reder, who was taking pictures 'for his personal use', had his camera taken from him. A. Faitelson writes about Himmler's order of 12th November 1941 forbidding the photographing of executions; cf. *The Truth and Nothing* ..., p. 29.

The Lithuanian population was almost entirely Catholic, deeply religious, and the influence of the clergy was pronounced. On Sunday all the churches were full and even the one year of the communist rule failed to put a dent in the religious behaviour. The priests were highly-educated people and were revered by the population. Many clergymen were successful authors and writers and their influence went far beyond the four corners of the church. It was for this reason that we were so anxious to hear what they had to say in church on this first Sunday without the communist regime checking up of every statement. There was absolutely no doubt that if the priests said just one word to discourage the population from committing crimes against the Jews, it would have a profound effect. What the partisans were committing was pure murder. It was not an act in defense of the country, no battle was raging. It was an act against defenseless people who, deep in their hearts, loved Lithuania but happened to be Jewish.

How disillusioned Mishell's family was to hear the tidings from their maidservant, a Lithuanian and Catholic, after she returned home from the mass! Asked whether the priest admonished the partisans not to attack the Jews, she replied,

> No, on the contrary, he praised them for their patriotism, for their devotion to Lithuania, and for their courage in fighting the communists. He praised the Nazis and Hitler as the liberators of Lithuania and urged the people to cooperate with the Germans. He even mentioned that some clergy is planning to send a telegram to Hitler promising to fight alongside the Germans against the Bolsheviks.

Asked what the priest said about the Jews, it turned out that he indeed mentioned them – as those who "cooperated with the communists against the interests of Lithuania." When the Mishells asked whether the priest dropped a hint about what is being done to the Jews in the town, what they heard from the servant was: "No, he only stressed that the true enemy were the Bolsheviks and it was important for the Lithuanian population to cooperate with the victorious German army." Thus, Mishell notes:

> The news was far worse than we had expected. Our last hope was now dashed. It seemed that a part of the clergy was ready to cooperate with Hitler. Of course, we did not know whether this was the attitude of all the clergymen, but for us what really counted was that the priests had not acted to stop the pogrom.[403]

---

[403] Mishell, op. cit., p. 29. In 2000, the Catholic bishops of Lithuania declared a Day of Repentance and Apologies. As we can read in their letter to the local community of the faithful, "We express our profound regret that some of the children of the Church showed a deficit of love for the persecuted Jews during the Second World War; that they failed to use all the possible methods in order to defend the Jews; and, in particular, that they appeared to be insufficiently resolute to influence those who were assisting the Nazis," after: "Winy Kościoła", *Gazeta Wyborcza*, 17th April 2000.

The pogrom in Kaunas, if we mean by it the riots in the streets and the overt murder of Jews, came to an end on the Sunday of 29th June 1941, but not in the least resulting from a condemnation of the crimes by the Catholic Church. Instead, the Germans themselves decided that the time had come to present themselves as providers of law and order. It was decided to subdue the "licence" of the Lithuanians and show who was the actual ruler in the city. This by no means meant the Germans quit the idea to "finally solve the Jewish question" in Lithuania. On the contrary, the Sipo and SD crews knew from the very beginning – just a reminder of what Stahlecker said – that the "self-cleansing actions" they inspired were for propaganda purposes and offered no guarantee of solving the issue of the annihilation of the Jews. The extermination was to be conducted in a gradual manner, strictly under German control, not exposed to the public. The concentration of local Jews in ghettos was designed as a preceding stage.

When one considers why it was in Kaunas that a pogrom of such a large scale took place, there are several relevant factors that call for being taken into account. The most important among them was probably the fact that Kaunas was the main hub of underground activity targeted against the Soviet rule between June 1940 and June 1941; moreover, the underground maintained contacts with the Lithuanian émigré community in Berlin. The other important factor that made anti-Semitic slogans so powerful in Kaunas and won enthusiastic support among some of the locals for disposing of the Jews was the iniquities and crimes of the communist system during the Soviet occupation – primarily, the deportation of Lithuanians carried out moments before the war broke out, from 14th June 1941 onwards. The contributions of persons of Jewish origin to the activities of the local NKVD would call for detailed explanation. Even if it was not significant in reality, it sufficed for heightening anti-Jewish sentiments. Moreover, one should not lose sight of the fact that Kaunas – as opposed from Wilno/Vilnius, for that matter – was home to no other ethnic minority than the Jews; this strengthened the conviction held by the local Lithuanians that Kaunas was their own and no-one else's city. Although Wilno, whose 1939 population of 209,000 included 65.5% Poles and 27.7% Jews,[404] was the scene of anti-Jewish riots in October 1939,[405] nothing resembling the Kaunas developments occurred there once the Germans entered the city in June 1941.

---

404 Cf. Wardzyńska (see footnote 8), op. cit., p. 21.
405 The anti-Jewish riots in Wilno broke out on the day the rule of the city was taken over from the Russians by the Lithuanians. As Henri Minczeles writes, the local Poles shouted, "Down with Lithuanians!", "Down with Jews!" and "Down with Soviets!"

If we were to endorse the opinion Kazimierz Sakowicz expressed about Lithuanians in his diary (in January 1943): "No other nation in the world has as many murders on their conscience,"[406] we might come to the conclusion that Poles would never be capable of committing such acts. Yet, the events that took place on 10th July 1940 in Jedwabne testify to something else.[407] In Wilno, however, the Poles did not take part in the Holocaust. Even though they rejoiced the liberation from Soviet rule, they, unlike the Lithuanians, never treated the Germans as their allies – on the contrary, they treated them as an enemy, and cooperation with the Germans was condemned by patriotic public opinion. There was also another reason, namely, the German's attitude toward Poles: the Germans were reluctant to engage in any arrangements with the Polish people, not least because the latter would be sorted out, too, in due time. This having been the case, Reinhard Heydrich's reply to the suggestion made to him by the command of the 17th Army (which operated in the south, in the Lvov region) that Poles with anti-Jewish and anticommunist inclinations could be used in "self-cleansing actions" is characteristic. The head of Sipo and SD issued on 1st July 1941 a special order in this respect remarking that although the Bolsheviks and Jews needed to be eradicated in the first place, actions will in future be taken against the Polish intelligentsia as well. For this reason, he advised against making use of Poles as an "element for initiating" pogroms.[408] In this context, the Jedwabne incident might have ensued

---

      One man was killed, and some 200 were wounded; cf. Minczeles, H., *Vilna, Wilno, Vilnius*: La Jérusalem de Lituanie, Paris 1993, pp. 376–7.

406 K. Sakowicz, *Dziennik 1941–1943*, ed. by M. Wardzyńska, Warsaw 2014, p. 64. The author of this diary, Kazimierz Sakowicz, witnessed the murders committed by the Lithuanians in Ponary near Wilno as supervised by the Germans; cf. Tomkiewicz, M., *Zbrodnia w Ponarach 1941–44*, Warsaw 2008.

407 What I am referring to is Gross's book published in Poland in 2000 as *Sąsiedzi*, which has been translated into several languages – the English version being *Neighbors. The Destruction of the Jewish Community in Jedwabne, Poland* (Princeton, NJ, 2001). In Poland, the publication triggered a national debate; I refer to this book in the Foreword as well. A two-volume collection *Wokół Jedwabnego*, edited by P. Machcewicz and K. Persak, Warsaw 2002, contains related essays written by historians, along with accounts and testimonies of witnesses and archival materials. Also, cf. T. Szarota, "Selbstreinigungsaktionen" Sipo i SD na Litwie i w Polsce a udział ludności miejscowej w Holokauście (na przykładzie pogromów w Kownie i Jedwabnem)", [in:] *Świat …NIEpożegnany*, Warszawa-Londyn 2004, pp. 686–701.

408 Krausnick and Wilhelm, op. cit., pp. 167, 207. For the text of the order, see *Die "Ereignismeldungen UdSSR" 1941 …*, pp. 64–65 (dispatch no. 10 of 2nd July 1941).

from the commander of the *Einsatzkommando* operating in that area not being aware of the said order, or from his insubordination.

A German offer to the Jews: continued pogroms or the ghetto

It can be assumed that it was only on 29th June 1941 that SS-Standartenführer Karl Jäger arrived in Kaunas. We have encountered this figure when reporting on the course of the Berlin conference with Heydrich before the outbreak of the German-Soviet war. German historian Hans-Heinrich Wilhelm has called Jäger "probably the most productive mass murderer in the recent history."[409] Twelve years older than Stahlecker, his superior, Jäger began his duties in Kaunas three days later, leaving, for the time being, Dr Ehrlinger in charge of the operations of Sipo and SD. As I already mentioned, Jäger was interrogated in the Federal Republic of Germany in 1959 and gave extensive evidence on that occasion. Before he committed suicide in his cell, he wrote farewell letters, of which fragments were subsequently published, along with his testimony.[410] He probably never supposed that historians would some day have the opportunity to compare everything he said and wrote in 1959 with the report he compiled and sent on 1st December 1941 to the commander of *Einsatzkommando A*. A copy of this report was found in Moscow and reprinted, in facsimile, as part of a collection of documents edited by Adalbert Rückerl.[411]

Let us first hear what Jäger had to say in his post-war story:

> When I arrived in Kaunas, executions of Jews were ongoing already, that is, there were some Jews already shot by firing squads and some were still being shot. These executions, it was said, were carried out by the Lithuanian auxiliary police. [...] On whose order these executions were done, I am not aware. Also, I cannot tell whether Ehrlinger or Wolf, together with their people, actively participated in that. They certainly tolerated it, as otherwise the executions committed by the Lithuanians would not be continued. I did not bring those executions to a halt, either, for it was [made] certain, through

---

409 Wilhelm, *Rassenpolitik und Kriegsführung* ... (as in footnote 316), p. 11. Wolfram Wette, author of Jäger's biography (cf. footnote 319), fully confirms this statement.
410 Ibidem, pp. 186–198. In his farewell letter, Jäger wrote: "I never deemed these executions of the Jews appropriate. [...] I was put in my position during the war contrary to my internal convictions. I never ordered that Jews be executed, never have given a command to execute. [...] I have not committed any crime, nor have I incurred any blame on myself", ibidem, p. 196.
411 *NS-Prozesse. Nach 25 Jahren Strafverfolgung: Möglichkeiten – Grenzen – Ergebnisse*, ed. by A. Rückerl, 2nd ed., Karlsruhe, 1972; recently, in Wette, op. cit. (as in footnote 319), pp. 236–245 (a facsimile copy).

Heydrich's speech on the occasion of the Berlin sitting, that Jews in the East must be executed... I saw in that statement made by Heydrich a binding order, instructing that after I took actions in the East, the Jews were to be shot by firing squads. This is why I took no steps against those executions. I did reject them inside myself, though, deeming them cruel and horrible that some people for the sole reason of their religion or race were killed or should be killed. Still, I should like to stress that I never gave an order to anyone belonging to my duty station that a certain determined number of Jews, at all, be put before firing squad. I had no need to do so, after all. All of that was going on out of its own impetus. I cannot possibly quote how many of the Jews had been executed by the time I arrived, or were executed in the first days [of my stay in Kaunas – T.S.]. However, there could be thousands of them...[412]

And now, let us see what the extant report signed by Jäger on 1st December 1941 says: "On my instructions and orders the following executions were conducted by Lithuanian partisans: 4.7.41 Kaunas–Fort VII – 416 Jews, 47 Jewesses, total 463; 8.7.41 Kaunas–Fort VII – 2,514 Jews."[413] True, the command was not given in this particular case to members of a Sipo or SD formation, but it was about the killing of local Jews, after all! Jäger did not assign a specified number of Jews to be liquidated. Within a few days, a special *Erschiessungskomando* numbering several dozen members and commanded by Lt. Norkus, a Lithuanian, killed a total of 2,977 people at Fort VII, whereas Stahlecker has estimated the number of victims of the pogrom that had been perpetrated for many days by hundreds of "partisans" at around 3,800.

Since from a certain moment onwards, the murders were committed in hiding and the "partisans", as all-powerful until recently as they were, disappeared from the streets of Kaunas, the population were given the impression that peace, law, and order finally prevailed in the city thanks to the Germans. The families of the Jews who had been arrested by the "partisans" saw an opportunity to intercede for them with the German authorities so that they could be released and go back home. The State Archives of Vilnius holds applications written in German by Jews to the Kaunas Sicherheitspolizei requesting the release of members of their families who had been caught in the street or arrested while at home. Two such recently published letters are dated 2nd July 1941 (the day Karl Jäger assumed his

---

412   Wilhelm, *Rassenpolitik und Kriegsführung* ..., pp. 190–191.
413   Jäger goes on to meticulously enumerate the dates and numbers of the Jews executed, i.e.: 9th July – 24 killed; 19th July – 26; 2nd August – 209; 9th August – 534; 18th August – 1,812; 26th September – 1,608; 4th October – 1,945; 29th October – 9,200; 25th November – 2,934; and, 29th November – 2,034.

office in Kaunas) but refer to the events of 25th/26th June and the doings of the "partisans" at that time.⁴¹⁴

Let us now take a look again at the "confession" of the head of *Einsatzkommando 3*:

> I was told on one of my first days in Kaunas that the Lithuanian lieutenant Norkus had driven into Fort VII some 3,000 Jewish men and had them executed by firing squad. From whom I received the dispatch, I cannot tell now. What I know is that I went to that Fort the following day. The executed Jews still lay in the yard. The view was horrible. [...] The way it looked at the site of the execution, there could be some 3,000 people... When back at my office, I called the said Norkus in and explained to him that he was supposed to relinquish such wilful executions in the future. With regards to performing any actions, which was supposed to extend to executions as well, he was supposed instead to consult SS-Hauptsturmführer Schmitz, head of the State Police, or Obersturmführer Hamann. What I told him later on was that he should take care about the burial of the previously executed Jews, in accordance with the rules.⁴¹⁵

Further in his argument, Jäger tries to give the impression that he essentially condemned the killing of innocent Jews. As he argued in 1959,

> I considered these executions of Jews, from the very beginning, to be a great injustice and a great crime. I felt that the matter was about collective responsibility with no underlying specified actions of the affected people, which would call for being punished... [...] Since those executions made me psychically exhausted and burdened my conscience, I was looking for some solution. This is why I wrote to Stahlecker and suggested that a ghetto be built in Kaunas, the justification being, namely, that all the Jews could not possibly be executed as some would still be needed to do the labour...

As we can then learn, Jäger visited Stahlecker's quarters in Pleskau and was promised by him that the suggestion would be forwarded to an upper decision-making level, himself considering the idea a good one. "Stahlecker drew attention, though," Jäger adds, "to the fact that the Security Service and the State Police must have ensured access to the ghetto at any moment, for even once the

---

414 A facsimile copy of one of these letters is published in *Einsatz im "Reichskommissariat Ostland"* ... (as in footnote 361), pp. 178–179. The request sent by Berkus Friedman, owner of a fur factory, to the head of the *Sicherheitspolizei* in Kaunas reads as follows: "On Friday, 26th June 1941 [Thursday, in fact – T.S.], for no reason at all, abducted from our dwelling [...] by the Lithuanian partisans were my wife Ida, aged 42, my daughter Ester, aged 16, my son Elijahu, aged two-and-a-half years, and my cousin Ester Slonimsky. As I have learned, they are kept in the prison at Mickievičius St. Since the abovementioned persons have not been members of any party and are loyal citizens, I kindly request that my innocent family be set loose."
415 Wilhelm, *Rassenpolitik und Kriegsführung* ..., p. 192–193.

ghetto is formed, executing the Jews will be required, for the reason of providing security by the Police..."[416]

A conclusion one might draw from these words is that Jäger wanted to save the Jews from death by building the ghetto for them, using for the purpose of argument the benefit of having a useful labour force. Yet, the formation of the ghetto was essentially about getting the Jews concentrated in a single place to enable their gradual annihilation and to leave the decision about the pace and sequence of killing them in the hands of the Germans. In his 1st December 1941 report, Jäger would overtly and proudly claim as follows: "Today I can confirm that our objective, to solve the Jewish problem for Lithuania, has been achieved by EK 3 [i.e. *Einsatzkommando* 3]. In Lithuania there are no more Jews, apart from Jewish workers and their families." He would go on to say, "I consider the Jewish action more or less terminated as far as Einsatzkommando 3 is concerned. Those working Jews and Jewesses still available are needed urgently and I can envisage that after the winter this workforce will be required even more urgently. I am of the view that the sterilization program of the male worker Jews should be started immediately so that reproduction is prevented. If despite sterilization a Jewess becomes pregnant she will be liquidated." In this same report, Jäger states that 137,346 Jewish people have, altogether, been killed in Lithuania.

Now, however, we are following the course of events in early July 1941. The day following the great massacre he had ordered to be carried out at Fort VII, SS-Standartenführer Karl Jäger called in five of the most prominent members of the Jewish community in Kaunas. His superior SS-Brigadeführer Walter Stahlecker joined the meeting as well. Avraham Tory, the Jewish lawyer and Zionist activist who managed to survive the Holocaust, thus noted down the speech Jäger delivered on that occasion in his diary:

> "The present situation – and the Jews know exactly what the situation is – cannot go on. Total disorder and unrest prevail in the city. I cannot allow this situation to continue. I will issue orders to stop shooting. Peace and order must return to the city. The Lithuanians have announced that they no longer wish to live together with the Jews; they demand that the Jews be segregated in a Ghetto. The choice is up to the Jews – either the present situation with the disorder and the bloodbath, or leaving the city and moving into the Ghetto." [...] "You must go to the Ghetto," said the general [i.e. Stahlecker – T.S.]. He pointed to Slobodka on the map. "Here will be the Ghetto. There is plenty of room for you there."[417]

---

416   Ibidem, p. 194.
417   The diary of Avraham Golub (Thory), translated from Yiddish to Hebrew, was published in Tel Aviv in 1988 by Dina Porat; two years later, Martin Gilbert prepared its

It is possible that Stahlecker thought about creating a ghetto in Kaunas already during the first talks he had in that city with Klimaitis, Šimkus, and Norkus, on 25th June 1941; it is possible that he indicated to the Lithuanians the district of Slobodka, that is, Vilijampolė, as the site of the pogrom. It is astonishing, in any case, that the local Jews were given almost the same reason behind the development of a ghetto as the Jews of Warsaw before them! In both cases, the enclosed district was meant to protect the Jews from the aggression of the locals who showed all too clearly through the pogroms they spontaneously organised that their coexistence with Jews was impossible. Towards the end of the aforementioned meeting with Jewish representatives in Kaunas, Stahlecker apparently lost control of himself, saying that all the Jews ought to be executed as they were all communists; he mentioned Lenin, Stalin, and a whole list of communist leaders. As one of the attending Jews named Rabinovych remarked that neither Lenin nor Stalin, nor several other figures mentioned by Stahlecker were actually Jews, the latter muttered something and said that they must have had some connection with the Jews, in any case.[418]

The date the Kaunas Jews were supposed to move to the ghetto was fixed at 15th July. Five days earlier, the Jewish Committee, which had meanwhile been established (led by Dr Elhanan Elkes, its members including Leib Garfunkel, Jakob Goldberg, and others), issued a memorandum to the German Security Police in an attempt at dissuading the Germans from building the ghetto in Vilijampolė. The authors explained that Vilijampolė was a small suburb area, populated until then by some 12,000 people, including 5,000–6,000 Jews and 6,000–7,000 Lithuanians. There were terrible conditions prevailing, with an average of three to five people populating rooms of less than 10 square metres in floor area. They pointed out that there was a shortage of running water and sewage facilities in the district, and not a single hospital, and that placing as many as 25,000 people there would pose a threat of epidemics.[419] Needless to say, the memorandum was

---

English edition, transl. by Jerzy Michalowicz: cf. Tory, A., *Surviving the Holocaust. The Kovno Ghetto Diary*, Cambridge and London, 1990; cf. p. 10.
418 Based on an account by Josef Goldberg, published in Yiddish and quoted here after: Dieckmann, C., "Das Ghetto und das Konzentrationslager in Kaunas 1941–1944", [in:] *Die nazionalsozialistischen Konzentrationslagern. Entwicklung und Struktur*, ed. by U. Herbert, K. Orth and C. Dieckmann, Göttingen 1998, p. 463.
419 *Einsatz im "Reichskommissariat Ostland"* ..., pp. 180–181.

sent to no avail. Interventions taken by the Jews with the Lithuanian authorities were futile as well.[420]

On 10th July 1941, the day the Jewish notables submitted their memorandum to Jäger, Dr Elena Kutorgienė noted in her diary: "It was announced that the Jews must wear a yellow six-pointed star and that they can be outside only until eight o'clock [in the evening]. The streets are frighteningly empty. The city is dead..." Two days later, she would add: "Jews walk about with the yellow star; they are allowed to walk on the pavement, not on the sidewalks. They may walk only in single file, not together, and they have to remove their hats for every passing German." A decree of 28th July 1941, signed by SS-Oberführer Cramer, acting as the *Stadtkomissar*, forbade the Jews to use the city's greenery or public benches, or means of public transport.[421] There was no longer any doubt that it was the Germans who were ruling the city of Kaunas.

---

420 Col. Jurgis Bobelis, commander of the Lithuanian army in Kaunas, assured he was not an anti-Semite and declared that the rule of the city was exercised by the Germans. Members of the Provisional Government considered the creation of the ghetto a successful solution for them. Bishop Vincentas Brizgas basically shared this view; cf. Dieckmann, C., *Deutsche Besatzungspolitik in Litauen* ..., pp. 332–333.

421 For the content of the decree, see: *Einsatz im "Reichskommissariat Ostland"* ..., p. 182.

List of Illustrations and their Sources

1. *"Topokrzyż"* symbol, *Krak*, December, 1937.
2. The article *"Nie naśladować Niemców!"*, *Polska Żyje!*, no. 41–42, 1940.
3. Signs at Paris establishments, S. Klarsfeld, 1941. *Les Juifs en France. Préludes à la Solution finale*, Paris 1991, p. 4.
4. A "butterfly" reading *"Ici maison juive"*, ibid. p. 5.
5. Jews show their service for their country, ibid. p. 5.
6. Report on the synagogue attacks, *Paris Soir*, 4th October 1941.
7. Demolished entrance to the Synagogue on rue Sainte-Isaure, S. Klarsfeld, *Les Juifs...*, p. 78.
8. Notice board reading *"Juden Viertel/Joodsche Wijk"*, Onderdrukking en Verzet. Nederland in Oorlogstijd, Arnhem-Amsterdam, Vol. III, p. 85.
9. A barbed-wire barrier at the border of the ghetto (under preparation) in Amsterdam, ibid., p. 87.
10. The *"razzia"* (roundup) – a hunt for Jews in Amsterdam, L. de Jong, *Het Koninkrijk der Nederlanden in de Tweede Wereldoorlog*, The Hague 1972, Vol. IV, part 2, ill. 96.
11. Report on the incidents in Antwerp, Institut für Zeitgeschichte – München, MA 677/3, c. 352 (A-21).
12. Welcoming the Germans in Kaunas – 25th June 1941, F.W. Seidler, *Die Kollaboration 1939–1945*, München-Berlin 1995, p. 9.
13. Lithuanian "partisans" driving Jewesses through the streets of Kaunas, *"Schöne Zeiten". Judenmord aus der Sicht der Täter und Gaffer*, eds., E. Klee, W. Dreßen, and V. Rieß, Frankfurt am Main 1988, p. 33.
14. The massacre of Jews at the "Lietukis" garage yard in Kaunas, ibid., p. 37.
15. Lithuanian "partisans" monitoring the course of the killings, ibid. p. 37.
16. A bloody harvest, ibid., p. 34.
17. A message written in blood on a wall: "Jews! Take revenge!", E. Oshry, *The Annihilation of Lithuanian Jewry*, New York 1995, p. 3.
18. R. Heydrich's report on the events in Kaunas, *The Einsatzgruppen Reports*, eds., Y. Arad, Spector, New York 1989.
19. SS-Brigadeführer Walter Stahlecker, *Die Deutsche Polizei*, 1942, no. 8.
20. The murderer poses for a photograph, *"Schöne Zeiten"...*, p. 31.

Geschichte - Erinnerung - Politik
Posener Studien zur Geschichts-, Kultur- und Politikwissenschaft

Herausgegeben von Anna Wolff-Powęska und Piotr Forecki

Band 1 Machteld Venken: Stradding the Iron Curtain? Immigrants, Immigrant Organisations, War Memories. 2011.

Band 2 Anna Wolff-Powęska / Piotr Forecki: Der Holocaust in der polnischen Erinnerungskultur. 2012.

Band 3 Marta Grzechnik: Regional Histories and Historical Regions. The Concept of the Baltic Sea Region in Polish and Swedish Historiographies. 2012.

Band 4 Lutz Niethammer: Memory and History. Essays in Contemporary History. 2012.

Band 5 Piotr Forecki: Reconstructing Memory. The Holocaust in Polish Public Debates. 2013.

Band 6 Marek Słoń (ed.): Historical Atlas of Poland in the 2nd Half of the 16th Century. Voivodeships of Cracow, Sandomierz, Lublin, Sieradz, Łęczyca, Rawa, Płock and Mazovia. Volume 1-4. Translated by Agata Staszewska, Editorial Assistance Martha Brożyna. 2014.

Band 7 Maciej Janowski: Birth of the Intelligentsia 1750-1831. A History of the Polish Intelligentsia – Part 1. Edited by Jerzy Jedlicki. Translated by Tristan Korecki. 2014.

Band 8 Jerzy Jedlicki: The Vicious Circle 1832-1864. A History of the Polish Intelligentsia – Part 2. Edited by Jerzy Jedlicki. Translated by Tristan Korecki. 2014.

Band 9 Magdalena Micińska: At the Crossroads 1865-1918. A History of the Polish Intelligentsia – Part 3. Edited by Jerzy Jedlicki. Translated by Tristan Korecki. 2014.

Band 10 Anna Wolff-Powęska: Memory as Burden and Liberation. Germans and their Nazi Past (1945-2010). Translated by Marta Skowrońska. 2015.

Band 11 Thomas Szarota: On the Threshold of the Holocaust. Anti-Jewish Riots and Pogroms in Occupied Europe. Warsaw – Paris – The Hague – Amsterdam – Antwerp – Kaunas. Translated by Tristan Korecki. 2015.

www.peterlang.com

www.ingramcontent.com/pod-product-compliance
Lightning Source LLC
LaVergne TN
LVHW042246070526
838201LV00089B/48